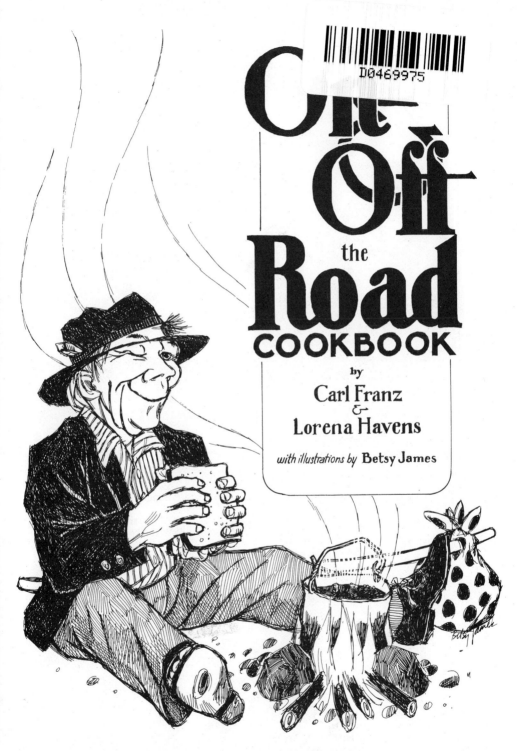

The Off the Road COOKBOOK

by
Carl Franz
&
Lorena Havens

with illustrations by **Betsy James**

John Muir Publications • Santa Fe, New Mexico

Published by John Muir Publications, Inc.
P.O. Box 613
Santa Fe, New Mexico 87501

Library of Congress Catalog Card No. 82-081875

ISBN 0-912528-27-3

First Edition July 1982

10 9 8 7 6 5 4 3 2 1

The last number to the right in the
above sequence indicates the
printing history of this edition.

Acknowledgements

This book has been stewing for years, but it was Ken Luboff's friendly push (or was it a shove?) that finally got it going; Lisa Cron, our publisher's alternative to nuclear energy, kept us moving with steady enthusiasm and encouragement; Joy Franz offered much needed help in editing and research; and Aladene Whitaker ran it all through her typewriter at unusual hours of the day and night. Many others contributed to the book in one way or another: *thank you.*

A special thanks to Betsy James, whose pen is as sharp as a vegetable knife.

For Steve and Tina: your friendship is a feast.

Contents

1 Meal Planning 13

A Tale of Chocolate 14
Some Questions & Answers 17
Typical Camp Cooking Styles 20
No Food At All 21
A Crust of Bread 22
Cold Cooking 23
The Gourmet Picnic 23
Heat n' Serve Cooking 24
Homestyle Camp Cooking 26
Meal Combinations & Variations 27
Cravings & Snacks 29

Vegetarians Vs. The Wilderness 32
Eating Well 34
Commonsense Nutrition 35
Calories & Protein Requirements 37
Vitamins & Supplements 38
Typical Menu Planning 39
How Much Is Enough? 41
Planning by Weights & Measures 43
Home Packaging 43
Weights & Measures 43
Food Comparison Table 46

2 Shopping & Provisioning 51

Lists 53
Stores: Where, When & How? 54
Food Co-ops 55
Supermarkets 56
Health Food Stores 57
Specialty Shops & Delis 58
Restaurant Suppliers 59
Shopping & Economizing Tips 59
Food & Shopping Suggestions 62
Beans 62
Beverages 63
Breads & Tortillas 65
Cereals 66

Cheese 68
Eggs 70
Dried Fruit 70
Lentils & Split Peas 72
Meat 72
Milk 73
Noodles & Pasta 74
Rice 75
Nuts & Seeds 76
Oil, Margarine & Butter 77
Soy Proteins 78
Spices & Herbs 80
Vegetables 82

3 Foraging 85

Myth Versus Reality 85
Casual Foraging 86
Survival Foraging 86
Hunting the Elusive Robin 86

Berries 86
Mushrooms 86
Whining & Dining 89
Mushroom Spaghetti 90

4 The Complete Camp Kitchen 97

Make Your Own Gear 100
Alternatives for Buying Gear 102
The Backpacker's Kitchen 103
The Suitcase Kitchen 105
The Colonizer's Kitchen 107
The Bare Bones Kitchen 107

Take It or Leave It? 108
Aluminum Foil to Zip-Loc Bags 109
RV, Van & Car Kitchens 129
The Portable Herb & Salad Garden 130
Containers & Cabinets 132
Awnings to Ventilators 136

5 Camp Kitchen Skills 139

The Seven-Pot Meal 139
The Moveable Feast 148
Cooking & Camping 150
Kitchen Improvements 152
Quick & Easy Ideas 152
Washing Dishes 153
Garbage & Litter 155
The Sleeping Bag Ice Chest 155
Drip Coolers 156
Cook Fires 157

Tin Can Stoves & Ovens 162
The Tin Can Lantern 164
Camp Stove Care & Feeding 165
Coleman Stove Maintenance 168
Staying Healthy 169
How to Purify Water 170
Diarrhea, Dysentery & Poisoning 172
Cramps 173
Burns 173
Infections & Wounds 173

6   Cooking Tips & Techniques 175

Simplicity & Reliability 176
Cooking Methods 177
Food Storage 179
Preventing Spoilage 179
Emily Post & the Outdoors 181
Small Touches 181
Variety 182

Glop: A Four-Letter Word 184
Spices & Herbs 184
Honey & Sweeteners 185
Cooking with Seawater 186
High Altitude Cooking 188
Substitutions 188
Final Thoughts 189

7   Recipes 190

Soups & Stews 192
Beans 196
Sandwiches & Tacos 200
Eggs 206
Fish & Seafood 210
Smoked Meat & Fish 212
Noodles & Pasta 215
Rice & Bulgur 220
Potatoes 226

Breads, Biscuits & Tortillas 230
Cooked Cereals 237
Sauces, Gravies & Dips 239
Vegetables 244
Drying Fruits & Vegetables 245
Salads 248
Dressings & Croutons 252
Snacks & Desserts 254
Beverages 257

Appendices 261

Recommended Reading 261

Equipment & Food Sources 262

Index 265

Introduction

"Carl, you aren't going to believe this," Lorena said one afternoon, "but I've just discovered the *perfect camp meal!*" I looked up from my improvised couch of sleeping bags and jackets.

"Oh, yeah?" I didn't bother to disguise the doubt in my voice. Years of fruitless searching for the Ideal Campsite and the fabled Lost Elephant Graveyard had tarnished excitement with cynicism. "What is it?" I yawned.

"It's very fast cooking," she said, dodging the question, "warm, filling, lightweight, inexpensive, flavorful, uses just one pot..." Lorena hesitated for a moment, "...and it's highly nutritious!"

I propped myself up on my elbows. This was beginning to sound pretty good. "Well, what is it?" I persisted, feeling vague rumblings of curiosity from my stomach.

"We'll have it for dinner," she hedged, rummaging through the cooking gear. I slumped back, eyes closed, exhausted from a day of casual hiking and fishing. "...flavorful and filling" was just what I needed. I dozed off, dreaming of grilled steaks and golden french fries...

"Come and get it!"

I jerked awake, nostrils twitching at the rich odor of hot garlic. Lorena approached with a covered skillet, placing it carefully beside me on a flat rock. Food at last!

With a dramatic flourish she whipped off the lid, revealing The Perfect Camp Meal!

"*Popcorn?*"

Lorena and I have a schizophrenic relationship with camp cooking. I will spend thirty minutes preparing an omelette and then set it aside without a thought when a trout rises in a nearby stream or a hawk soars within range of my binoculars. Lorena is even more easily distracted. It often takes true hunger to tear her away from a life-long study of cloud formations and tree tops to prepare a meal.

Some campers see cooking as a complete chore, others find it enjoyable and even entertaining. Our experience, based on everything from backpacking trips in Guatemala and Mexico to boating in British Columbia and Alaska, is that camp cooking is a constant challenge. It is also a challenge that we prefer not to meet head-on. As Lorena put it after one of those long, hard days in the outdoors we'd all like to pretend don't happen: "When cooking ceases to be enjoyable, I tend to cease cooking." For that reason, this book deals with the realities of camp cooking—including garbage and dishwashing—not just armchair advice.

Some of our camping trips are relaxed van and car tours, allowing us to make use of fresh foods and a wide range of kitchen gear. On other trips, however, we will carry a week's food on our backs or a month's provisions in a kayak. Like most people, we can't afford the expense or inconvenience of having special foods and cooking equipment for each type of trip we make. Our menu, as well as our kitchen, must be practical no matter how or where we camp—and Lorena considers a house to be just a campsite with walls, roof and windows.

Many outdoor cookbooks are loaded with novelty cooking techniques and recipes based on imagination rather than the meal-to-meal realities of camp life. "Build a Nifty Solar Cooker from 17 large tin cans, then take one small buffalo or a mess of fresh squirrels and..." Other books treat food strictly as fuel and calories, leaving flavor, texture and eye appeal to chance.

Our approach is simple: food is vital to our health and good humor, whether we're camping in a remote wilderness or living at home. Camp cooking isn't a novelty or a fad, it's a basic skill that can enhance your outdoor experience.

This book stresses common sense, economy and convenience in camp cooking. There's no reason to completely disrupt your eating habits or your budget when you head out, whether it's for a weekend hike, a week-long canoe trip or an RV expedition. This Scout-like approach to camp cooking requires only a few things from you to be successful: a sense of humor, patience and a respect for what you eat. We hope you find, as we have, that it's well worth the effort.

Carl Franz and Lorena Havens
Steamboat Slough, Washington

The On & Off
The Road Cookbook

Chapter 1
Meal Planning

As originally conceived in the illuminating, obstacle-leveling logic found in the bottom of an Herradura tequila bottle, our upcoming kayak expedition to Baja California would be a model of excitement, an outdoor adventure of classic scope and simplicity. Three people, two men and a woman, of ordinary stature and stamina, pitting themselves against two thousand miles of treacherous seas and barren coastline in standard manufacture kayaks, equipped with off-the-shelf gear and provisions, a borrowed Boy Scout compass and fuzzy Xerox copies of several survey charts from the *USS Ranger*, circa 1881. In short, an expedition to gladden the hearts and minds of the most armchair-bound cynic; a trip of a lifetime, a voyage of discovery, a...

"Pipedream, if you ask me," Lorena snorted. "Based on too many hours in the Public Library when you were a frustrated, sixth-grade explorer."

My brother scowled at the sweeping oval I'd penciled on our large-scale map of Mexico, the proposed route of our epic Sea of Cortez Circumnavigation Expedition. "I've only got six months off work," Rob complained. "Couldn't we try something just a little less, uh, *ambitious?*" I caught an exchange of significant glances between him and Lorena, the all-too-familiar "Humor him until the boys in white arrive."

"Let's be reasonable," Lorena suggested, adopting a reasonable tone of voice that had laid waste to many other Grand Plans—common sense chipping relentlessly at dreams, fantasies, side trips, treasure hunts and wild goose chases. As she reached for the pocket calculator, bane of all those born to worship Lady Luck rather than New Math, I desperately tried a retrenching maneuver, a strategic withdrawal that would leave my basic position unscathed.

"We can hire local fishermen to portage us in their *pangas* past the boring spots," I blurted, "and bury food caches along the coast to reduce our load. We'll forage for seafood and distill our own water and..."

"Figuring two thousand miles in six months that is..." a long accusing finger stabbed at the calculator, "exactly ten-point-nine-eight miles per day not counting..." she glanced at a sheet of densely scribbled figures lying among a pile of nautical reference books, "...your average diurnal tidal movement along the eastern Baja *or*," Lorena's eyebrows raised significantly, "your equinoctial wind shifts in the Spring."

She took a noisy sip at her mint tea, cleared her throat, then added, "Given these factors I calculate that our *minimum* required paddling to be, offhand, about fifteen-point-five miles per day. You know what that means?"

"Yeah, let me guess. It's too damned far, right?"

If Necessity is the Mother of Invention, then Compromise must surely be the illegitimate offspring of Frustration. My original goals were reduced from thousands of miles of sea travel by kayak to mere hundreds; air drops of supplies were pared down to extra plastic bags of food stuffed into already bulging corners. All the drama, the romantic hustle and bustle of expedition planning and preparation, the scrutiny of dusty manuscripts, the urgent communiqués to far-flung benefactors and equipment designers were reduced to a cluttered kitchen table in a converted adobe garage in lower Santa Fe.

Beneath the feeble glow of a 60-watt generic lightbulb, and to the low moan of a sub-freezing wind that rattled cracked windows, we got down to the nuts and bolts of genuine expedition planning. While the neighbors battled over Saturday night's pizza and TV programs, we grappled with hundreds of decisions in a long process of negotiation, evaluation and debate that made Salt II look like a schoolyard squabble.

I was beginning to understand why great explorers continued on in the face of starvation, injury, disease and mutinous bearers. It was out of *relief* at having left behind the tedium and torture of organizing the expedition.

"Let's figure out the chocolate." Lorena's voice was firm and confident, having just won the hour-long bloody Battle of the Cashew Pieces by a slim margin, defeating my Toasted Almonds and Rob's Cracker Jacks by sheer bullying. My mind still reeled under the avalanche of nutritional data she'd hit us with, from fat-based caloric yield to microgram trace mineral content and complementary protein relationships. The conclusion of her argument was an impassioned Clarence Darrow-style harangue that brought tears to our eyes as we were made to understand the essential *goodness* of the less expensive (17.4% cheaper) broken raw cashew pieces. I could hardly wait for morning to come so that I might rush out to the Whole Foods Co-op and embrace these wonderful nuts in person.

"Chocolate?" Rob said. "That ought to be easy. How many candy bars can you eat in one day?"

"Twenty-five or thirty," I answered.

Rob gave an overly patient sigh. "Okay, wise guy, I forgot. How many candy bars do we *need* for one day?"

After a somewhat spirited discussion we compromised on five candy bars each per day. The logic was simple: chocolate gives quick energy and a mild caffeine lift that can be very helpful while paddling a heavy kayak. Chocolate has some food value and is good for morale. Five bars apiece was a generous ration but why suffer?

Lorena bent over the calculator. "Five candy bars at two ounces apiece times three people multiplied by one hundred and eighty two days..." her finger hesitated over the Total button, then plunged recklessly down. "That comes out to..." Lorena poked repeatedly at the button, a look of disbelief on her face. "Five thousand four hundred and sixty ounces?" Her fingers flicked at the tiny keyboard. "Three hundred and forty-one-point-two-five *pounds* of chocolate?" We sat in stunned silence.

"Doesn't leave a whole lot of room for food and water," Rob said glumly, visions of midnight chocolate feeds vanishing before his eyes.

"Let's try this from the other end," I suggested, trying to erase from my mind an image of a pallet-load of candy bars being dropped from a forklift onto our kayak. "How much chocolate can we afford to take, in terms of weight and bulk?" I looked over at Lorena, our official Load Mistress. Given a shoehorn and an extra morning, she could double the present payload on the Space Shuttle.

"About twelve ounces," she said without hesitation.

"A day?" Rob asked. "Just twelve ounces a day?"

Lorena gave him a wry smile. "No, that's twelve ounces *total*. For the entire trip. That's four ounces apiece. One candy bar every month. Split three ways. We're badly overloaded as it is."

Rob gave us a bleak look. "Well let's cut down on our cashews. We have to have more chocolate!"

"Can't," Lorena said flatly. "They have more food value. In comparison to *candy*," she uttered the word with a thinly disguised loathing, "cashews have forty-nine-point..."

"They do not!" I shouted, throwing my pencil onto the table.

"Do too!" Lorena answered.

"Says who?" Rob countered, wringing the top of another beer with a savage twist and plunging his hand deep into a box of Cracker Jacks.

"Hold it! Hold it!" I raised my hands in a signal of peace. "Let's leave chocolate until later and do something else. What else is urgent?"

"Sunflower seeds!"

"Fishing lures!"

I lowered my head onto my arms. It looked like a long night.

Planning the food and meals for a camping trip involves a formula slightly more complex than the equation describing a controlled nuclear reaction. Even after long years of practice my hands tend to tremble and clutch at my temples when I find myself confronted with an outdoor adventure and a blank shopping list. I never fail to be amazed by campers who can say with confidence: "Well, for lunch on Day 4 we'll have 2 ounces of Swiss cheese, a cup of onion soup and 3 sesame crackers and on Day 9 we'll breakfast on eight inch pancakes with..." By Day 9 on our trips I'm not sure that we won't be reduced to gnawing tree bark or raiding other camps.

It all depends, you see, on just how much food we can cram into our packs and still manage to stay on our feet. "We'll be back when we get hungry" has been the plan on more than a few of our expeditions. What this approach lacks in organization and nutritional common sense is often made up by a delicious feeling of excitement and anticipation.

The trip begins with a typical bout of gluttony ("We've got to cut down on some of this weight!"), followed by erratic attempts at rationing and self-denial. The 'Lifeboat Mentality' takes over on the third day, when each member of the party watches the others suspiciously for signs of chewing and the communal food bag is guarded as jealously as the treasure of the Sierra Madre.

An experienced cook juggles many factors when planning the meals for a camping trip, including mode of travel, food costs, availability of fuel and water, weather and the size of the group. Long practice over a cookfire and an ability to anticipate what will actually happen while camping rather than merely guessing, can give a well-seasoned cook an almost magical aura of competence and clairvoyance.

Going snow camping? Don't put your granola in those flimsy plastic sacks; they'll surely freeze and break.

A scorching desert exploration? Better do something with those chocolate bars or they'll turn to sticky goo before noon.

Kayaking in late summer? Pack the cooking oil close to the bottom of the boat or the 'greenhouse effect' of the sun's rays through the fiberglass deck will superheat the container and risk a very messy rupture.

These small details, however, are not nearly as overwhelming as how much flour shall we take? How many spoonfuls of coffee will serve six people on a seven day trip? Or should we forget coffee entirely and take instant juice and brewer's yeast? The answers to these questions can easily boggle the mind, until the only reasonable solution seems to be "Forget it! Let's go to Disneyland!"

The following questionnaire should help guide you through the confusing maze of meal planning. Read it through and consider how the suggestions and experiences of others can be applied to your particular trip, food preferences and feelings about cooking. There are many approaches to successful camp cooking. With a bit of patience and a lot of good humor, I'm certain you'll discover one that suits you best.

Meal Planning Questionnaire

Do you really care about cooking and what you eat?

There are reasons other than laziness and weak moral fiber for not wanting to cook. Many people resent time spent cooking in the outdoors because it distracts from the experience of hiking, contemplating nature or just lying around in the sun chewing on fern tips. Unless your trip will be especially rigorous or long, it is quite likely that careful planning and

shopping can eliminate cooking entirely — or to whatever degree you wish to avoid it. (See *Cold Cooking* later in this chapter.)

Once you've mastered camping, whether it's RV touring or cross-country trekking, you'll probably find cooking to be a challenge rather than a chore. Knowing how to cook expands your horizons greatly, especially if you camp out for long periods of time, when an ability to turn simple foods and foraged delicacies into nourishing meals can literally make or break the trip. But until then...don't worry about it too much. As long as you eat enough to stay healthy you'll do fine.

How is your budget? Fat? Skinny?

Economizing can be as difficult as dieting and requires a constant attention to detail. Compact high-energy foods can put a big hole in your pocketbook. Cooking homestyle in camp, on the other hand, allows you to prepare less expensive but highly nutritious foods. Why pay for costly processing such as freeze-drying if you can easily substitute more economical foods? If money is limited, your best bet is homestyle cooking, with cold-cooking as a backup. (See *Homestyle Camp Cooking*.)

What type of camping will you be doing? Van? Backpack? Boat?

We spend less time on meal planning when going by vehicle or large boat than we do if hiking or kayaking. The reason is simple: extra food isn't a burden if we have a van or boat to do the dirty work of hauling. When the trip is over, extra supplies just go home with us. Hiking is another story. There's nothing I hate more than coming out of the woods with five pounds of food on my back.

When weight and bulk aren't critical we take as much fresh produce as possible: potatoes, summer squash, sweet corn, oranges and other treats that backpackers only dream of as they gnaw at the granola bag. (See *Typical Camp Cooking Styles* for examples of our meal planning in a variety of camping situations.)

Will your trip be physically demanding or relatively relaxed?

I don't consider myself to be a fanatic about good nutrition, but if my body will be sorely tested in the outdoors, it only stands to reason to eat the best food I can. The pay-back is obvious and almost immediate, not only in the way you'll withstand a wearying hike or strenuous bout of paddling but in mood and general outlook. Poorly fed campers are like irritable porcupines. In genuinely trying circumstances your judgment and coordination can be adversely affected by a poor diet. Macho types who push too hard without eating properly are a hazard to themselves and their companions.

Eating well shouldn't be overlooked even if your outdoor activity is restricted to turning the pages of a bird guide or flexing a fishing rod. Although you'll probably get by on just about anything, you'd might as well get the best food you can for your money. (See *Eating Well: A Balancing Act* and the chapter on *Shopping and Provisioning*.)

What will the conditions be where you camp? Snow? Rain? Scarce fuel and water?

This is one of the most complex questions, since it includes such factors as fuel, water and weather. My reaction to the weather is simple: when it's cool or wet I must have a fire or a stove, if not both. That means I might as well cook something at the same time. If the fire will be kept up constantly, a familiar situation when beach camping in the Northwest, we'll have beans, panbreads and other slow-to-prepare dishes.

In extreme conditions such as snow camping, fuel must be rationed and quick-cooking foods are more practical. Friends who camp on glaciers in Alaska find that freeze-dried foods are a good compromise between nutrition, ease-of-preparation and fuel. Instant soups, noodles, quick-cooking grains and hot cereals are also good, especially if you can wrap chilly fingers around your cup or bowl.

In the desert, the limiting factor in cooking is often water. This makes cold cooking a useful option, or dishes that don't require a lot of soaking or boiling. We prefer a combination of cold and hot foods while in the desert. One cooked meal a day satisfies us, usually prepared in the afternoon or, when hiking hard, early in the morning to give plenty of energy.

Will your camping trip be a few days? Weeks? Months?

The complexity of meal planning for an extended camping trip seems to increase geometrically. Quantities, even of spices, become mind-bending.

There will be moments when you tear at your hair and shout, "We can't possibly eat all this!" Short trips — less than a week — are obviously going to be much easier to plan. You'll cram a list onto one sheet of paper, do the shopping with a single cart and the bill won't look like the down payment on a new condominium.

What about those longer expeditions, however — the three-week canoe voyage you've dreamed of for years, the twenty-five day mountain crest hike or the open-ended, back road, RV touring and exploring you've put off too long? Why is meal planning so difficult for these trips?

The answers are simple: very few people buy more than a few day's food at one time. Stores are just too convenient and besides, why bother? We seldom deal with food storage on such a scale, especially the hazard of spoilage: stick it in the refrigerator and forget about it! Packaging: who would have thought it would take hours just to divvy up the Spanish peanuts, seal the bags and separate them into some kind of coherent order?

Planning for a long expedition, especially if it's your first one, demands research and organization. Read over *Shopping* and *Recipes* and *think* about them. Nutrition can't be overlooked either, so give close thought to what foods you now enjoy and know how to cook. Are they 'nutritionally dense' (lots of food value per ounce) or are they 'empty calories'?

On expeditions, variety must often be traded off for convenience and to hold the lid down on weight and bulk. This is where a careful reading of *Recipes*, with all of the many variations in ingredients, can really help you out. Rice, for example, can be prepared in more ways than I can count. Plan your variations with great care and your staples won't be boring.

Typical Camp Cooking Styles

If it's true that a quick peek at a person's bookshelves will reveal a good deal of information about their character, humor and personality, what can we learn by rummaging through their kitchen cupboards? Are your spice containers of uniform size, arranged in alphabetical order from left to right? Or does your spice cabinet look like our friend Steve's, a bewildering and overflowing collection that rivals the Istanbul bazaar? Is it significant that I don't own a measuring spoon but have five distinctly different spatulas?

Learning from and imitating other cooks is one of the quickest shortcuts to successful camp cooking. I constantly ask others about their style of eating and cooking in the outdoors, how they solve problems, what mistakes they've made and corrected, their favorite trail foods, best source of cookware, and so on.

Most of what I learn is quite simple: a friend recently reminded me of canned cooked meat (not Spam, which I learned to hate in the navy, but

corned beef). It had been years since I'd voluntarily faced a can of cooked meat and I was surprised to find that I actually liked the stuff, especially when wrapped inside a hot flour tortilla and garnished with grated cheese and mustard. It made a very satisfying evening meal after a long stumbling hike in the dark.

Lorena and I constantly review our camping menu. What was our least favorite camp food on a four day hike with very limited water? Plain raw sunflower seeds; I felt like a test animal in some misguided 4-H project, forced to chew mealy seeds when I really craved a crisp salty snack with lots of flavor.

A friend who must have had a similar experience offered this recipe: toast raw, shelled peanuts in a heavy skillet over a fairly hot fire, dusting liberally with salt, garlic powder and mild chili powder. Cook until scorched, cool, then eat. He says it is vital to the flavor that the nuts actually scorch, not just toast.

The following cooking and meal planning styles vary from the mildly ridiculous to the almost sublime. I've personally abandoned No Food cooking in response to my body's insistent demands on foods. The Gourmet Picnic, on the other hand, is tantalizing but tends to cost too much and gives me all too vivid dreams. Somewhere, depending on the type of trip and your general humor, is safe and reliable middle ground.

No Food At All

Going without food while camping might seem to be pushing beyond common sense. With the growing popularity of fasting, however, both as a form of dieting and for spiritual enrichment, it is inevitable that some people will take to the outdoors with very empty stomachs. A friend raves about a four day trip he did without food, hiking up a desert canyon. He spent most of his time at a small creek, drinking a great deal of water and watching wildlife.

The hazard of such fasting, as my friend learned, was a recurring dizziness whenever he exerted himself. He took the sensible approach: he quit hiking and devoted his time to resting and meditating.

In situations where a clear mind and strong body are vital to your safety and even survival, fasting is not the way to go. If you fast in the outdoors, do it in the company of friends or from a secure base camp. In all cases, an emergency reserve of food should be close at hand. Some people experience strong and unpleasant side effects while fasting. You may want a meal on short notice.

A Crust of Bread

There's something undeniably romantic about stuffing a crust of bread and a few apples into our pockets and setting off to wander in the wilderness. It's a casual, devil-may-care approach that appeals to my spirit ... but not necessarily to my stomach. A friend and I did this type of camping regularly during high school. We knew how to cook (after a fashion) but had no real 'outdoor' gear other than leftovers from earlier Boy Scout careers.

Our routine was quite simple: We'd stuff matches and a few candy bars into our pockets, along with a salt shaker and, if we were feeling very domestic, a piece of aluminum foil. The next step was to decide where to go camping. We'd hop an early evening Greyhound bus heading east and somewhere in the darkness on the western slopes of the Cascades, tap the driver on the shoulder and ask to be let out. I think I enjoyed the driver's reaction to such unscheduled stops as much as the mystery and excitement of finding out where we'd landed when the sun came up the next morning.

We'd find a reasonably level and sometimes dry spot in the forest, climb into our thin cotton sleeping bags and swat mosquitoes until dawn. Hunger would then drive us to the nearest river or creek and we'd spend a few days or even a week, frantically catching trout to roast on alder sticks. Berries sometimes filled out our menu.

On one occasion, after several days under a large boulder in a relentless rainstorm, we hiked nine miles to buy a can of dill pickles with our remaining pocket change. We ate cold trout and pickles, followed by a refreshing swallow of pickle brine for dessert.

Modern camping, including cooking, tends to trade off spontaneity for comfort and security. We defend ourselves against the Elements with more and more sophisticated equipment, relying on technology where common sense is often more appropriate. Food is just one example: we may become so obsessed with eating exactly on schedule and just the right balance of calories, carbohydrates, proteins and so on, that we lose something of even greater value—the ability to "get up and go!"

Have you ever turned down an invitation to go camping with, "Sorry, but I just can't get it together that fast. Maybe next time?" I've used this line myself, and kicked myself later for not grabbing "a crust of bread" (and some cheese, salami, an onion or two, a chocolate bar...) and hitting the trail.

Cold Cooking

Cold cooking offers a sensible and nutritionally sound alternative to hot meals or foods prepared in camp. Cold cooking is especially useful on short outings and impromptu camping trips, when puzzling over what to eat can get in the way of actually going outdoors.

The idea is simple: take foods that don't require cooking or even warming. (Hot beverages are an exception. They can break the cold food routine with very little preparation.) Avoid too many snack and junk foods; one of the hazards of altering your normal eating routines and diet while camping is a tendency to dip heavily into the potato chip bag and candy bar stash. Cold cooking can be as nutritious and satisfying as regular hot meals, but you'll have to be inventive at times.

The list of possible foods is almost endless but includes such cold staples as cheese, canned meats and seafoods, peanut butter, yogurt, granola, sausages, nuts, seeds, butter, breads of all types, dried fruit, fresh vegetables and fruit, smoked fish and meat, instant drinks, bean sprouts, etc. I also like to include condiments such as fresh or canned chiles, mustard, relish and chutney. Add candy bars, hard candies and other treats and you should find that cold cooking satisfies your needs and cravings for trips of up to two weeks.(After a few days, I usually begin experimenting with cooked foods, even if it's just heating cheese sandwiches on top of hot rocks.)

Many foods can be prepared at home and taken to eat cold while camping. Bean and macaroni salads are among our favorites; they keep well and are very nutritious, as well as filling. A number of suggestions for cold foods can be found in *Shopping* and *Recipes*.

If you don't want to cook at all, even at home, consider provisioning at a local restaurant. Lorena and I made a weekend hike sustained by cold pizza. It kept us going quite well and required only thirty minutes of waiting and beer-sipping to 'prepare'. I couldn't face pizza for a month afterwards though.

A friend swears by cold hamburgers in the wilds, about half a dozen per day. His advice is to go easy on the catsup; it has a tendency to make the bun very soggy.

The Gourmet Picnic is the no-holds-barred approach to cold foods. We 'go gourmet' infrequently, mainly because it tends to be a budget-busting indulgence. The trick to making a gourmet picnic a memorable treat is to pull out all the stops. Don't go halfway. I prefer to prepare a main dish at home — some morsel like a small prime rib roast — and round this out with fine cheeses, caviar, pastries, marinated mushrooms, palm hearts and other high-camp fare. For those who refuse to cook at all, a visit to a delicatessen can provide cold roast beef, smoked salmon and whitefish, salads and other basic survival foods.

A Gourmet Picnic isn't complete without a tablecloth (preferably snow-white linen), serving dishes and the appropriate stemware. Pick a scenic mountain top, island or gravel bar and spread out the feast. Candles are nice, and in no case should anyone be allowed to swill their Gran Marnier from a Sierra cup.

There are innumerable variations in cold cooking. One of the most basic I've seen was a friend who ate nothing but granola. Lorena and I were hiking in Guatemala with this fellow, alternately amused, appalled and envious of his simple fare. His meal planning formula was simple: X ounces of granola per day times Y number of days, with a few extra fistfuls tossed in to compensate for a climb to over 11,000 feet. Like other granola fanatics I've known, he had a moody disposition and powerful molars.

Mealtime, traditionally a restful and energizing interlude on our camping trips, became as tense as a game of pot-limit poker. Our friend watched with poorly concealed disgust and envy as Lorena and I dragged out the usual odds & sods of our quickly planned provisions: fresh cucumbers, a bottle of Quetzalteca (a foul anise liquor of dubious origins), some more-or-less whole wheat cakes discovered in a local marketplace, a lump of goat cheese, an onion... By the second meal our companion developed a bad case of spaniel-eyes, mooning over our food with all the subtlety of a CARE poster. When we relented, however, he dove into the granola bag with a haughty, "I don't need any of that stuff!" This dismal scene was repeated, meal after meal, and undoubtedly contributed to my present prejudice against granola and related products.

The advantages of cold cooking are easy to see: it is quite economical, especially if you eat wholesome rather than processed foods; it reduces meal planning time to a minimum; food storage is simplified; cooking gear, utensils, clean up and KP are almost eliminated; and last but not least, it enhances your appreciation for 'real' cooking while providing a common sense alternative to being chained to a cook fire.

Heat n' Serve Cooking

Convenience foods, particularly freeze-dried and instant, (soups, noodles and casserole main dishes), occupy the middleground between cold cooking and homestyle camp cooking. Although we personally prefer cooking 'from scratch', instant and quick foods are useful in the outdoors, especially when the conditions are tough (snow camping, climbing and other adventures along the brittle edge of comfort, safety and common sense).

Some prefer 'heat n' serve' cooking for its predictability: if you've tasted one packet of instant noodles you've probably tasted them all, with minor variations. Freeze-dried meals reduce meal planning and eliminate surprises, though at no small cost.

Cost, in fact, is one of the main reasons we avoid freeze-dried foods. Careful planning, shopping and home packaging can mean great savings for those who put their own meals together.

Heat n' serve foods can be a good introduction to more involved camp cooking, since you'll still need a stove or cook fire and at least one pot for heating water. With the addition of a small skillet, the heat n' serve kitchen approaches what we use for homestyle camp cooking.

Many of the recipe suggestions in this book are so quick and easy that they compete with processed heat n' serve type meals. Noodle soups are a good example. Buy a packet of plain, quick-cooking, Oriental style egg noodles. Prepare them according to the directions (usually less than two minutes of boiling) or pour boiling water over them, cover, wrap well in a towel or T-shirt and set aside for ten to twenty minutes (until tender). If you eat meat, a few shreds of jerky can be added when you cook the noodles. While the noodles cook, mince a tablespoon of onion. Drain the noodles and serve garnished with the minced onion, a generous pinch of fresh or dried parsley, a chopped or sliced hardboiled egg, soy sauce, sesame seeds (well toasted), Parmesan cheese or whatever.

Even if you use all of the optional ingredients listed here, this meal shouldn't involve more than ten minutes of preparation. Compare it in cost, flavor, appeal and general sense of satisfaction to a dish of pre-spiced instant noodles.

Reserve Food: We use instant foods as back-ups and emergency reserves. Even dedicated cooks are tempted to go to bed hungry when faced with a soggy fire on a windy night. Heat n' serve dishes also make good snacks, especially in cold weather. We've carried some instant packaged foods as reserves for so long that the labels have worn away from countless miles in a backpack and kayak. It is important to remember, however, that reserve foods, like first aid kits, are rarely used until you need them very badly.

Homestyle Camp Cooking

Homestyle cooking in the outdoors is based on the simple notion that eating well is an important part of the camping experience. The rich smell of fresh coffee and the sensuous pleasure of pouring honey over a stack of hot pancakes can create a mood and memory as powerful as any outdoor view.

Our friend Steve carries this one step farther: he recalls campsites by the food eaten there, remembering the details of a meal with the clarity of a mountain climber describing the cracks and crevices of a particularly challenging peak. "Oh, yeah, that was the place we fixed Spanish rice, wasn't it? I had those capers I bought in Portland, and you fixed..."

Lorena and I spend a great deal of time camping — three to six months of the year, on an average — and sometimes more. We have tried many approaches to camp cooking, from eating as little as possible to cooking 'three squares' a day, week after week. Our meal planning and cooking routines have now stabilized, and though each trip has its own quirks, our eating in the outdoors is based on a few simple requirements.

Flavor: First of all, our camping meals must taste good. This might sound obvious, but believe me, if you've ever sampled what some cooks serve in the name of nutrition or convenience, you'd know that flavor is often the first sacrifice made over the camp stove. A good rule of thumb is: *If you wouldn't serve it at home, don't serve it in camp.* I know that raging appetites can tolerate strange concoctions, but such meals should be considered exceptions, not the rule. I've eaten onion soup accidently made with a 'stock' of Red Rose Tea and lived to tell the tale. These little disasters make good stories but poor regular fare.

Quick and Easy: Another requirement is that the meal or dish be relatively quick and easy to prepare from readily available materials. When Lorena and I go camping we put a lot of energy into cooking, but we try to make it brief and intense. Any meal takes twice as long to prepare in the outdoors as in a home kitchen and I want some free time to savor being in the woods or on the beach. We have a basic menu of reliable recipes that can be cooked on a stove or campfire, with variations in taste and texture provided by spices, condiments and extra ingredients.

One-Pot: Our favorite backpacking and kayaking meals tend to be one-pot, with nutritional balance provided by tortillas, bread, simple salads, cheese, nuts, etc. We do our best to make these one-pot dishes as distinct in flavor, texture and appearance as we can. For example, I add ginger and a large portion of sesame seeds to a fried rice to give an Oriental flavor. Then the next day, Lorena might prepare the same basic dish, substituting lots of garlic and Parmesan cheese for the ginger and sesame seeds. This second rice is prepared almost exactly as the first, but looks and tastes quite different.

When camping from a vehicle or in a large boat, these same rice dishes become the main course in a slightly expanded meal.

Old Favorites: If you already know how to cook you've undoubtedly got a few favorite dishes. Are any suitable for camping? Can they be modified and, most important, simplified? Baked casseroles are a favorite economical home-cooked meal, but will your camp kitchen include an oven? If not, can the dish be prepared on top of the stove or fire according to one of our 'quick' methods for rice and noodles? (See *Recipes*.)

The more complicated a dish is, the less versatile it will be for camping. If you find yourself complaining, "I just can't make this without... (capers, rye flour, saffron, etc.)" then the dish probably isn't appropriate for camping, at least not on a regular basis.

Novice cooks would do well to pick one or two staple dishes, practice cooking them until their basic preparation is routine, and then creatively modify these recipes according to individual taste.

Combinations

Combinations of cooking styles can relieve much of the burden of cooking full time in camp. For example, when Lorena and I do a short hike or van camping trip of two or three days, we often don't cook on the first day out. Our meals will be cold or we'll reheat a dish we prepared at home — or bought in a deli or restaurant. This gives us a maximum amount of free time for setting up camp, reading or wool gathering.

The next morning, however, I'll try to fix fresh eggs with toast or tortillas. Unless the weather is very hot, we'll have a mid-afternoon meal of steak (for me), a one-pot casserole and roasted fresh vegetables. Lorena will balance out her vegetarian meal by loading her baked spud with sour cream, yogurt or grated cheese or fry tofu in butter and soy sauce.

Breakfast on the third and final day will be fried leftover potatoes and vegetables, with eggs if any are left. Lunch will be a general foraging through the remaining snacks and cheese.

On other trips we might cook for a few days, then fall back on a supply of cold foods, a combination of cold and hot food, or a bout of home-assembled instant meals.

Variations

Let's assume you're planning a two-week canoe voyage or van camping tour. Although you might not eat noodles every third day at home, while camping you must be willing to sacrifice a certain amount of variety for convenience. Besides, time seems to stretch magically while outdoors. If you are quite active, three days will often feel like a week. Here are several very simple and reliable noodle dishes that taste quite good, are quick and easy to prepare, don't cost much and aren't messy to clean up after:

1. Boiled or quick fried noodles (see *Recipes*) with butter and garlic.
2. ...with garlic and tomato sauce or tomato powder.
3. ...with cheese; either grated cheddar, Parmesan or blue, but only one, not a combination.
4. ...with olive oil or butter and mushrooms (canned, dried or fresh).
5. ...with minced or flaked parsley, oil and clams (canned, or dried or canned shrimp).

These are typical noodle dishes that we use all the time, both camping and at home. On a backpacking trip I'd use #5 on the first evening, to get rid of the weight of the canned clams or shrimp. The can should be packed out, but if the weather is reasonably cool, I'd transfer the clams and broth to a tight plastic bag before setting off.

If you're like us and enjoy leftover dinners for the next day's breakfast you've just solved the problem of ten separate meals.

If I could condense all of our meal planning advice into one Golden Rule it might be: Don't take meal planning too seriously or you'll lose your appetite as well as your sense of humor. Stay loose and flexible and accept from the beginning that you can't plan for everything. How many times have I stopped suddenly in my boot tracks, smacked myself in disgust on the forehead and cried out, "Oh, no! I forgot the Chinese mustard!"

Meal planning can be as complex as a game of chess or it can be a bore. To avoid tedium (not just while you're still at home hunched over a food list but also in camp as you yawn over Meal Seven's standard fare), try new combinations and variations of your regular menu. When I was a kid my mother started a family tradition of having Saturday's dinner be a breakfast, usually pancakes and fried eggs.

On a fishing boat in Alaska our cook once got so drunk that he slept for thirty-six hours — then woke up, completely turned around and confused — and prepared a full ham dinner at 4 a.m. The crew later agreed that it was a great improvement over our usual breakfast of overcooked boiled eggs and scorched toast.

Variety

The search for variety in your camping meals can often lead to unnecessary confusion and frustration. Americans have been conditioned to think that eating the same meal twice in one week is a sign of hardship or laziness. "Gee, we had meatloaf last Friday!" would sound quite odd in most parts of the world where a few basic foods make up the bulk of a person's lifetime diet. For novices it's also better to cook a few dishes well than several dishes poorly.

There are advantages to repeating meals that usually outweigh any uncalled-for complaints from those you are feeding. Planning and shopping are greatly simplified (and the cook inevitably does these chores in addition to actual preparation of the food). You'll not only be able to buy in larger and bulk quantities (greater economy) but packaging and storage will be much easier.

Simplification also extends to your kitchen gear: We used the same pots, pans and utensils on a two-month kayak trip as we did on a five-day hike — and a month-long van outing. On the other hand, if we'd tried to prepare a much wider variety of dishes we would almost certainly have found our basic kitchen gear inadequate and frustrating.

Variety doesn't have to be thrown out the window. In fact, by following our recipe suggestions and cooking tips later in this book, I doubt that you'll ever feel restricted by your camp meals. And once you've mastered all the basic elements of camp cooking, from selecting the right brand of breakfast cereal to hauling water in leaky buckets and coping with cranky stoves, you'll be well prepared to try your hand at more complex and innovative dishes.

Cravings & Snacks: A Bite in Time

Sudden changes in your daily routine, especially the increase in physical exercise that most campers experience when they head outdoors, may cause intense food cravings. After a long day of skin diving, hiking or gathering firewood, I can count on a merciless attack of the Killer Munchies an hour after dinner. When the munchies strike, nothing is safe: stale tortillas with mustard, cold oatmeal with jelly, smoked fish, crackers, candy bars, the honey jar ... lick it to the bottom ... pass the catsup and chiles ...

On one long camping trip in Mexico, I became obsessed by chocolate bars. The *idea* of chocolate bars, that is. I hadn't eaten candy since I was a kid and hadn't even thought of taking any with me. Then we came upon a remote village. I'll never forget my intense feeling of relief when I spotted a dirty glass jar filled with stale hard candies in a tiny three-shelf store. I cackled with glee as the old woman behind the counter wrapped those precious nuggets in a twist of newspaper.

When routine foods can't quite satisfy your needs, don't fill the void with expensive and nutrition-low junk foods. Take the Scout approach and *Be Prepared*: cheese, nuts, fresh and dried fruits, juices, smoked fish or meat jerky. Eat these foods first, then allow yourself to dip into the sack for things like gum drops and pretzels.

Snacks are useful for more than just casual cravings, especially if you're backpacking or boating. That last two-mile stretch of rugged trail or hour of frantic paddling to reach a perfect campsite can leave you incapable of anything more than unwrapping some delicious treat and rolling into a sleeping bag for the night. Moments such as these will be much less of a hardship if you have a really tasty and nutritious snack on hand.

Constant snacking isn't a vice, especially while exerting yourself physically. Forget that childhood brainwashing about not eating between

meals; steady snacking gives steady energy, rather than the tiring 'high-and lows' that come from gorging at widely separated mealtimes.

By indulging yourself more on snacks, *when you really need them,* you'll save on food (and money) in the long run and be healthier.

Wish List

Uncontrolled snacking can make serious inroads on your food supply and budget, especially if anyone in your family or group has a ferocious appetite. Whenever I hear the furtive rustle of a paper bag, I immediately think of my brother on one of his notorious midnight commando-snack raids. Blood may be thicker than water but in Rob's case it is thinner than the sugar level in his veins. I sleep with one hand on my personal munchie bag when he's along and remind him with dire daily threats of the consequences should his self-control snap again.

If there are stores nearby, or you've stocked up in advance, heavy cravings won't be a problem. But what if you're at the end of a fifty-mile dirt road or three-day's paddle from a store? You're out of luck; start daydreaming about food and jot down a 'Wish List', cataloging cravings, favorite foods and flavors, criticisms and ideas for new meals and even vague dislikes. It is amazing how easily these feelings are forgotten once you return home. The practical value of such a list will become obvious when you plan the food for your next trip.

Economizing

Snack foods — wholesome or junk — tend to be more expensive than staples. Many people therefore mistakenly buy cheap food, especially cheap snacks. An expensive bar of high quality chocolate goes a lot farther than one that is basically just sugar and flavorings. Tuna fish is a favorite snack and although it isn't cheap, a can of good quality tuna will make several sandwiches or tacos, a tuna salad or a large tuna and noodle casserole. Or just open the can and eat it with your fingers.

Economizing on snack foods is difficult but not impossible. The obvious solution is to have fewer irresistible munchies along. The self-denial approach often leads to feelings of martyrdom in the woods and scenes of eating mayhem once you're within striking distance of a store or restaurant.

Our method of saving while satisfying our cravings is to use staple foods as snacks whenever possible. My brother and I found that of all the food treats and desserts we used on a long desert van and hiking trip our favorite, hands down, was warm flour tortillas smeared liberally with honey. These honey tacos were sweet, flavorful and filling. We ate them as a dinner dessert, midnight snack and even as a quick breakfast. At home, faced with a wide variety of dessert possibilities, we would never have come up with such a simple and satisfying solution.

One of my favorite camping snacks is just cold boiled potatoes, garnished with salt and pepper and eaten with a green onion or canned jalapeño chile.

I'm also a maniac for mustard, the hotter the better. Imagine that you're five days into a trip and suddenly feel a vague but gnawing hunger that threatens your very sanity. You may well need a quick dose of mustard. Sprinkle a few spices into a cup of cold leftover noodles, potatoes, beans or even rice. Add a good dollop of reconstituted dry mustard (my favorite is Coleman's). If you've got a fresh onion add a teaspoon, well-minced. Stir and set aside for an hour, or, if you must, eat it at once. The carbohydrates will satisfy your craving and the mustard and spices will appease taste buds.

Honey can also be poured on — brace yourself — cold beans or leftover cooked staples. Rice pudding, for example, is nothing but soft-cooked rice with milk, cinnamon and sweetening. Noodles with jam sounds awful but in the privacy of a mountain meadow you might be surprised at what a cheap, satisfying dessert it can make.

Spices, condiments and 'additives' can often be stretched far beyond the normal quantities added to a dish. A pinch will often do where half a teaspoon is called for. This also applies to snack foods. One wonderful mouthful of raisins will flavor an entire pot of oatmeal or garnish a full dish of fried rice. Rice, in fact, makes a great filler for sweet snacks: try mixing cold cooked rice with dried fruit that has been well-minced and softened in boiling hot water (or milk). Drink the sweet fruity broth as a beverage and

mix rice, fruit and honey together, shape into attractive lumps and serve with a dash of cinnamon and/or nutmeg. Call it fruitcake.

Vegetarians Vs. The Wilderness

Lorena was the first person I met from that strange and slightly dotty tribe called Vegetarians. Foods that I had always viewed with suspicion and distrust, if not downright loathing—spinach, brussels sprouts, collard greens, whole wheat flour—she embraced with unrestrained glee and appetite. While I shopped in the meat and potatoes department of the grocery store, Lorena could be found in the nearest health food shop, rummaging through subversive products like torula yeast, Vegex and triticale.

Her frequent admonition, "Don't put any meat in mine!" never failed to cause my rear molars to grind in frustration. Every meal became a confrontation: "How can I possibly cook stew without stew meat?" was answered by, "Just leave out the meat!" Compromise came reluctantly, in the form of double dishes of food identical in all ingredients except for one item: the meat. We had two spaghetti sauces, 'with' and 'without'; two stews, with and without; two omelettes, with and...

The final crunch came at the end of our first long camping trip together, a several week idyll on a Mexican beach. Lorena casually pointed out that I'd almost become a vegetarian, eating only occasional fish and oysters rather than my usual steady fare of hamburger, steaks and the lucky roast or two. Like most people, I considered the word 'vegetarian' to be synonymous with 'health nut' and took offense at the label.

"We've been out here for over a month," Lorena added. "I bet you can't remember the last time you ate meat."

I thought hard. "I had some barbecued chicken on the way south, up by Mazatlán. But that's not *meat*. Chicken is...well, chicken is like fish. It's different, somehow. Chickens don't bleed enough to be meat."

Lorena gave a disgusted laugh and went back to repairing the broken mesh in our hammock. I continued staring into the surf, puzzled. "Was I a latent vegetarian? If fish wasn't meat and chicken was marginal..."

In the years following this scene, Lorena and I came to an agreement, through circumstance and compromise, to be 'practical vegetarians'. (As a basic carnivore, however, I call myself a 'reluctant vegetarian'.) This translates to mean that if our camping trip will be so long and arduous that it requires foraging to maintain good health, she will eat fish and shellfish. This was tested to the limit on a remote Caribbean coast. Our diet of beans and tortillas, with the odd bowl of oatmeal now and then, had to be heavily supplemented by lobster, conch and barracuda.

On the other hand, I now make an effort to eliminate meat from my favorite recipes, reserving it for side dishes. I might fix a stir-fried rice, for example, with a small chunk of broiled meat as a treat for myself—but cooked separately, not mixed into the rice. This took time to adjust to, especially after Lorena informed me that I couldn't stir a vegetarian dish with a meat-greasy spoon or fry eggs in bacon fat.

"Lard isn't meat!" I cried, "It's..."

"Pig fat!" Lorena cut in, adding, "And lay off the chicken bouillon cubes too!"

It is ironic that the very term 'vegetarian' creates an often angry and irrational response from the average person. Eating meat is seen as healthy, balanced and common-sense whereas not eating meat is weird, nutritionally risky and unsatisfying. In the ensuing controversy the following fact is obscured: a vegetarian or near-vegetarian diet is the most practical way to eat while camping. Some simple realities about meat (from a meat lover), are:

• Meat requires refrigeration or processing (canning, smoking, etc.) to be available regularly in the outdoors.

• Meat is expensive when compared to foods such as cheese, nuts, eggs, dried fruit, etc. (I include dairy products and eggs in a vegetarian list of foods though in the strict sense of the term they are animal, not vegetable). Freeze-dried meat is particularly costly and most people report it unsatisfying as a regular food.

• Meat and dishes containing it must be handled carefully to avoid food poisoning, especially in warm weather. I demonstrated this to myself by eating a plateful of leftover meat with noodles on a long hike in the desert. Six hours later I was flat on my back—when I wasn't on my knees, turning my stomach inside out. It took me days to recover my strength. I was lucky to be within close reach of drinking water or the situation could have been very tricky.

What special problems confront vegetarians while camping? Ironically most vegetarians have a much higher awareness and interest in nutrition than the average meat-eater. This gives the vegetarian an advantage, since the nutritional approach to meal planning can be complicated. Balancing proteins, calories and essential amino acids may send you raving to the nearest McDonald's.

An awareness of good nutrition, however, shouldn't be allowed to become a preoccupation. My main complaint with special 'vegetarian meals' I've been served in the outdoors is that the cook attempted to do too much. The dish might be so loaded with highly nutritious ingredients that it comes out heavy and unappetizing, or it will be such a complex recipe that camp conditions make it almost impossible to cook properly. Simple dishes are easier to prepare, more reliable and often more satisfying, day after day, than elaborate concoctions better suited to relaxed preparation at home.

Sudden radical changes in your surroundings (from well lighted kitchens to open-air campsites) can throw even the most reliable cook off the rails. Vegetarians often suffer when suddenly cut off from health food shops and whole foods co-ops. Fresh produce is a staple for most vegetarians — and a luxury for the average camper. Tofu, an excellent meat substitute, does not travel well in a backpack (use a good plastic container, rinse and recover with fresh water daily). The cook who depends on tofu at home may face a vista of endless cheese-based dishes before the trip is over.

A common reaction when familiar cooking routines are disrupted is to fall back heavily on snack foods and munchies. This is acceptable for a short time, but after a few days you'll want something more substantial than whole wheat crackers and cream cheese for breakfast or the ever-present granola bag.

Our advice — whether you are a reluctant, practical or dyed-in-the-wool vegetarian — is to use a little humor in your meal planning.

The recipes in this book lean heavily toward a vegetarian approach to camp cooking, but whenever possible we have indicated variations that can 'lighten' a dish. Pancakes, for example, can be made with all whole wheat flour, wheat germ and soy milk. These will be very nutritional — but to my taste, too heavy. Use half whole wheat and half unbleached white flour and forget the wheat germ and soy milk. Are these pancakes a little too frivolous? Add the wheat germ and try again.

Eating Well: A Balancing Act

If the following discussion of balancing foods and juggling complementary proteins reminds you of a Barnum & Bailey circus, I sympathize.

Keep in mind, however, that most of us balance our diets without thinking about it. An egg sandwich, for example, is a beautiful nutritional blend of grain (the bread), eggs, and fat (the butter or margarine). If you like fancy egg sandwiches, a dab of mayonnaise, a slice of onion and a lettuce leaf expand the meal's food value. So why all the hoopla about nutrition if it's this simple?

There are several reasons why campers should take more than passing interest in the nuts and bolts of good nutrition. An improperly balanced diet is very inefficient. It wastes money and is literally heavier — in pounds of food eaten — than an efficient balanced diet.

Because meat, seafood and many dairy products are luxury items for campers (and for many of us at home) we must learn to eat well without them or use them in very limited quantities. This is easy to do but takes a little thought and planning.

A comment in *Diet for a Small Planet* really brought home to me the advantage of thinking about what we eat while camping. The author noted that two ounces of turkey prepared in a meal of grains, black-eyed peas or peanuts, was equivalent to eating a ten-ounce steak. Turkey and peanuts doesn't drive me wild with anticipation but what about smoked turkey with noodles in a casserole? Noodles are lightweight and inexpensive and two ounces of turkey, even smoked, isn't that expensive. Combinations such as these can be revelations to those who travel light and on a limited budget.

Many people find it difficult to eat well and regularly while camping. It's often a case of 'feast or famine', with a lot of junk food snacking for good measure. This leads to highs and lows in physical energy, in mood and general humor. The wisecrack, "We have to get home in time to recuperate from our vacation," usually comes as a result of over-exercise and under-nourishment.

There can be immediate and subtle long-term benefits in paying more attention to what you eat while camping. What you learn about food in the outdoors can easily be applied to your diet at home. After all, if you have a tasty, balanced menu that is economical and enjoyable while camping, why not expand it to full-time? The recipes in this book represent the basic core of our own diet, whether we're kayaking, van touring, or sitting at home writing a book. Today, for example, we'll be eating homemade whole wheat flour tortillas, noodle-cheese-vegetable casserole and smoked cod. This is identical to many of our camping menus.

Here, then, are some basic facts about nutrition that should make it easier for you to plan your menu. For more detail I strongly suggest that you consult one or more of the source books listed in the Appendices under *Recommended Reading*.

Good Common Sense Nutrition in a Nutshell

Energy and Food: The food energy that fuels our bodies is measured in terms of calories. In order for calories to be burned up, rather than excreted or converted to a spare tire around your middle, other nutrients are also needed. Of these, B vitamins are very important. There are three major sources of calories:

Carbohydrates (sugars of all types and starches)

Fats (butter, oil, margarine and others)

Proteins (meat, seafood, dairy products, vegetables, grains, etc.)

Carbohydrates are the body's major fuel source. They are quickly converted to energy. Highly processed foods, in fact, are too quickly converted (or stored) to be really beneficial. Junk foods are often called 'empty calorie' foods. They are high in calories but too low in real nutrients to be efficiently converted to anything but fat and a quick sugar 'high'.

Unrefined sources of carbohydrates (such as whole wheat bread) burn slower and give sustained energy. Fats and proteins also slow down the digestion of carbohydrates, allowing them to be used more efficiently.

Fats are what I call 'fun foods': anything dripping with butter, especially cheese sandwiches or tacos. Fats give about twice as much energy per ounce as carbohydrates and proteins. They can also be stored, as you may regret if you are storing more than your share and can't squeeze into last year's shirt.

Fats are satisfying to eat because they tend to slow down digestion, leaving us with a contented, full feeling. But we eat too much fat: One to three tablespoons of polyunsaturated oil a day (unrefined safflower is best) is all we need. If you prefer margarine, it should have liquid oil as its main ingredient. No wonder so many people are overfattened.

Protein is what the body is made of, our basic muscles, tissues, organs and assorted 'innards'. Proteins themselves are made of amino acids. If a food has all of the essential amino acids we need to sustain ourselves, it is called a 'complete food' or 'complete protein'. Natural sources of complete proteins are limited: meat, fish, dairy products and soybeans. A 'balanced diet' is a matter of matching up incomplete protein foods in dishes or combinations that make complete proteins—while also being tasty and appealing. Our turkey and peanuts, for example, has limited appeal but is nutritionally balanced.

Balancing proteins isn't difficult. Food groups that complement each other (balance out proteins) are:

Grains with .... eggs and dairy products
legumes (beans, peas, etc.)
meat

Legumes with ...... eggs, dairy products
grains, nuts
meat

Vegetables with .... eggs, dairy products
grains (especially rice and millet)
seeds and nuts (especially sesame, brazil)

Remember: By themselves, meat, seafood, dairy products and soybeans are already complete and balanced.

How Much Food Energy?

The crux of the matter, especially for those who will be travelling far or working quite hard, is how much food do we need and just how little can we get by on safely? And second, how in blazes do we measure all these things?

Let's take the second question first, since it is the easiest to answer. Lorena and I use what we call the 'Backhanded' approach to nutrition and meal planning. Look at a respected diet book (not a faddish Top Ten bestseller). Make a list of foods that overweight people are warned away from. These will be good foods for camping (with such obvious exceptions as junk foods) — dense with calories and nutrients.

My favorite aid to nutrition is a fifty-cent booklet commonly known as a 'Calorie Counter'. Run down the calorie, protein, fat and carbohydrate columns quickly, looking for relatively high figures. Eliminate junk and highly refined foods and you're well on your way to recognizing foods that are 'nutritionally dense'. If you're low on money, scratch out the expensive items and you've got a basic shopping list.

See our *Meal Planning and Nutrition Table* at the end of this chapter. Books listed in *Recommended Reading* also provide detailed (often to the point of stupefaction) tables of food content.

Back then, to how much food, how many calories, how many grams of fat, protein and carbohydrates? Here are some suggestions, taken from several respected sources listed in the Appendices:

Suggested Daily Calorie Intake

To maintain only:

Men under 45 years ... 11 calories per pound of body weight
Women under 45 years 10 calories per pound of body weight
Men over 45 years .... 10 calories per pound of body weight
Women over 45 years .. 9 calories per pound of body weight

For normal exercise and activity, increase your basic maintenance calorie figure by 50%.

For light exercise, increase the new total by 10-20%.

For medium exercise, increase by 30%.

For heavy exercise, increase by 50-75%.

Using myself as an example: body weight for under 45 years of age: 160 x 11 = 1760 calories a day just to stay alive and reasonably happy. If I held my intake to 1760 and exercised, I'd lose weight slowly but steadily. This, in fact, is the key to sane dieting.

For normal activity, however, I increase my intake: 1760 + 50% (880) = 2640 calories a day. Adding another 10% for such light exercise as walking gives me about 2900 calories a day, for medium exercise — backpacking — about 3432 (2640 + 30% or 792 calories), and for heavy stuff such as ocean kayaking or climbing: 2640 + 50% (1320) = 3,960 calories a day.

One of the ironies or hazards of increasing your calorie intake while camping is that you soon become used to eating more than normal. During a six month combined kayaking and beach camping expedition, I developed an appetite as awesome as a white shark's — and trimmed down to 142 pounds at the same time. Within three months of returning home, without restraining myself or counting calories, I quickly shot up to 168 pounds. At that point I realized that my high energy camping diet was much too rich for my low energy writer's routine.

Because most people are at least slightly overweight to begin with, I'd go easy on the extra calories while camping. Don't short yourself, however, in a frenzied attempt to lose weight in the outdoors. Slimming takes time and a combination of too few calories and heavy exertion can be dangerous to your health.

In addition to counting calories it is very important to calculate your intake of protein.

Protein Intake:

Multiply body weight times .36 grams (mine is 160 pounds × .36 = 57.6 grams a day, or about 2 ounces).

As you increase your rate of exercise, increase your intake of protein and fats in proportion to carbohydrates. Again, this measure provides steadier, prolonged energy. Because proteins and fats take longer to digest, however, they should be taken in relatively small quantities throughout the day. 'Pigging out' is a very inefficient way to fuel your body; steady snacking is much better for you in all respects.

Nutritional Supplements and Vitamins

Our balancing act hasn't yet taken into account such vital factors as minerals and vitamins. I'm not going to suggest that you round out each meal with a fistful of pills and capsules, but the fact is most of us don't get all the minerals and vitamins we need for peak health. The following suggestions are simple, economical and shouldn't cause your friends to tease you for being a 'health nut'.

B Vitamins: Brewer's yeast and torula yeast are highly concentrated sources of these essential vitamins. Yeast can be hidden in all types of dishes, from soups and gravies to bread and beverages. It is said that a high intake of B vitamins makes the body less attractive to mosquitoes. Yeast is very lightweight and keeps well—two more good reasons to use it.

Vitamin C: Powdered vitamin C is sold in health food shops. It is much cheaper than capsules or pills and can be dissolved easily in water or juice. Vitamins C and B are water soluble and daily doses will replace vitamins flushed out by the body. This flushing also prevents toxic build-up, which can be a problem with Vitamins A, D, E and K.

Vitamin A is good for eyestrain, a common problem while camping and boating.

Vitamin E and **granular lecithin** combine with food to help it burn more efficiently. Vitamin E is widely held to promote healing.

Vitamin D, the so-called Sunshine Vitamin, is one that we who live in the Northwest should take regularly, for lack of the real thing.

Minerals of all types are vital to the body. Vegetable broth and powdered kelp are good mineral sources and both blend well in cooked dishes. Vegetable broth is also an excellent salt substitute.

Salt is getting a bad reputation but if you exert yourself heavily, especially in warm weather, you must have plenty of salt. Symptoms of salt deficiency are easy to recognize: dull headache, nausea, weakness, muscle cramps and a general rotten feeling. Sip seawater, dissolved salt or swallow salt tablets.

Calcium is very good for cramps of all types, from muscle spasms to menstrual cramps. (See *Camp Kitchen Skills: Staying Healthy*.)

A Typical Daily Menu

One of the greatest hazards of careful, methodical meal planning is that the cook will suffer from preparation overload and disappear screaming into the bushes, leaving friends and family to pry open cans of noodle soup and boxes of saltines for dinner.

Where do you start, or better yet, where and when do you *stop* planning meals and actually begin shopping, packing up and cooking? Right now or at whatever point your mind begins to boggle at factors such as nutritional value, weight, bulk, packaging, perishability, cost, economy... *Remember*, you're going camping, not on a one-way trip to the stars.

Day One

The next step, now that we've cleared the air and relaxed a bit, is to decide what to have for breakfast on Day One. Eggs are my favorite choice. Eggs can be carried whole, in the shell, or cracked into a sturdy container. If the weather is cool I'll simplify meal planning by eating eggs for as many consecutive breakfasts as is practical. Eggs are not boring, especially if you play around with omelettes, egg sandwiches and other fireside concoctions.

If variety is important or the eggs run out, there's always granola, cooked cereals and pancakes.

Lunch is a meal I hate to cook. Long lunch breaks on the trail tend to turn into early camps for the night. While driving or boating, preparing a hot lunch often means a major re-shuffle of gear, stove and the inevitable piles of disorganized odds and ends. Lunch in our camps tends, therefore, to be leftovers or a rather lavish snack. Cold salads (with vegetables, beans, macaroni, potatoes or grains) are nice.

Whatever your choice of food for lunch may be, don't allow it to go by unnoticed just because you're behind schedule or are too tired to dig into the food containers. Skipping lunch can bring on a bad case of the 'droops' that will only get worse as the day progresses.

Lunch can also be spread out over a period of several hours, as a series of small snacks. This is not only energy-sustaining but cuts down on the cook's chores and dishwashing.

Supper is our largest and most lavish camp meal, though from a strictly nutritional standpoint we'd be better off eating more at breakfast and less later in the day. The fact is, however, that we just can't break the late meal habit, though we compromise by trying to eat before sundown. After we've been out for a few days we use dinner leftovers for breakfast. This reduces time spent cooking and insures a hearty morning meal.

My favorite supper, whether we're hiking, kayaking or van camping, is a one-pot noodle dish. It is quick to prepare, hearty and quite nourishing. Novices will find that noodles are much easier to do well *consistently* than almost any other main dish food.

Well, you've planned Day One and now face Day Two, Three, Four...At this point you might be tempted to just repeat Day One for as long as you can bear it. It is true that hunger is your best defense against boredom with what you eat. Anyone who has done a 30 or 60-day camping trip can testify that *any* meal looks and tastes great after weeks in the outdoors. If you feel inclined to expand your menu, however, look at the *Recipe* chapter in this book. There are enough variations there to keep you going for quite a long time.

How much is enough?

Most people worry too much about running out of food while camping. This leads to extra bits and pieces of food that soon add up to a considerable surplus. I am guilty of this myself and have rarely made a camping trip without carrying home some extra food. Although you expect to have a raging appetite in the outdoors, in reality you'll often be too tired to cook everything you'd planned so carefully at home.

A dinner of spaghetti, cooked dried vegetables, pudding and bread sounds great as you write out the menu in the comfort of your favorite easy chair, with a 100-watt bulb lighting the page and a calculator at hand to add up the food value of the meal. But in the woods, with a flashlight stuffed in your mouth and wind stinging your face, you might suddenly realize that barely warmed up spaghetti and bread will do just fine, and save the rest for a better day.

"Can't somebody finish this off?" is a familiar plea from a camp cook who has prepared too much food and is faced with leftovers or force-feeding. Most people over-eat, both at home and while camping, so don't feel guilty if the bottom of the pan is licked clean before everyone is totally gorged.

We plan on one large meal a day, a second more modest meal (usually breakfast or lunch) and a steady rate of in-between snacking. 'Three squares' a day in the outdoors leaves you forty-five minutes of daylight for hiking, kayaking, fishing or photographing your favorite leaves and stumps.

Portion Control

'Portion control' is very difficult to achieve, especially under the wildly varying conditions that exist on most of our camping trips. One day I'm 'sort of hungry' and prepare half a cup of rice; the next day I'm 'mildly famished' and double the ration of noodles. The only solution is to plan for the average. If the average isn't quite enough or just a bit too generous, you've learned a lesson that can be applied to your next meal planning session. If a picture is worth 1,000 words, then a simple mistake (and 'mistake' is really too harsh) rates at least half a chapter of any advice we can offer.

Inventory your food.

No matter what your approach to meal planning, keep a detailed inventory of the foods you take with you. This will be your most valuable tool toward refining your provisioning skills. We have a file of old lists, faded, sweat-stained and some nearly illegible, dating back to almost-forgotten hikes in Mexico and boat trips to British Columbia. These lists include a post-trip section listing leftover and undesirable foods as well as things we wished we had more of.

These records, as haphazard as they may be, show clear trends in our eating that might otherwise be overlooked. We may note, for example, that we took too much rice. The next time we plan a trip we'll ease up on the rice supply. No cookbook or friend can give us this sort of practical information since it reflects *our* eating habits.

Lorena and I spent three full days assembling, sorting, weighing and listing the provisions for a 15-day boat trip. This was our most fanatical meal planning session to date and left me feeling as though I'd undergone electro-shock therapy.

We hoped to supplement our diet heavily with foraged food, mainly seafood, and that made it especially difficult to anticipate the quantities of staples we'd need. What if the fishing were poor? What if one of us was hurt or sick and we had to hole up? These were questions that couldn't be answered in advance — but questions that also seemed to urge us to take more food.

When our final 15-day list was completed we loaded the provisions into string bags. A fish-weighing scale quickly told us the sad news: our total was about 33 pounds (from noodles and flour to soy sauce, spices, cheese, etc.) Dividing this by 15 days and adding in the seafood we expected to forage told us we had too much. It even *looked* like too much. (I always rely somewhat on 'gut feelings' when planning a menu.)

We decided to reduce our larder by one third, down to 22 pounds. Since spices and condiments don't weigh all that much to begin with, our efforts focused on the bigger bags: rice, beans, flour, honey and even coffee. It took another full day of tearing our hair but we pared it down.

Two weeks later, after a very enjoyable trip, we returned to our starting point and inventoried our leftovers. Although we'd run out of a few things, especially beverages, and could have used more beans and flour, there was enough food remaining to scratch by for another week. We dug out our original inventory, noted the changes and scratched out the heading "For Two Weeks" and made it "Three Weeks". We now had a realistic and well-tested inventory that could be used as the basis for meal planning for other boat trips as well as hiking and van excursions.

Open Larder or Pre-packaged Portions

There are two basic approaches to packing and storing the food for your camping trip: the pre-measured and packaged meal method and the 'open larder' method. The former smacks of careful planning and organization, the latter of a less rigid, improvizational eating style. As you might have already guessed, we go almost entirely with the open larder approach.

There are several reasons why we prefer the larder method, not the least of which is that it's less work than meticulously anticipating what your every bite will be while camping. The open larder method allows you to improvise and vary the ingredients in a recipe. It also makes it simple to adjust the quantity of food you eat from one meal to the next.

Our experience has shown that an open larder approach helps stretch food supplies, especially when it is possible to forage for fish, seafood or berries. Flour that might have been loosely intended for pancakes can become batter for frying, the crust of a simple pie or the gravy to pour over a baked fish.

While kayaking long distances in Baja with little chance of replenishing our food stocks, we became very miserly as our 'cupboards' grew more and more bare. To conserve food, Lorena would periodically inventory our provisions and then allot certain amounts from our reserve food bags to replenish our 'kitchen bags'. The kitchen bags were for immediate, day-to-day cooking. This gave us a very clear picture of how much food we were eating and how much — or little — we had left.

When it became obvious that our food wouldn't last out the trip, we immediately increased our seafood foraging. The day would often begin with a meal of leftover grilled fish or several lobster tails (this was true suffering!), a couple of big flour tortillas and a small glob of honey. Lunch would be more cold cooked seafood, a bit of dried fruit, nuts and a tortilla. Dinner was a miserly portion of noodles, rice or beans with tortillas, seafood again and a few teaspoons of dried vegetables and cheese. In this situation, pre-planning and packaging our meals would have been impractical and inconvenient.

Weights & Measures

Short cuts to meal planning can be as elusive and treacherous as the Northwest Passage. Whenever Lorena says, "I've worked out an interesting system of meal planning" I know that at the least it will involve Numerology, Astrology and/or Pyramid Power. Such theories must, of course, be field tested and it was a recent 'breakthrough in meal planning' that sent us into a remote Oregon wilderness carrying 24 small pecan pies. On our backs. In retrospect this sounds ridiculous but some blinding logic sent us up the trail with those pies. At the end of the day, I lay helpless in the tent, racked by severe muscle spasms in my lower back and steadfastly refusing to eat any of the cursed pastries. I resolved to find a genuine shortcut to provisioning for the outdoors.

Meal Planning by Measuring Cups

If you don't have a set of measuring cups, use glass jars or tin cans of a known volume. To backtrack one step, let's assume that you haven't yet bought the food for your trip and will be shopping in a bulk foods co-op. Look at the recipes in this book and others to decide what basic meals you'll be eating. Jot down a list of their main ingredients and a multiplier number to indicate how many times this dish will be repeated. A typical entry might look like this:

1 cup dry noodles x 3 meals = 3 cups dry noodles

Take your measuring cup or container to the co-op, dip out three cups of noodles (elbow noodles fit into cups and small containers easily) and you're on your way. Repeat this with cereals, granola, dried fruit, etc.

Measuring spoons are better than cups for small things like herbs, spices and dried vegetables. If your trip will be long, check the *Meal Planning and Nutrition Table* at the end of this chapter to get an idea of how many cups of instant coffee can be made from half a cup of crystals, how many tablespoons of oil are in a pint and so on. "Oh, the hell with it, it's not that important!" holds true only if you have unlimited carrying power. It all adds up, usually much faster than you'd have believed possible.

For those who shop at regular stores and must buy packaged foods, the *Table* will give you an idea of how many cups of a staple food are in a pound. Before you visit the store, calculate portions by cups and convert this to pounds. When you get home again and begin sorting and re-packaging, you might want to double check your measurements.

If you've never cooked while camping or plan a long trip, I heartily recommend that you actually test recipes and portions at home. No recipe can anticipate every person's appetite and taste preferences. If a half cup of dry rice looks like enough to stuff a horse when cooked up, you'll probably be able to get by with a quarter cup per meal.

Scales can be very useful for meal planning, especially when used in combination with measuring cups, spoons and our *Table*. Dieter's scales are sold in drug and discount stores. Most go up to a pound or two, since they are used for small portions of food. For larger weights we use a fish scale, commonly called a 'de-liar'. These come in various sizes and qualities but even the cheap ones are surprisingly accurate.

As you measure and weigh out your foods, try to keep a clear detailed list for later reference. This will save you a lot of work when meal planning for future trips. Once you know that half a cup of dried kumquats weighs X number of ounces or grams and will serve Y number of people you'll never have to calculate the basic weight and measure for that particular food again.

Some people go so far as weighing entire meals and can mentally calculate the dry weight of a recipe at a glance. Such skill takes time to develop but it pays big dividends when preparing for a camping trip, especially on short notice.

Pre-Packaging

Your food will have to be packaged and re-packaged, depending on where you bought it and how much you'll be taking camping. We tend to put foods into as few containers as possible. This is the 'open larder' method again and requires re-measuring of the foods as they are used. The pros-and-cons of putting each meal's ingredients into separate bags have already been discussed but our own experience has shown that the open larder generally works best for long trips and for more experienced cooks.

Pre-mixing ingredients can reduce your containers and save work in camp. A dried lentil stew, for example, can be prepared at home with your own blend of dried vegetables and spices. Again, it is best to carefully test home-mixed ingredients to be absolutely certain you haven't made some error. What if you get a queasy stomach and decide that the soup would taste better without garlic and black pepper? My preference is to prepare dishes 'from scratch' but this does take more time and concentration.

Meal and Nutrition Table

In compiling this table (which gave two people gray hair), we noted discrepancies between figures given by different sources. Rather than cut it too fine, we have rounded off some figures and accepted contradictions. A pound of flour, for example, can yield 4 cups one day and 3½ the next. It all depends: on the humidity, the texture of the flour (settling reduces volume) and who does the measuring. When planning a long trip and large quantities, try to sample each food by weight and volume, then make your provisioning inventory based on your own figures, not ours.

In converting from ounces and pounds to grams we have rounded off the figures to avoid complicated fractions. One ounce actually equals 28.35 grams. We have used 28 grams for convenience.

(continued overleaf)

Food Comparison Table

Food	Measure	Weight	Calories	Grams Protein	Fat	Carbo-hydrates
Beans						
Beans, pinto, dry	1 cup	190g/6.75 oz.	663	44	2.3	120
cooked	1 cup	95g/3.4 oz	330	22	1.1	61

Remarks: Beans double (or more) when cooked. ½ cup dry beans = 1 cup cooked = 2 modest portions. 1 pound dry beans = 2 1/3 dry cups = 6 cups cooked. 1 quart dry beans = 1.7 pounds; 1 gallon dry beans = almost 7 pounds.

Food	Measure	Weight	Calories	Protein	Fat	Carbo-hydrates
Peas, split, dry	1 cup	200g/7 oz.	696	48	2.0	120
cooked	1 cup	200g/7 oz.	230	16	.6	42

Remarks: Split peas and lentils triple in volume when cooked. 1 pound dry = 2¼ dry cups = about 7 cooked cups or 12 to 14 modest servings. A cup of cooked peas or lentils will make 2 to 3 cups of soup or stew.

Food	Measure	Weight	Calories	Protein	Fat	Carbo-hydrates
Soy protein, dry		28g/1 oz.	90	21	trace	4.0
Tofu, soybean		100g/3.5 oz.	72	7.8	4.2	2.4
curd		454g/16 oz.	327	35.4	19.1	10.9
Grains						
Flour, white, en-riched, sifted	1 Tbsp	8g/.3 oz.	29	.8	.1	6.1
	1 cup	110g/4 oz.	400	11.6	1.1	84
Flour, wholewheat	1 cup	120g/4.3 oz.	400	16	2.4	85
	3¾-4 cups	454g/16 oz.	1510	60.3	9.1	322
Flour, soybean, high fat	1 cup	100g/3.5 oz.	356	43.4	6.7	36.6

Remarks: Sifting fluffs up flour. Flour can be compacted in strong storage containers. 1 pound sifted flour = 1 quart. 5 pounds unsifted = 1 gallon.

Food	Measure	Weight	Calories	Protein	Fat	Carbo-hydrates
Bread, white	1 slice	23g/.8 oz.	62	2.0	.7	11.6
Bread, wholewheat	1 slice	23g/.8 oz.	56	2.0	.7	11.0

Remarks: Whole wheat flour and bread has more vitamins and minerals, plus fiber, than white.

Food	Measure	Weight	Calories	Protein	Fat	Carbo-hydrates
Gravy, brown, homemade	4 Tbsp	72g/2.5 oz.	164	1.2	14	8.0

Food	Measure	Weight	Calories	Protein	Fat	Carbo-hydrates
Rice, white, raw						
enriched	1 cup	191g/6.75 oz.	692	14	.8	150
cooked	1 cup	150g/5.4 oz.	164	3.0	.2	36
Rice, brown, raw, short grain	1 cup	200g/7 oz.	720	15	3.8	150
cooked	1 cup	150g/5.4 oz.	178	3.8	.9	38

Remarks: Brown rice is richer in vitamins than white rice. Short grain brown rice cooks better than long grain. 1 pound dry rice = 2⅛ dry cups = 10 cooked cups. 1 cup dry rice = 3½ cups cooked or 6 servings.

Food	Measure	Weight	Calories	Protein	Fat	Carbo-hydrates
Noodles, enriched,						
raw	1 cup	110g/4 oz.	405	13.7	1.3	83
cooked	1 cup	140g/5 oz.	207	7.0	.7	42

Remarks: 1 pound of 1 inch macaroni = 3½ to 4 dry cups = 10 cooked cups. 1 cup raw = 2 to 3 cooked cups or about 4 servings.

Food	Measure	Weight	Calories	Protein	Fat	Carbo-hydrates
Bulgur wheat, raw	½ cup	112g/4 oz.	396	12.4	1.6	84.8

Remarks: ½ cup raw bulgur can be cooked with 1 or 2 cups water to yield about 4 servings. The more water used, the thicker and heavier the cooked bulgur will be. Bulgur is *very* compact.

Food	Measure	Weight	Calories	Grams		
				Protein	Fat	Carbo-hydrates
Oats, rolled, dry	1/3 cup	28g/1 oz.	111	4.0	2.1	19.3
cooked	1 cup	236g/8.5 oz.	148	5.4	2.8	26

Remarks: 1 cup dry oatmeal = 4 cups cooked. 1 pound = 5 dry cups = 20 cooked cups.

Food	Measure	Weight	Calories	Protein	Fat	Carbo-hydrates
Granola, Pillsbury	½ cup	56g/2 oz.	240	6.0	8.0	38
High Protein Granola (Laurel's Kitchen, page 115)	½ cup	56g/2 oz.	244	9.6	13.2	26

Remarks: Commercial granolas run heavily to oats, an inexpensive grain.

Food	Measure	Weight	Calories	Protein	Fat	Carbo-hydrates
Grape Nuts	½ cup	56g/2 oz.	200	7.4	.6	46

Dairy Products, Fats and Oils

Food	Measure	Weight	Calories	Protein	Fat	Carbo-hydrates
Milk, whole, dry, instant	1 Tbsp	7g/.25 oz.	35	1.8	1.9	2.7
	1 cup	100g/3.5 oz.	499	26.3	26.8	38.2
Milk, whole, dry, regular	3¼ cups	454g/16 oz.	2227	120	125	173

Remarks: 2 to 3 Tbsp regular dry milk + 1 cup water = 1 cup fresh milk. 4 to 5 Tbsp instant dry milk + 1 cup water = 1 cup fresh milk. 16 oz. of either regular or instant dry milk makes about 30 cups of fresh milk but instant is bulkier (5 ¾ dry cups per pound) than regular (3 ¼ cups). Dry milk can be compressed in strong containers to save space.

Food	Measure	Weight	Calories	Protein	Fat	Carbo-hydrates
Creamer, non-dairy	1 tsp	2g/.07 oz.	11	.1	.7	1.1
		454g/16 oz.	2497	22.7	159	250

Food	Measure	Weight	Calories	Protein	Fat	Carbo-hydrates
Cheese, cheddar		28g/1 oz.	112	7.0	9.1	.6
		454g/16 oz.	1792	112	146	9.6

Remarks: 4 oz. of most soft cheeses is a piece just slightly smaller than a cube of butter. 4 oz. = 1 generous cup of shredded cheese. 2 oz. will make a sandwich.

Food	Measure	Weight	Calories	Protein	Fat	Carbo-hydrates
Cheese, Parmesan, grated	1 Tbsp	5g/.2 oz.	23	2.1	1.5	.2
		454g/16 oz.	1783	163	118	13.2

Remarks: 2 ounces hard Parmesan = 11 Tbsps grated = ¾ cup.

Food	Measure	Weight	Calories	Protein	Fat	Carbo-hydrates
Yogurt, whole milk	1 cup	246g/9 oz.	153	7.4	8.4	12.1
Butter	1 Tbsp	14g/.5 oz.	108	.1	12.2	trace
	1 cup	227g/8.1 oz.	1625	1.4	184	.9

Remarks: 2 cups of butter or margarine = 1 pound = 4 sticks. 1 stick = 1 cup = ¼ pound = 8 Tbsp.

Food	Measure	Weight	Calories	Protein	Fat	Carbo-hydrates
Margarine	1 Tbsp	14g/.5 oz.	120	0	14	0
	2 cups	454/16 oz.	3840	0	448	0
Oil, safflower, soy-bean, sesame, cotton-seed	1 Tbsp	14g/.5 oz.	120	0	14	0
	1 cup	218g/7.8 oz.	1927	0	220	0

Remarks: Values for other oils will be slightly lower. 1 pound of oil = 2⅛ to 2½ cups.

Food	Measure	Weight	Calories	Protein	Fat	Carbo-hydrates
Eggs, fresh, large	1 egg	54g/2 oz.	88	7.0	6.2	.5
Eggs, dried, whole	2 Tbsp	14g/.5 oz.	82	6.6	5.8	.6

Remarks: 1 dozen extra large eggs = 756g/27 oz.; 12 medium eggs = 588g/21 oz. Egg shells account for about 12% of total weight.
2 Tbsp dried egg + 2 Tbsp water = 1 fresh egg. 6 ounces dry egg = 1½ dry cups. 1½ dry cups + 1⅞ cups water = 12 fresh eggs.

Meat and Seafoods: Ready to Eat

Food	Measure	Weight	Calories	Protein	Fat	Carbo-hydrates
Beef jerky		10g/.4 oz.	38	4.2	1.7	1.4
		454g/16 oz.	1725	191	77	63.5

Food	Measure	Weight	Calories	Grams		
				Protein	Fat	Carbo-hydrates
Beef, corned, canned	1 slice	28g/1 oz.	60	7.1	3.4	0
		454g/16 oz.	960	114	54.4	0
Beef, dried, chipped	2 thin slices	28g/1 oz.	57	9.6	1.8	0
		454g/16 oz.	912	154	28.8	0
Caviar, canned, pressed	1 round tsp	10g/.4 oz.	32	3.4	1.7	.5
Salmon, smoked		56g/2 oz.	100	12.3	5.3	0
		454g/16 oz.	798	98	42.2	0
Salmon, pink, canned with liquid		114g/4 oz.	161	23.4	6.7	0
Sardines, canned in oil, drained		85g/3 oz.	173	20.4	9.4	0
Tuna, canned in water with liquid		114g/4 oz.	144	31.8	.9	0
Vegetables						
Carrots, dehydrated		100g/3.5 oz.	341	6.6	1.3	81
		454g/16 oz.	1547	30	5.9	368
Onions, dried, flakes	½ cup	32g/1.1 oz.	112	2.8	.4	2.6
	8-9 cups	454/16 oz.	1588	39.5	5.9	372
Potatoes, dried, flakes	4½ cups	454g/16 oz.	1651	32.7	2.7	381
reconstituted and mashed	1 cup	210g/7.5 oz.	166	4.2	4.6	27.5
Remarks: 1 cup dehydrated flakes = 100g/3.5 oz.; 4¾ cups cubes = 1 pound; 1 cup granules = 200g/7 oz.						
Sprouts, fresh, Mung bean	1 cup	60g/2.2 oz.	21	2.3	.1	4.0
Fruit						
Apples, dried, raw	1 cup or 15-20 slices	85g/3 oz.	234	.9	1.4	61
	5½-6 cups	454g/16 oz.	1247	4.5	7.3	326
Remarks: Dehydrated apples have about 3% moisture content and dried apples about 30%. Food values run 20 to 30% higher for dehydrated apples.						
Banana flakes, dry dehydrated and flour	½ cup	50g/1.75 oz.	170	2.0	.5	44.5
		454g/16 oz.	1542	20	3.6	402
Dates, dried, pitted	10 medium	80g/2.9 oz.	219	1.8	.4	58
	1 cup	178g/6.4 oz.	488	3.9	.9	130
	2½-2¾ cups	454g/16 oz.	1243	10	2.3	331
Remarks: 1 pound of figs = 2¾ cups; 1 pound of prunes = 2 1/3 cups.						
Raisins, seedless	3 Tbsp	28g/1 oz.	80	.8	trace	22
	1 cup	145g/5.2 oz.	419	3.6	trace	110
Remarks: 1 pound of raisins = 2½ to 3 cups, uncooked.						
Nuts, Seeds, Peanuts and Popcorn						
Peanut butter	1 Tbsp	16g/.6 oz.	93	4.4	7.9	3
	1 cup	258g/9.2 oz.	1490	72	130	44
Remarks: 1 pound of peanut butter = 1¾ cups.						

| Food | Measure | Weight | Calories | Grams | | |
				Protein	Fat	Carbo-hydrates
Peanuts, roasted, with	1 Tbsp	9g/.3 oz.	52	2.4	4.5	2.0
skins, chopped	1 cup	144g/5.1 oz.	838	38	72	30

Remarks: Peanuts are legumes (like beans, peas), not nuts. 1 pound in shell = 2¼ cups of nut meats.

Food	Measure	Weight	Calories	Protein	Fat	Carbo-hydrates
Cashews, roasted	26 small nuts	28g/1 oz.	159	4.9	13	8
	1 cup	140g/5 oz.	785	24	64	41
	3¼ cups	454g/16 oz.	2545	78	207	133
Sunflower seeds, shelled, kernels	2 Tbsp	18g/.6 oz.	102	4.4	8.6	4
	1 cup	145g/5.1 oz.	812	35	69	29
Sesame seeds, unhulled	2 Tbsp	18g/.6 oz.	101	3.3	8.8	4
	1 cup	145g/5.1 oz.	816	27	71	31
Popcorn, popped, plain	1 cup	14g/.5 oz.	54	1.8	.7	10.7
unpopped	1 cup	196g/7 oz.				

Remarks: ½ cup of kernels gives 14-16 cups of popcorn.

Beverages

Coffee ground: No appreciable food value but sure tastes good. 4 Tbsps dry grounds = 1 ounce =¼ dry cup. 1 pound of grounds yields about 64 Tbsps.

Instant: 1 tsp = 2 grams or .07 oz.; ½ cup = 28g/1 oz. Instant coffee can be greatly compressed by gentle grinding, crushing or blending.

Postum, cereal beverages	1 tsp = 3 grams and 1 cup = 5-6 oz.					
Teas	Most teas weigh about equal to ground coffee, measure-for-measure.					
Yeast, brewer's, debittered, powdered	¼ cup	33g/1.2 oz.	91	13	trace	12

Sweets and Munchies

Food	Measure	Weight	Calories	Protein	Fat	Carbo-hydrates
Honey	1 Tbsp	21g/.75 oz.	64	trace	0	17.3
	1 cup	338g/12 oz.	1034	.7	0	264
Sugar, white	1 Tbsp	11g/.4 oz.	46	0	0	12
	1 cup	200g/7 oz.	770	0	0	200

Remarks: 1 pound of sugar = 2½ cups or 2 cups of superfine sugar.

Food	Measure	Weight	Calories	Protein	Fat	Carbo-hydrates
Jam, all types	1 Tbsp	20g/.75 oz.	55	.1	.1	14.2

Remarks: 1 pint of jam = 1½ pounds.

Food	Measure	Weight	Calories	Protein	Fat	Carbo-hydrates
Chocolate bar (Hershey, plain)	1 bar	58g/2 oz.	302	4.7	19.4	32.4
Tiger's Milk Bar, Carob-Coated	1 bar	56g/2 oz.	250	9.0	8.0	35
Granola Bar, Nature Valley, Coconut	1 bar	24g/.86 oz.	122	2.0	6.1	15.2
Breakfast Bar, Carnation, Peanut Butter	1 bar	43g/1.5 oz.	205	6.0	11	22

Odds and Ends

Liquids, whole grains, legumes: 1 pint = 2 cups = 16 oz. = 454 g
1 cup molasses (blackstrap) = 12 oz. = 336 g
1 cup cane molasses = 8 oz. = 224 g
1 cup maple syrup = 8 oz. = 224 g
1 cup dried apricots = 4 oz.
1 cup prunes with pits = 6-7 oz.
5 cups shredded coconut = 1 pound
2 2/3 cup carob flour = 1 pound
1 oz. salt = 2⅜ Tbsp
1 pound salt = 2⅜ cups
1 oz. of Baking Soda = 2 Tbsp
1 Sierra cup = 10 ounces = 280 g = 1¼ measuring cups
4 oz. powdered milk + 1 quart water = 1 quart milk
1 pound powdered milk + 4 quarts water = 1 gallon fresh milk
2 cups evaporated milk + 2 cups water = 1 quart whole milk
1 pound walnuts in shells = 1 2/3 cups nutmeat
1 Tbsp Baking Yeast = 1 package or cake of yeast

Weights and Measures - Liquid

1 tsp	=	60 drops			=	5 g
3 tsp	=	1 Tbsp	=	1/2 oz	=	14 g
2 Tbsp	=	1/8 c	=	1 oz	=	28 g
4 Tbsp	=	1/4 c	=	2 oz	=	56 g
5 Tbsp + 1 tsp	=	1/3 c	=	2 1/2 oz	=	76 g
8 Tbsp	=	1/2 c	=	4 oz	=	114 g
10 Tbsp + 2 tsp	=	2/3 c	=	5 1/3 oz	=	151 g
12 Tbsp	=	3/4 c	=	6 oz	=	170 g
16 Tbsp	=	1 c	=	8 oz	=	227 g
1 c	=	1/2 pt	=	8 oz	=	227 g
2 c	=	1 pt	=	16 oz	=	454 g
4 c	=	1 qt	=	32 oz	=	908 g
4 qt	=	1 gal	=	8 lb	=	16 c

c	=	cup	oz	=	ounce	gal	=	gallon
tsp	=	teaspoon	pt	=	pint	lb	=	pound
Tbsp	=	tablespoon	qt	=	quart	g	=	grams

Chapter 2
Shopping & Provisioning

Although I love to cook and eat I've never been able to dredge up much enthusiasm for food shopping. As soon as I enter a supermarket I fall under the influence of every known merchandising trick, reeling from one food display to the next like a drug addict running amok in a pharmacy. Often I can be found in the produce department, usually near the mushrooms, turning slowly in circles, repeating "toilet paper yogurt aluminum foil pinto beans..." as I mindlessly fold and refold a tattered and illegible list.

The importance of careful shopping is perhaps best appreciated when things go wrong and careful organization and pre-trip planning fall into mindless chaos. I shudder to think how many 'last minute stops' at a store before embarking on an overnight hike have created loads that would drop a Himalayan Sherpa to his knees.

A shopping style can be as distinct as a person's style of cooking. Lorena, for example, follows 'List plus 25%'. If we need one pound of rice she buys a pound and a quarter. "We may run out!" is her standard justification for over-stocking. If I respond, "But we never run out," her answer is automatic: "That's because I always get enough." Obviously it is up to me to trim 25% off the list before she reaches the shelves.

My own shopping style has been compared to one of Fidel Castro's epic speeches: I begin with a carefully prepared 'text' (my list), ticking off item after item, until I am gripped by sudden inspiration and begin an endless ad-libbing: "Anchovy paste! Why didn't I think of it! Freeze-dried macadamia nuts! Of course! A box of rice cakes!"

Aimless shopping can be tolerated if your budget and cupboard are vast, but for most campers the cost and weight of food are of great concern.

I look in awe upon campers who prepare detailed lists weeks in advance, carefully combing newspapers for money-saving coupons and notices of special sales. These people know to the last penny what they'll be buying and how many grams of cheese and tortillas can be made into so many tostadas on the third night of the outing.

Most of us don't have the time or energy to cut so close to the bone. On a recent desert camping trip, I found myself elected to help shop for food. There were five of us and we planned to be out for about ten days. Simple arithmetic told us we would need: three meals a day times five people times ten days equals . . . 150 meals? I felt as though a dentist had peeked into my mouth and said, "You need about a hundred and fifty fillings; shall we begin immediately?"

Our shopping technique for that trip was a modification of the 'smash and grab' burglary: "You take the left side of the store and I'll hit the right." We went through a large whole foods cooperative like locusts, working without lists or other restraints. Our companions waited impatiently outside, revving the truck engine to remind us that time was short. We had a few seconds to review our purchases before the cashier rang up the bad news, and managed to eliminate a few glaring duplications and over-indulgences (Do we really need six pounds of raw cashews?).

Confusion mounted as we packed the bulging bags and already splitting cardboard boxes into the truck. Because space was limited and our gear extensive, the food ended up on the bottom of the pile. In the days to come we abandoned all attempts at civilized eating and merely gnawed our way from the tailgate forward. Meals were as simple as shouting, "Dive in!" We'd each go for a favorite box like a rookie player chasing a fumbled football.

Although I don't advocate such a carefree (or, if you prefer, 'careless') approach to every camping trip, it does add a flavor of zaniness that can be quite entertaining.

Lorena and I once participated in an unusual backpacking trip where each person bought their food in complete secrecy and revealed it to the others meal by meal. Our menu ran heavily to snacks and side dishes, but was never boring. I recall endless green olive and cream cheese sandwiches. This style of shopping and eating is ideal for times when careful planning may actually become an obstacle to making an impromptu camping trip.

Lists

A shopping list might seem obvious to those who shop regularly and know by long practice and experience just what foods are needed and when. A good list, however, isn't just a scribbled row of entries: honey, soap, rice, juice, etc. — but an actual inventory, including weights, volumes and even brand names.

The more restricted you will be in terms of budget and weight, the more detailed your list should be. These seemingly petty details will be your best defense against the dreaded Shopper's Syndrome, when a bewildering variety of brand names, colorful packages, unit price labels, special sale offerings and other typical distractions confront you in the supermarket. (In bulk and whole foods co-ops this Syndrome is set off by a *lack* of such distractions, when nothing is labelled and every choice has to be made on such outmoded factors as the food's appearance, smell, heft and general appeal.)

I go so far as to include reminders, warnings and threats on my shopping list: "whole wheat flour, 2 lbs., no more! *Don't overdo pancakes!*" This last comment tells me that we will not need extra flour for pancakes as it is already in the 2 pound figure. I usually panic and buy extra, assuming incorrectly that we forgot pancakes in our meal planning calculations.

Obey your list, reminding yourself that once your canoe or motorhome is stocked up, there'll be time to fill in any urgent gaps.

One of the most astounding shopping disasters I've been witness to happened in preparation for a long trip to Alaska. I was working on a ten-man fisheries research boat bound for a five month voyage into the Gulf of Alaska. Although this wasn't a camping trip in the strict sense of the word, it qualified in many people's minds if only because we were constantly wet, cold, miserable and caught few fish.

Shortly before we were due to take on provisions, the cook vanished, never to be seen again. He left only a long list of foodstuffs and several empty bottles of Canadian whiskey. The search for another cook was quick and frantic; the man barely had time to unpack his seabag before the skipper ordered him to buy the season's food.

"What shall I get?" he asked me, the youngest and greenest man aboard, my shopping experience limited to helping my mother carry a few bags home from the local Safeway. There was such a note of desperation in his voice, however, that I felt compelled to give a few well-intentioned words of advice.

"Why don't you take that list we found in the cook's bunk and, well, just sort of play it by ear." The new cook's hand went instinctively to his ear, tugging it insistently to dislodge an inspired solution to his problem.

"It is a very messy list," he said. "Maybe it isn't finished."

"Just double everything then!" I advised, receiving a mysterious flash of inspiration that would very nearly send us both to the Unemployment Office. "How can you go wrong?"

The cook, an honest man who had only recently immigrated from Norway, was only too eager to take my advice. The list was very difficult to read, the brand names unfamiliar, the captain was breathing down his neck ...in short, maybe this kid had a point.

The Day The Food Came immediately entered into local lore, along with the Gale of '65 and other fabulous natural disasters. The skipper was pacing the deck when I arrived, doing an excellent imitation of Captain Bligh, while the cook darted frantically from pallet board to pallet board, checking off tons of canned and packaged foods against a thick sheaf of manifests. A semi-truck was parked on the dock; behind it the driver of a large freezer van scowled impatiently as he waited his turn to unload. I felt a distinct sense of impending doom.

The cook greeted me with a high pressure stream of hissed Norwegian and backed me into a corner of the galley. I judged by the amount of eyeball bulging from his darkly flushed face that he was on the verge of a massive apoplectic stroke or homicide, and threw my arms out in the international gesture for mercy.

He calmed suddenly, slumping at the galley table with his head buried in his hands. An explanation soon followed: he had taken my advice and doubled the previous cook's list, sending it immediately to the food wholesaler approved by the captain. There was just one hitch: according to other crew members, the first cook had concocted the list while well under the influence of demon rum. We had taken a very garbled rough draft of a list he had intended to *pare down* to approximately 150 day's provisions for ten very hungry men and doubled the already over-generous quantities.

"Dot iss nine tousand meals!" the cook shrieked. "Nine tousand! NINE TOUSAND!" He seemed as dismayed by the number as the thought that he'd have to cook them, all by himself.

"Hey, cook!" The Captain loomed in the doorway. "We got about six hundred boxes of cupcake mix here." He chewed at the words slowly, as though digesting ten penny nails. "Where do you want 'em?"

"Cup...*cakes?*" The cook's confusion was genuine and total. My heart fell; didn't they eat cupcakes in Norway? He turned slowly toward me, drilling a shaking finger into my newly purchased 'halibut shirt'. "Put dem in da kid's bunk, by golly! Ja! Now I got me a helper!"

It was going to be a very long boat ride.

Stores & Food Suppliers

Careful shopping involves more than a simple comparison of food prices, especially when preparing for a long or arduous trip where every ounce has to be counted—and often carried on your back. Appropriate foods assume great importance: shall I go very light with freeze-dried meals and forget the expense? Or put together my own meals with cheaper bulk foods from the local food co-op or health food shop?

Food Co-ops

If your idea of a food co-op is a funky storefront plastered with radical political posters and crowded with long-haired vegetarians, you're probably fairly accurate — and perhaps reluctant to shop there. In the interests of good eating and economy I suggest you give co-ops a try. (At the very least they are good places to watch people.) Once you get used to the co-op's relaxed style, you'll probably find the local supermarket about as exciting as the Post Office.

Food co-ops (often called 'whole foods stores') are well suited to camper's food needs. Most staples are sold in bulk or very simply packaged. This makes it easy to buy the quantity you need, not what some distant marketing executive has decreed you must have, expensive wrapping and all.

When preparing for a long van camping trip, we needed a large supply of dried fruit. By advising the local co-op well in advance, we were given a price even lower than the normal bulk discount. This saved us money and simplified our shopping and packaging. The fruit was weighed, in bulk, and given to us in our own shopping bags.

Cheese can also be cut and wrapped in the weights you'll need if you notify them ahead of time.

Because most co-ops encourage shoppers to provide their own food containers, you won't be seen as a dangerous nut if you walk in with a load of bags, boxes, bottles and baskets. Take your cooking oil container to the bulk dispenser, fill it up and you're ready to pack it away.

I take a measuring cup along and dip out exact quantities of rice, meal by meal, pouring the grain directly into the same plastic bags that will be stowed in my pack or the kitchen box. I've never been very good at shopping by weight (how many portions are one and a half pounds of dry noodles?) When I can literally lay my hands on the food, shopping is much easier.

Most co-ops offer working memberships. A few percent off of a large grocery bill can be well worth your time.

Supermarkets

As food companies respond to an increasing demand for products that are nutritious as well as tasty, supermarkets have become more convenient when outfitting for a camping trip. Our local supers have everything from dried banana chips and brewer's yeast to imported cheeses and high quality cereal beverages. Unless freeze-dried foods are needed because of strict weight and fuel considerations, there is no reason why any trip, from an overnight hike to a month-long canoe voyage, couldn't be provisioned in one of these stores.

My biggest problem when shopping in supermarkets is finding and recognizing new and improved products. Because Lorena and I do a good deal of camping in Mexico and tend to shop in food co-ops while in the U.S.A., I am often surprised to find foods now in the supermarkets that were previously sold only in specialty stores, outdoor shops and health food outlets. The variety and quality of dried soups, sauces, meat substitutes, whole grains, condiments, snacks and beverages have improved dramatically in the past few years. However, the prepackaged food in a supermarket (as well as freeze-dried) will almost always have more additives and preservatives than their counterparts in a food co-op or health food store.

Health Food Stores

Although health food stores are now common in suburban shopping malls, they still suffer from an association with 'health food nuts' and diet faddists. Swallow your prejudices; the local health food store stocks foods that are very useful for campers.

An amazing amount of research and development money has gone into products loosely categorized as 'health foods'. These foods are often 'nutritionally dense'; in other words, you get a lot of food value per ounce and per dollar. The fact that these foods aren't laced with chemicals and preservatives is an added bonus.

Some common health food products come immediately to mind that deserve attention from campers: instant soups, instant sauces and gravies, soy protein meat substitutes, high energy drink mixes and diet supplements, low sugar and sugar-free instant puddings and dessert mixes, carob candies, concentrated vegetable broths and seasonings, wholesome snack foods and munchies, unprocessed yogurt and peanut butter, dairy products and much more.

Larger health food stores also offer good breads, fresh eggs, tofu and even produce. A chain-owned health food store in our area has regular sales on bulk dried nuts and fruit and other camping staples.

Specialty Food Shops and Delis

My usual shopping tactic when time is not a consideration is to 'cruise the deli' for special treats, condiments and snacks. I won't buy on this trip (well, maybe a half pint of olives and a tiny piece of lox just to keep my strength up), but will make a note of prices and compare them against the food co-op and supermarket. Prices for specialty foods vary considerably and, for a long trip, comparative shopping can mean substantial savings. I recently spotted almonds in a delicatessen that cost 50% more than identical nuts in a food co-op. The deli's salami, however, was a much better buy than the supermarket's and not loaded with preservatives.

So-called 'ethnic' food stores are excellent sources of new foods and condiments, but I tend to distrust exotic dishes when prepared by All-American cooks. Whenever a friend says, "I'm going to fix you a Vietnamese dinner that will really blow your mind!" it's more often my stomach that takes the shock.

Using great self-control, walk the aisles to see what is available. In a Mexican food store I found a familiar but forgotten standby that few gringos know about: instant refried beans. Add hot water and you've got bean dip, taco filling, soup stock or good old refrieds.

Restaurant Suppliers

Restaurant and institution food suppliers are located in most fair-sized towns (look under Restaurant Equipment and Supplies in the phone book). Those that sell 'cash and carry' can provide real bargains in packaged foods, especially if you are preparing for a long expedition or will be feeding a large group. Most items are of 'institutional size', in other words, *large*. Gallon cans of nuts, coffee, hot chocolate; large boxes of dried milk and non-dairy creamer, dried potatoes, vegetable soup mix, etc. The selection will be familiar to anyone who has eaten on a chow line in the military, a prison or large school.

Shopping at a restaurant supplier can be mind-boggling. The instant potato package that says "Serves 100" is common and it takes careful calculation to avoid over-buying.

Read the labels and if you aren't sure of a product, pass it by until you're more confident. We once bought a bargain can (the size of a small drum actually) of almonds that proved to be less than a treat when opened: the almonds were for "dessert toppings and baked goods." This translated to mean bland, colorless and tasteless and not worth eating.

Ask about special deals on damaged goods; some suppliers sell dented cans and torn packages for a song. You might not really need 5,000 tea bags but if the price is right...?

Shopping & Economizing Tips

When the time comes to take list and money in hand, I follow a few simple Commandments that have comforted and guided shoppers since time immemorial. These are:

• Never shop when hungry or thirsty. You'll unconsciously try to satisfy your immediate cravings by filling the cart with food and drink. This may sound unlikely to some, but believe me, it's a genuine hazard.

• Unless you are a very practised and confident shopper, make a special shopping trip for your camping food.

Because I am easily distracted I refuse Lorena's requests to "grab half a gallon of milk" or otherwise confuse the basic issue: to stock up for the outdoors. This narrow-mindedness helps me concentrate on keeping weight down, buying exact quantities, etc. When I get home the bags of food can go directly into a pack or whatever corner of the house we've designated as a staging area for the trip. Cross-checking of lists is easier, and if costs are being shared the receipts go directly to Accounting (a paper bag of scribbled notes and receipts).

• Carry a pocket calculator (two are even better — but this smacks of fanaticism). Since I inevitably punch the Clear button halfway through the

list, I also jot down prices on my list, which is firmly attached to a clipboard. In a second column I note food weights. When the list reaches $84.72 for 37 pounds 13 ounces of food for an overnight fishing trip, I immediately know that it's time to retrace my steps, paring down here and there.

• If your budget has to be squeezed hard, find a store offering generic brand foods. Go there first and search carefully for bargains. Now visit the dried and bulkier

foods: beans, rice, cereals, flour and so on. Buy larger and cheaper items first and you'll indulge your desires to fill the cart before running the gauntlet of the costly treat and delicacy aisles.

• Check labels carefully for information on servings. In my experience such information isn't just worthless but downright misleading. "Serves six" on a package of dried soup usually means that on a cold windy night you and five former friends will jealously share what one or two people could gulp down by themselves. It makes me feel gluttonous to admit it but I can usually eat two to four of 'their' servings with no trouble.

• Avoid foods you've never prepared or are unsure of. A friend learned this one the hard way on a three-week river-rafting expedition. Food was divided into categories and each member of the group set off to buy Staples, Produce, Munchies, etc. This is a risky way to shop but time was limited and with six mouths to feed, the job was just too much for one person.

As later reconstructed by the survivors, events went about like this: The youngest member of the party, who I'll call Bill, drew Staples. He didn't know how to cook but had firmly held notions of what was good and wholesome. While pondering a bin of short grain brown rice in a whole foods store, he happened to fall into conversation with another shopper. She knew a great deal about food and with missionary zeal, converted him on the spot to the joys of bulgur and falafel. (Bulgur is cracked wheat that has been parboiled and dried; falafel is cooked chick peas, ground and dried.) He bought enough to last the whole trip, a very large bag of each. Back on the river the food was quickly stowed and the boats launched.

River rats have a tradition of eating well. Weight and space are not big problems and a cast iron skillet or dutch oven is often standard kitchen gear. Excitement and anticipation ran high and at the first night's camp everyone pitched in to create a memorable meal. With appetites honed to a sharp edge by fresh air and hard work the rafters gathered 'round the larder. Bill handed the cook a bulging grain bag.

"What's this?" the cook asked suspiciously. Bill hesitated.

"Bulgur?" he said, "and falafel?" Blank stares prompted him to add, "Highly nutritious stuff." To rather tight-lipped questions, Bill could only shrug and say, "You cook it just like rice. *I guess.*"

Three weeks later one of the group, considerably diminished in weight, was heard to rant in a McDonald's parking lot: "Bulgur is vulgar but falafel is awful!"

• Always buy the best quality food you can afford. Like many 'old saws' the saying that "only the rich can afford low quality" is especially true in regard to camping foods. The cheapest noodles, for example, take longer to cook (using more fuel and water) than higher quality, aren't as nutritious and are less pleasing — especially if they come out as a gluey mess that even the finest sauce can't conceal.

Think of expensive foods as being packed with flavor and nutrition. A compact but comparatively costly cheese such as Gruyere goes much farther, both in flavor and enjoyment, than bland processed American cheese.

On a very tough hike up a desert mountain I found that most of my weight allotment (fill pack until knees tremble, deduct five pounds and set off) was taken up by water. This meant a reduction in clothing and food. My solution was simple but tasty: salty Greek olives, a very hard garlic salami, extra sharp smoked cheddar cheese, Swiss chocolate and fresh whole wheat pita bread (in addition to some basic staple foods such as granola, dried milk, soup). All of these 'luxury' items cost more than I normally care to pay for food. On the mountain, however, they went a long way and in the end were probably as economical as cheaper, bulkier foods.

A friend addicted to wilderness boating and eating summed up the question of cost versus quality like this: "Trying to fix a good meal with low quality food is like trying to hack a seaworthy canoe out of a rotting log."

• "Let's hit the supermarket and see if there's any last minute things we can use." This simple suggestion is loaded with more hazards than a storm shrouded reef.

"Last minute" usually means "unnecessary" and is nothing but smoke to camouflage our fear of running out of peanuts or chocolate fifteen miles from the nearest store. If you must go back to the store, try this: measure the space you have left in your backpack, canoe or van. Mentally divide this by half to allow for miscalculations; an hour from now you'll suddenly recall that you've forgotten your socks or teapot.

Now locate some handy container about the size (or smaller, never larger) than this empty space. If you're backpacking, it'll probably be a small lunch-bag sized space; in a motorhome it could be as large as a sea chest. Take this container to the store, fill it to the brim (or less), then turn directly for the checkstand and the exit. You are full up, done, completely provisioned and outfitted. Not one thing more!

Food & Shopping Suggestions

Beans

I have always admired beans. They are very durable; come in a variety of shapes, sizes, colors and flavors; are satisfying to eat and highly nutritious; stow easily in pack or canoe and don't cost much. For all this, beans are misunderstood and abused by most cooks, relegated to throat-searing pots of *chili con carne*, followed by ribald choruses of "Beans! Beans! The musical fruit...."

Beans are a very simple food but unfortunately they are not as simple to cook as most people assume. "Let's whip up a mess of beans" usually means a pot of mealy, underdone (but somehow overcooked at the same time) pellets leading to gastric disturbances that a friend rudely describes as 'bean breath'.

I was lucky to learn the ins-and-outs of beans from a Mexican woman who has been cooking for almost seventy years. The following tips are based on her advice, with a few ideas from our own experience thrown in for good measure. (Also see *Recipes: Beans*.)

Buy the best quality beans; they will cook faster and taste better than low quality beans, which are often last year's crop (or older). This saves cooking time, fuel and water.

Pinto beans are our personal favorite for camping. Black beans can be tricky to cook and white 'navy' beans aren't as versatile. Pintos make fine soups, refrieds, chili or Mexican style 'pot beans' (cooked in broth). Red kidney beans and small Japanese aduki beans are very good, too, and we carry them for variety on long trips.

Because even the best beans take longer to cook than any other staple food, we tend to reserve them for lazy days around a campfire and for boat and vehicle camping. A pressure cooker cuts cooking time, but I greatly prefer the flavor of slow-cooked beans.

Cooked beans will keep for a surprisingly long time, even in warm weather. The secret is to cool the beans as much as possible and reheat them to a full boil at least once a day. In hot weather, we wrap our aluminum billy pot in wet cloths and stow it in the shade, preferably exposed to a breeze. Beans (and other vegetarian dishes as well) can be kept for several days by this method.

If your beans ferment or taste sour they can still be safely eaten as an emergency food. On a trip where food was too scarce to throw out, we heated slightly spoiled beans for several minutes and seasoned them with very liberal doses of chile powder. (Beans cooked with meat, eggs or seafood of any type should not be eaten unless freshly prepared. Flesh spoils much quicker than vegetables and can easily cause food poisoning.)

Leftover beans can be difficult to transport. Lorena solved the problem on a long hike by drinking the broth and packing the cooked beans into a strong plastic bag. That evening she poured hot water over the beans, added seasoning and mashed them lightly with a fork to release more flavor.

Canned beans are useful for boaters and vehicle campers, but I'd opt for a can of refried beans. They are much more concentrated (less broth), and can be used for dips, sandwich or taco fillings, omelettes, soups and even baked concoctions (layered with cornbread and hot chiles). I like to take a small can of bean dip for a first-or second-day backpacking meal of bean tacos with cheese, fresh minced green onion and bean sprouts.

Beverages

Our bodies require a rather amazing intake of fluids. Although two quarts of water per day is the 'survival' minimum in hot weather, most campers will want more. I can quaff a gallon a day with no trouble when hiking or paddling, even if the stuff comes out of a ditch. (Tips on purifying water are given in *Camp Kitchen Skills: Staying Healthy*.)

Beverages enhance the flavor of your water and can provide valuable nutrients, not to mention a welcome psychological boost. 'Coffee breaks' are as important in camp and on the trail as they are in the office and factory; a chance to catch your breath, tighten your bootlaces and puzzle over the map while your hands cradle a hot cup.

We pack a variety of beverages while camping, especially on longer trips when heating and drinking water becomes a major form of relaxation and entertainment. Coffee is my overall favorite but Lorena prefers herbal teas, vegetable broth with brewer's yeast and other arcane potions that defy casual identification.

Coffee and teas containing caffeine can give a much needed lift in the morning and on tough outings, but both are diuretics — they make you pee more. If water is rationed there's no point in pouring it in one end and out the other. I have reduced my incurable addiction by substituting decaffein-ated coffee for about 75% of the grounds, with the remainder 'real' coffee.

Once I passed beyond withdrawal (and that's no joke — caffeine is a drug and a sudden reduction can cause headaches and vague nausea) I found this mixture had advantages over full strength coffee: calmer nerves and stomach, and no slump at the end of the day. Hard exertion speeds up your body's metabolic processes and a strong cup of coffee can literally jolt you right out of your hiking boots.

For energy, Lorena prefers brewer's yeast with hot water, vegetable broth and a dash of soy sauce, or ginseng tea.

We also carry small amounts of instant coffees (perhaps flavored if they aren't more than 50% preservatives and Agent Orange), tea bags (we like an herbal mixture as a nightcap, such as Sleepytime by Celestial Seasonings), freeze-dried juices, cereal beverages (Postum, Pero and others), hot chocolate (Swiss Miss is good and not laced with chemicals), bouillon cubes, vegetable broth, instant soups, miso, etc., etc. This is quite a list but if you take just enough for a few servings of each, the total weight and bulk won't be much. Organizing and packaging are another matter — we put our beverages into plastic Zip-Loc® bags and stuff these into a Beverage Bag. (See *Spices: The Spice Rack*.)

When water is scarce we almost always mix it with something flavorful and, hopefully, nutritious. This can be as simple as a spoonful of honey mixed into a cup of hot water or 'Y&B' (brewer's yeast and vegetable broth). Dried fruit or vegetables can be soaked in hot or boiling water to make an interesting beverage-snack. I do the same with smoked fish and meat jerky, adding a dash of bouillon or broth for 'body'. Lorena prefers miso (fermented soybean paste — tastes far better than it sounds) with dried seaweed. You can almost feel that seaweed racing through your veins!

Beverages can easily become meals. We might whip up a cup of broth and then fill it out with pieces of dried tortilla or bread, cold leftover rice or noodles, a blob of butter, a spoonful of minced fresh onion...

Desert and beach campers must often endure brackish and mineral-bitter drinking water. While camped in Baja for several months we almost got used to water that tasted like the dregs of an old aquarium, mainly by doctoring it with a wide variety of beverages and flavorings. For salty, brackish water, add lemon or lime juice (as much as you can) or a small shot of vinegar to a quart of water. (Adjust according to taste and salt content of the drinking water.) Lime juice or vinegar will give the water a more satisfying taste and quench your thirst faster.

Powdered drink mixtures designed for athletes can be useful for campers. We carry Gookinaid® while kayaking and desert hiking. Lorena likes it but I can't really decide if it helps or not (the drink is supposed to replace vital salts and minerals lost through sweating).

We begin a hike or boat trip with at least one canteen each of grape juice for quick energy. As the level drops in the canteen we top them off until the 'juice' is only tinted a light purple. It still tastes faintly like grapes, however.

Alcoholic beverages are a luxury on most trips, though I have gone camping with folks who considered them a staple. For those who must go light I suggest strong drink: 151 proof rum is my choice, administered in teaspoon-sized doses and diluted with hot tea or cold water. Pure 190 proof grain alcohol, known as The White Death, Popskull, and other less polite nicknames, is best taken in a camp cocktail, never in a straight shot.

Drinking at high elevations can knock your feet right out from under you, especially at the end of a tough day of hiking or climbing. Use alcohol very cautiously, if at all. Nothing takes the edge off a fine mountain sunrise like a skull-cracking hangover.

Wine can be carried in plastic bags and bottles, but I prefer to leave it at home. There's something about Chablis poured from a Zip-Loc® bag that offends my palate.

Breads and Tortillas

The Staff of Life has propped up more than one nutritionally shaky camping trip. Whenever I provision by the 'Snatch & Grab' technique I pass very close by the bread, cracker and tortilla department of the store. Bread is a very good food (if you eat wholesome types) and psychologically reassuring. If you've ever been on a camping trip where the bread ran out or was forgotten you know what I mean: a look of wide-mouthed panic and a frantic, "Whattaya mean? *No bread?*" is the standard reaction.

Most familiar sliced breads don't travel well. When squashed into the bottom of a backpack or jammed into the bow of a canoe, sliced bread quickly turns to bread crumbs, perfect for feeding to birds but difficult for campers to enjoy.

Buy heavy, durable breads, preferably unsliced or sliced very thick. Dense breads withstand abuse and are much more nutritious than fluffy, highly processed breads. Bread rolls and bread sticks are good and come in convenient one-portion sizes. No arguments over who eats the heels.

My favorite camp breads can be loosely categorized as 'ethnic'. A Mexican friend ironically calls them 'UnAmerican breads'. These include tortillas, chapattis, pita, hardtacks, bagels and basic, manna-like breads common throughout the world. Most of these breads can be prepared in advance or in camp.

The ability to bake bread probably ranks with such elemental skills as Kindling Fire and Brewing Beer. I consider bread-making an essential outdoor skill, especially for those who plan extended trips into remote country. Even if you can manage the cost and logistics of food drops or caches, it is impractical to include loaves of bread or fresh bagels; they just won't last. You must learn to prepare bread from scratch, using raw materials. (My attempts to bake wilderness bagels, however, caused a Jewish friend to warn that further efforts would bring down the Wrath of Jehovah, if not a general Plague and Pestilence.)

Some campers have made a lifelong study of the powdermilk biscuit, others go for Yukon bannock or Pecos griddle cakes. Lorena and I prefer whole wheat tortillas (corn tortillas are very difficult), panbread and fried biscuits. Tortillas can be any shape, size and thickness (round, of course, is the most common) and actually cook best over open fires rather than stoves. Panbread is that old standby, pancakes, converted with imagination into various lumps, loaves, cakes and dumplings.

Startling Bread Facts: All breads are variations on a basic combination of flour or meal and water. The variations, however, have filled innumerable books. (We consider gravy, for example, to be 'liquid bread'.)

Once you've chosen a basic bread and mastered the technique of preparing it in camp, you'll have ample opportunity to experiment. Just be patient; like most so-called 'simple' foods, bread is simple to botch up and demands careful attention.

Cereals: Granola to Mush

I've never been much of a breakfast cereal fan. Faced with a bowl of cold granola or a blob of steamy oatmeal I think wistfully of a 'truck driver's breakfast': fried eggs, crisp bacon, hash brown potatoes, a few greasy sausages, maybe a side of grits with a thick pat of butter and coffee as strong and bitter as brake fluid. Oh yeah, and lots of toast with grape jelly. Unfortunately, you need a truck to haul the ingredients...

Granola might well be called New Age Wheaties or Breakfast of Campers; the sound of jaws grinding through nuts, seeds and toasted grains is as much a part of the current wilderness experience as the methodical munching of beavers in a stand of tender cottonwoods. Lacking the necessary teeth and temperament, I couldn't face granola until I discovered that a large dose of hot milk would soften it to proper gumming consistency.

To save money and wear and tear on my dental work, I buy the plainest granola available at a food co-op (supermarket granola costs much more) and then jazz it up myself. I add raisins, dried banana chips, a dash of cinnamon, and if I'm feeling reckless, a few toasted cashews. Lorena goes whole hog: filberts, walnuts, chunks of dried pineapple, wheat germ, coconut and God-knows-what-else.

Making your own granola from scratch is even more economical, but in my experience it isn't worth the trouble and potential for disaster. A batch of granola represents a fair investment in raw materials and nothing is worse than having to eat your mistakes, day after endless day. It takes skill and careful attention to blend and roast a variety of diverse ingredients, especially granolas made with honey.

Unfortunately, few prepared cereals are as convenient and nutritious as granola. Of the standard cereals I prefer Grape Nuts.® They are quite compact and when prepared with hot milk, banana chips, raisins, honey or maple syrup, Grape Nuts are tasty and reasonably nutritious.

Cooked cereals offer much more variety and economy. The least processed are also the most nutritious and, in my opinion, the most flavorful. 'Instant' cereals, including oatmeal, really aren't much easier to prepare than regular cooked types and their texture tends toward wallpaper paste, especially if prepared carelessly.

Cooking disasters with mush — a very appropriate term — are common. Lumpy messes that congeal like cement on dishes and utensils, resisting the most abrasive scrubbers, have converted more than a few camp cooks to the joys of fried rice for breakfast. (See *Recipes*.) To minimize such problems carefully test your cereals before committing yourself to eating them regularly. We once bought a large quantity of a bulk cereal called Bear Mush.® It was economical, very compact and we both liked the name.

Unfortunately we were never able to prepare the mush without large lumps. We tried everything, including wildly beating the boiling water with a fork as a second person added the dry mush in a carefully controlled stream. The result: unappetizing lumps. The flavor was great but not worth the overall hassle.

Cheese

"A hunk of cheese and a crust of bread" is probably the original camping meal. If Heidi could dash up and down the Swiss Alps on such simple fare it stands to reason that modern hikers and outdoors people can benefit from eating more cheese.

Cheese is one of the first things to be purged by dieters — always a good sign that a food is rich in calories and fat. If that isn't enough to convince

you, cheese is a complete protein and has as much protein as fish. It also comes in convenient lumps, blocks and slices and is easy to divvy up with a dull knife. When cheese is eaten with beans, spuds, nuts and grains, it balances the protein in these foods and provides good amounts of calcium.

What else? Well, cheese will keep for months without refrigeration if properly packaged and... it tastes good. Let's hear it for cheese!

Cheese (and all dairy products) is an excellent substitute for meat. If you want to ease your way into vegetarian cooking, cheese is invaluable. Carnivores usually find cheese satisfying and filling.

Spoilage worries many campers, especially those who forget that cheese was invented long before the Kelvinator. We have carried cheese for as long as six months without refrigeration in very warm weather (including the lowlands of Mexico). Properly cured cheese improves in flavor with age and although it often becomes quite hard it can be grated and shaved for cooking.

We prefer sharp or extra sharp cheeses for camping. The flavor goes farther and aged cheeses contain less water. If the trip will be quite long, however, we'll buy a large block of mild cheddar and 'sharpen' it ourselves to save money.

Mold will eventually appear on the cheese so the fewer cuts the better. Bigger hunks also retain moisture longer, giving them a more pleasing texture. (Hard dried cheeses are almost indestructible, however, and will survive repeated dunkings in water.)

To preserve cheese, wrap it in pieces of clean cotton cloth, paper bags, unwaxed wrapping paper or, you guessed it, cheesecloth. This wrapping absorbs oil and moisture from the cheese and protects it from mold. Cheese kept in this manner will last for weeks, though you'll want to lightly scrape away surface mold before using it.

To keep cheese even longer and to age and sharpen it yourself, soak a clean cotton cloth in vinegar (or add a few shots of household bleach to a quart of water and soak the cloth), wrap the cheese and allow the cloth to dry. Wrap another light cloth or absorbent paper around the cheese and pack it away.

Do not keep your cheese in plastic bags. Plastic traps moisture and speeds up spoilage.

Inspect the cheese at least once a week, especially in hot weather. Cheese is like stored apples: one day all the chunks will look fine, the next day one or more show signs of heavy mold. A light layer of mold is protection for the cheese, so just trim the piece you want to use. However, if the mold is thick, especially in deep cracks, clean away the worst of it and repeat the vinegar or bleach rinse. We also dunk the cheese itself in vinegar or mild bleach solution (water purifying tablets work too) from time to time and allow it to dry in the sun.

Cheese that has aged to rock-hardness will rarely melt well when cooked. Shave or grate it as finely as you can and mix evenly into the dish being prepared. A few tablespoons of well-aged cheese should flavor a full pot of rice or noodles.

Blue cheese is an excellent concentrated flavoring for salads and casseroles. A piece no larger than an egg should be enough for four or five dishes, if not more.

Parmesan is very important to our camp menu; we use it for just about everything, from scrambled eggs and tortilla pizzas to salads, casseroles and even soups. I like very hard and strong Parmesan. It goes a long way and doesn't require careful handling — I might toss a lump into my pack without bothering to wrap it.

Specialty cheeses combined with meat should be handled as if they were meat, not cheese. Spoilage can be a hazard with these cheeses and for that reason I use them only in cool weather or make sure they're eaten up quickly.

Herb cheeses are very nice for camping and their flavor is often all you'll need to spice up a dish of rice, noodles or potatoes.

Calculating how much cheese to take on a trip can be difficult. Half a pound of cheese provides about 100% of the average person's daily protein requirement. (Processed cheeses are less nutritious.) On a long trip a half-pound daily ration of cheese would undoubtedly begin to stick in your throat. We usually eat lots of cheese for two or three days and then taper off, adding smaller amounts to cooked dishes. Start with milder cheeses, then switch to stronger flavored and longer lasting types.

An ounce of Parmesan or extra sharp cheddar daily per person is a good minimum ration for flavoring and protein balancing.

Eggs

Fried eggs with hashbrown potatoes is my idea of the perfect outdoor breakfast. It is even more perfect with bacon, but since Lorena insists that I wash out the skillet after using bacon — and before frying her egg (Whoever heard of eating one egg anyway?) — I have learned to accept the less perfect version. Eggs are an excellent camping food: easy to prepare, nutritious and inexpensive.

The latter holds true even if you buy 'real' eggs. When you discover the superior flavor and freshness of good eggs from a food co-op or health food store, you'll never want to buy a 'factory' egg again.

Unfortunately, eggs break easily. I have broken them in my backpack, in the van and even in the store. Broken and cracked eggs spoil quickly (think of them as meat). Inspect every egg and cook any that are damaged or lopsided immediately.

When backpacking I carry fresh eggs for one breakfast and as many hardboiled eggs as I can manage to gulp down for lunch, usually half a dozen. On the second day I use leftover eggs in a deviled egg concoction, an egg salad or crumble them up to feed to the birds.

To minimize loss from breakage, crack fresh eggs into a plastic jar with a tightly sealing lid. Use the eggs within one or two days, depending on the air temperature. If you're hiking, stow the eggs well away from your back. Body heat can cause spoilage.

Dried eggs are very good in breads, gravies, sauces, casseroles, desserts and other dishes. I cannot stand them prepared as real eggs, especially scrambled. This is undoubtedly a result of facing powdered eggs in a Navy chowline more times than I care to remember. Powdered egg omelettes are best disguised with spicy sauces or left at home.

Fruits: Dried

Dried fruits are much more than nutritional snacks; in many camping situations they are a valuable staple food. We depend on dried fruits on arduous hiking and kayaking expeditions. They are compact, very durable and can be eaten right out of the bag or prepared in a variety of cooked dishes, including such main dinner courses as fried rice (add raisins, dates and pineapple).

Dried fruits provide large amounts of carbohydrates and natural sugars, making them an excellent source of quick energy. Dried fruits are better for you than candy or processed sweets and they're much cheaper.

We buy most of our dried fruit at food co-ops and health food stores. Supermarkets may have dried fruits in bulk but they usually aren't bargains. Exceptions are sales on locally dried fruit (especially in California) and raisins.

The price per pound of fruit assortments may be tempting, but we've found it more economical and convenient to buy individual dried fruits. Assortments seem to run heavily to dried apples. I find dried apples rather uninspiring and by coincidence they are less nutritious than some of my favorites. Check prices carefully as you shop: dates, for example, are generally a good bargain, especially if you buy date pieces. (Some exotic and very tasty dates are expensive, however.)

Dried pineapple is our first choice for quick snacks and treats. After the second hour of paddling a heavily loaded kayak into steep head-on seas, nothing sounds better than a slice of dried pineapple. This is used as a blatant bribe/reward, as well as for energy.

Date pieces blend well into cooked dishes, especially the morning mush. Dried figs, bananas, apricots and raisins complete our selection. All are easy to eat and cook and cheaper than exotic fruits such as mango and papaya.

Pack your dried fruit carefully, especially if you'll be boating or hiking in damp country. Moldy dried fruit won't hurt you but the flavor won't win any prizes. On long trips we sun-dry our dried fruit at least once a week.

If mold appears, bathe the fruit in a mild solution of vinegar, bleach, iodine or water purifying tablets. Let it soak for several minutes, but beware of leaving it in the bath too long or you'll have to re-dry the fruit for several hours or more. Rinse the fruit (optional) and dry well in the sun. This purifying bath should retard the growth of mold but if all else fails, cooking the fruit in main dishes should disguise any moldy flavor.

The temptation to gorge on dried fruit is a major hazard. 'Out of sight, out of mind' is the answer: pack all but a one or two day stock of dried fruit in a reserve bag and stick to the rule that the reserve won't be used ahead of schedule. I never let my brother, Rob, inspect the dried fruit for mold ("Hey, this one looks weird. I'd better taste it!") or even allow him to handle it ("There's seven dates here. Why don't I eat this odd one and make it an even three apiece?").

On long trips and group outings we set aside a small part of each person's daily ration for the general cooking 'fund'. This allows the cook to add a generous portion of raisins to the oatmeal without having to beg or extort a contribution from each person.

Drying your own fruit is an enjoyable and economical alternative to store bought. It's also much easier than you might think. (See *Recipes: Drying Fruits & Vegetables*.)

Lentils and Split Peas

Dried lentils and split peas are nutritionally very similar to other legumes such as beans. Their main advantages — which are big ones — are faster cooking times than beans and general ease of preparation. Both lentils and split peas have rich, satisfying flavors that often appeal to those who don't care for other legumes.

I always associate a thick pea soup with the outdoors, perhaps because it was standard fare on boats I worked on in Alaska. At the first sign of a big southeasterly storm roaring up the Gulf of Alaska, the cook would prepare a cauldron of pea soup — Southeast Stew. I learned to enjoy the stew but dreaded seeing it on the galley table since it inevitably meant tough weather ahead. With a thick pat of butter or cheese and a stack of hard Swedish crackers, pea soup makes a full meal in any situation.

Lentils and split pea soup mixes are sold in most stores, but it takes only a few minutes to prepare your own. Add dried vegetables, dried vegetable broth and spices to the legumes, mix well and bag up.

On long trips we periodically set up 'rest camps' to recoup our strength or to enjoy the scenery. A pot of pea or lentil stew on the back of the fire eases the cooking burden considerably and stretches food supplies. This works well in group situations where it is difficult to get everyone together at the same time for a meal. Hungry campers can grab a bowl of soup before their appetites set off an extravagant snacking spree.

Meat

Fresh meat is a treat while camping, but because of potential for spoilage, as well as cost and weight, I indulge my carnivorous impulses only

on short trips and remain a reluctant vegetarian on others. Canned meats are more practical — just don't read the fine print on the label or the list of additives and preservatives may wipe out your appetite immediately.

Since I eat meat infrequently I enjoy it to the maximum when given the opportunity. Fortunately, my favorite cuts are among the least expensive. Chuck steaks and roasts, for example, are ideal for barbecuing: fat enough to create sizzling clouds of smoke (and those delicious carcinogens) yet tender if slow cooked. Leaner cuts tend to be tougher and less flavorful.

Stew meat is another bargain. Buy the boneless, already cubed variety. It can be stewed or, as I prefer it, skewered on wire or green sticks and prepared as shishkabobs. (Steaks can also be skewered, either whole or cut into strips and cubes.) In general, cheaper cuts of meat benefit by stone-age cooking methods: a searing hot fire with lots of smoke will really bring out the flavor of the fat and meat.

One of the best barbecues I've tasted was in northern Mexico. A group of cowboys invited me to share their Sunday dinner: several pounds of beef and bone that appeared to have been cut with a chain saw were simply tossed into the coals of a large oak wood fire. When medium-charred the meat was retrieved, brushed off, and served with fresh flour tortillas, sweet cream and hot chiles. It was an unusual and very tasty meal. (For more on meat, see *Recipes: Smoking Fish & Meat, Jerky*).

Milk

In dried and condensed forms milk is ideal for camp cooking. Milk can be used at every meal, from granola to gravy, in desserts, breads, drinks, casseroles or what-have-you. Adding whole dried milk to a variety of dishes is a very simple and inexpensive way to balance out what may otherwise be an incomplete protein (see *Meal Planning: Eating Well: A Balancing Act*). Milk can be especially important for vegetarians.

Powdered milk has to be one of the most useful and convenient mass-produced foods available for campers. Although 'instant' dried milk is more popular, dried whole milk (not instant or non-fat) is more nutritious.

If you'll be camping in hot weather, protect your dried milk from the sun and heat. Several weeks of high desert temperatures gave our dried milk an odd and disagreeable taste, like scorched plastic. If space is not critical, leave the milk in factory-sealed packets.

Canned milk might seem too heavy or bulky for camping but we sometimes take condensed milk on short hikes. This milk makes good desserts (see *Recipes: Snacks & Desserts*) and is welcome on breakfast cereals. Some people pour condensed sweetened milk on bread and crackers. It takes all types...

Canned whole milk and super-pasteurized whole milk have a long shelf life and are useful for boaters and car campers.

Non-dairy creamer can be substituted for milk. It's richer flavor and thicker consistency make it well suited for soups, dessert toppings, beverages and sauces. Our favorite brand, Farmer Brothers, came from a restaurant supply store.

Quite a variety of highly nutritious soy milks are available at health food shops. These milk substitutes are excellent foods but I have never been able to acquire much of a taste for them. Try soy milk in cooked dishes, perhaps with a mixture of dried whole milk. Considering food value and compactness, dried soy milk is worth learning to like.

Noodles and Pasta

In a recent interview in *People* magazine, James Beard, noted cook and author, declared, that pasta is now "in." Judging from the furor among athletes and outdoor types over 'carbohydrate loading' and the news that even professional boxers are gorging platters of spaghetti before their fights instead of raw steaks, this indeed seems to be the Year of the Noodle.

Cynics might charge that this furor is a calculated pasta maker's media blitz, but in our experience noodles are an excellent camping food. Their major drawback is the amount of water needed for cooking. However, by using our technique for Quick Fried Noodles (see *Recipes: Noodles and Pasta*), you'll find that most pastas can be prepared faster and require less fuel and water than almost any main dish food.

The best pastas for camp cooking, especially if water is scarce, are thin noodles or small elbows and other tiny shapes (look in Italian food shops). I generally use elbows; they go well in salads, soups and casseroles. (Spaghetti and fettucini noodles are much more compact, however.) I avoid large noodles because they take longer to cook and require more water to prevent lumping up.

Whole wheat noodles and other wholesome pastas (spinach flavored, tomato, etc.) are sold in food co-ops and health food shops. Although they may be somewhat more nutritious than other pastas, I find them more difficult to cook properly and less pleasing in texture. Test them carefully before buying large quantities. In situations where water is severely rationed I would sacrifice some nutritional value for a quicker cooking pasta.

Oriental style noodles are now very popular in the U.S. Packaged ramen noodles are inexpensive and very quick to prepare. I prefer them to the American style noodles-in-a-cup, which seem to taste of the plastic container and preservatives.

Bulk oriental noodles are sold in some food co-ops and specialty food shops. It is quite simple to make up your own flavorings for these noodles. I really enjoy them as a quick hot lunch. They take little more preparation than a cup of tea and provide fast energy as well as a morale boost. Lorena and I enjoy competing to see who can whip up the quickest and tastiest cup of noodle soup.

Rice

Rice is well-suited for one-pot camping dishes. When water is scarce rice can be cooked with some salt water, a factor that saved us a good deal of fresh drinking water on long ocean kayaking trips. Cooked rice can be eaten cold or used in soups and salads. This is important for arduous trips where cooking opportunities may be infrequent.

Rice is high in carbohydrates and we often eat it for breakfast. By adding hot or cold milk, honey and cinnamon you've got Mexican *atole*, a high-energy treat that requires little time or mental energy to prepare. Leftover *atole* can be carried in a vacuum bottle or canteen. It might not be bacon and eggs, but it's a nutritious alternative to more elaborate meals. (See *Recipes: Beverages: Atole.*)

As for the white-versus-brown rice argument, I can only say that once you learn to cook brown rice properly, you'll probably prefer it over white rice. I do enjoy white rice, however, especially steamed, with a simple topping of butter and soy sauce or garnished with sesame seeds and cheese. Brown rice takes longer to cook and therefore uses more water and fuel.

Converted rice is nutritionally in between white and brown rice and cooks faster than both. I don't like the texture of converted rice, however, and use it only when fuel is strictly rationed.

Rice is a classic example of a food that doesn't quite mesh with an All-American cooking style. Anyone who can get excited over gooey steamed rice smothered in brown cornstarch gravy has a stronger stomach than mine.

To do rice justice prepare it in ways that are simple and reliable. Some time-tested recipes based on oriental and Mexican rice dishes are given in *Recipes*. Once you've mastered rice you'll probably find, as we have, that it is more useful and versatile for camping than potatoes.

Quite a variety of prepared rice dinners are available at supermarkets and whole food stores. A friend simplifies his camp cooking to an extreme by eating Rice-A-Roni every day, along with a liberal selection of sweets, cheese and canned meats. It's not too inspiring but it certainly gets him into the woods with a minimum of preparation.

Nuts and Seeds

Nuts and seeds are among the most nutritious foods available for campers. Nuts and seeds are compact, durable and can be eaten in combination with almost any other food, either raw or cooked. (Tavern customers have been known to live on beer nuts for months at a time.)

Better yet, some of the most nutritious nuts and seeds — peanuts, sesame and sunflower seeds — are among the cheapest. More expensive nuts, however, — mainly cashews — are so good for you that you almost can't afford *not* to eat them. Nuts and seeds are rich in protein, oil and vitamins, and provide energy over an extended period of time.

Nuts and seeds are much better buys at whole foods stores, although health food stores and supermarkets with bulk food and snack sections may have occasional sales. Raw nuts and seeds are cheaper yet, and by toasting them yourself, interesting flavors and combinations can be dreamed up (see *Recipes: Snacks, Desserts*).

By buying bulk raw nuts and making your own trail mixes, you'll save a considerable amount of money and get a snack more suited to your own particular tastes. My favorite, which won't be found in any supermarket, is heavily garlicked sunflower seeds mixed with slightly scorched sesame seeds, raisins, and just a dash of cayenne. It's got flavor to spare.

Butters can be made from many nuts and seeds other than peanuts. Sesame, sunflower, cashew and almond butters are sold in most health food stores. They tend to be a bit gluey in texture but you can't beat them for compactness.

Nuts and seeds can be baked into breads, cookies or 'energy bars', but I prefer to carry mine in individual packets. I might find myself standing beneath a towering redwood, admiring the rich golden evening light, when a sudden desire for a brazil nut strikes. Somewhere in my pockets, perhaps slightly damp and lint-covered, will be just the nut I need to complement the scene. As you may have guessed by now, I find 'mixes', whether of nuts, fruit or dried vegetables, to be boring.

Dry roasted nuts are quite tasty and much lighter than unprocessed nuts. I buy them on sale or in the Generic Section of the supermarket. After much sampling, I prefer the unsalted variety; they seem to have more flavor than salted nuts and are probably better for you.

Be very careful when packing and storing nuts, especially in a food cache that may not be used for several weeks. Nuts and seeds tend to pick up other flavors. You haven't lived until you've eaten several pounds of onion-flavored walnuts. Keep them cool, dry and out of the direct sunlight.

Nuts and seeds are the natural foods of creatures with strong stubborn teeth. Do your best to pack such treats out of reach. We have been raided by rodents too many times to ignore the potential damage and food loss. We even had mice stowaways on a kayak trip.

This is amusing — now, on dry land — but when we were ten days from the nearest town and had two sets of sharp teeth gnawing through plastic and wood we took it as a serious threat. We were eventually forced to unload the boat completely, anchor it in waist deep water, then tediously inspect and repack each item of gear to flush out the rodents. This took many hours. It was somewhat humorous the first time... and not at all funny the second.

Oil, Margarine and Butter

Oil and fat are vital foods and nothing demonstrates their importance like a really tough outdoor trip. On a long ocean kayaking voyage Lorena and I became head hunters. Fish heads are loaded with tasty fat and we all but danced around the fire when blessed with a huge snapper head, spitting and snapping over hot mesquite coals. Lorena's only inhibition was the eyeballs, though she did watch as I gobbled them down.

The body's need for fat can lead to wild food cravings that raise hell with your larder if allowed to go unchecked. Fat-rich foods are an obvious solution, but it's often cheaper and more convenient to eat more butter, margarine and cooking oil.

Margarine is a favorite for many camp cooks: inexpensive, it comes in convenient containers, has good flavor, doesn't melt in your pack except in the hottest weather, and spreads nicely on bread and tortillas. (All-vegetable margarine keeps better than margarine made with milk solids. Check the label.)

In the long run, however, I prefer cooking oil, especially unprocessed safflower or corn oil (from health food or bulk food stores). My logic is this: unless I'm camping in consistently cool weather, I know that one day the butter, margarine or lard will melt and my leakproof container will leak. I have been angry at lard in particular for melting inside a huge reserve bag of food we used while boating. Two pounds of liquid lard (or butter or margarine) will coat approximately ten square miles of gear and clothing. Oil, on the other hand, is already liquid and never pretends to be otherwise.

The problem, then, is to find oil-proof containers that will survive rough use. We use plastic bottles from REI (Recreational Equipment Co-op. See *Appendices*) with screw-top lids. They have endured years of camping and though they look scroungy by now with minor oil spills and soot coating their surfaces, these containers can be depended upon. (All the same, we wrap them inside a plastic bag for added protection.)

Oil is a camping staple but butter is a flavor treat. We begin a trip with fresh butter and, if at all possible, canned butter to break out for special occasions. Unfortunately, canned butter is difficult to find in the U.S. Look for it in delis and ship's chandlers.

Butter will keep much longer than most people realize and even when stale or slightly rancid it is still edible. We stretch butter even further by mixing it with oil or margarine. Like olive oil, a small amount of butter goes a long way.

Butter Buds is an interesting new product: packets of so-called 'dried butter' that can be reconstituted with water. It comes out quite runny but is good for cooking and dips. We eat Buds sprinkled dry on popcorn or noodles.

The distinctive taste of olive oil is reason enough to include it in our camp kitchen, if only an ounce or two for salads and an occasional sauce. Stretch olive oil by mixing it half-and-half with cooking oil. On long trips we drop half a pint of strong Greek or Spanish olives into a one quart plastic bottle of safflower oil. We keep this oil in reserve and by the time we need it our taste buds are sensitive enough to call it 'real' olive oil. When the oil is gone the olives make a fine treat.

All fats and oils can be stretched by using non-stick frying pans. Frying is actually a poor way to consume oil as heat reduces its nutritional value. Leftover oil is often dirty and always messy. Use a very lightly oiled coated pan and watch it closely to avoid scorching.

Adding fat and oil to casseroles, breads, soups and gravy is much more efficient than frying. Butter and margarine can be smeared on food or melted into cooked dishes. Oil dressings are good, but salads in the wilderness are all too rare. (Exceptions are grain salads such as tabouli, and cold bean sprout and noodle salads; see *Recipes: Salads.*)

Conserving oil can be nutritionally risky, but on long expeditions you may have no other choice. On a boat trip, for example, we had to go for several weeks without replenishing our food supplies. By using a non-stick frying pan and careful rationing, we reduced our oil consumption to half a quart a week. Most of this oil went into tortillas and breads. Any fried dish was followed by soup or casserole — without washing the oil residue from the pan. This is true miserliness, but by eating a great deal of seafood (those delicious heads!) we were able to complete our trip in fine health.

Soy Proteins

I call textured soy proteins and soybean meat substitutes 'phoney

baloney', though none I've eaten bear much resemblance to baloney *or* meat —or to soybeans, either.

Why bother with these foods? Soy proteins, especially the dried variety (known irreverently by some as 'kibbles') are highly nutritious, compact, lightweight and durable; in other words, good for camping. I much prefer dry soy products; they're easier to spice up than canned varieties and their texture is more pleasing. Canned soy foods are useful, however, as sandwich spreads and taco fillings.

Once you've leaped the psychological hurdle and accepted soy proteins, you face an even tougher problem: how to cook the stuff? Because reconstituted soy food looks somewhat like ground meat, many cooks innocently cook it like meat. The result is usually very disappointing: soggy patties that crumble like old cookies and casseroles that lay very low in the pan, prompting unkind remarks from suspicious friends.

Because Lorena has been a vegetarian all of her life (though recently converted to the joys of fresh seafood) and soy foods offer a partial solution to the problem of eating well on long outdoor trips, I have had ample opportunity to experiment 'in the field'. My first breakthrough came when I absentmindedly left a skillet of soy 'burgers' on the campfire while mixing myself a health drink of rum and branch water.

These patties, which normally came out soggy and lifeless, were overcooked to perfection; in fact, they were quite good! I now make my patties thin and fry them in very hot (but not smoking) oil or butter. Don't flip them too often or they'll break.

The next improvement was gradual but dramatic: I learned to use lots of garlic and spices, especially oregano or sage (associated in most people's minds with meat dishes), liberal quantities of minced onion, raw egg, flour or oatmeal, and chopped nuts and seeds (sesame, cashew, walnuts and pecans). The trick is to mix everything as you reconstitute the dried soy food. This gives it time to pick up flavor and makes it easier to adjust the final moisture content. Runny soy food is very difficult to work with. For patties and casseroles, a final liberal coating of cheese, dried onion, bread crumbs or tomato sauce is nice.

Choosing a dried soy food is difficult, mainly because it bears little resemblance to anything you've eaten before. Uncooked soy food doesn't taste very good so you won't really know what you've got until you've cooked it. In general, I've found that most people prefer types that are not too chunky or heavily factory-flavored.

Chicken-style soy food comes immediately to mind; we carried it on a long hot trek through the Sierra Madre. We broke the old rule that says don't trust an untested food on a tough trip and we were suitably punished. The large textured lumps were less like chicken than tough marine growths I've scraped off sailboat hulls. The flavor was strong, with far too much cumin, and by the time we'd rinsed it from our mouths, strange and ominous gas rumblings were coming from our stomachs. Steve's final verdict, after forcing down yet another hearty portion, was, "I feel like the Goodyear blimp with hiking boots."

This experience was with a cheap brand of soy food. Higher quality types with fewer additives shouldn't cause problems.

Soy foods are cheapest in food co-ops. Because their customers really use these foods, they tend to stock the better, tastier types. Ask someone for a suggestion and buy a sample.

Supermarkets and health food stores carry packaged soy foods, usually fancy boxed, prespiced, 'add water and cook' types. They are a good introduction to soy foods but tend to be expensive. Try them, and when you find a favorite, duplicate it using bulk soy foods and your own spices and condiments.

Spices, Herbs and Condiments

Too many outdoor cooks overlook the potential of spices and herbs and lay heavy hands on the salt and pepper. By adding just a few spices to your provisions, you'll not only be able to create new flavors, but will avoid the camping rut where "everything tastes fine but everything tastes the same." Spices add flavor, interest, color and even texture. Considering cost and weight, they are exceptional bargains.

Lorena and I have found that on long camping trips our craving and appreciation of new and strong flavors grows by the day and week. Nothing quite compares to the aroma of a rich curry on a cold desert night. A clammy rain-lashed tent can be transformed by lifting the lid on a pot filled with a pungent garlic sauce. A simple pinch of dill or caraway seed in an otherwise ordinary cabbage salad makes the difference between good-but-forgettable and, "Hey, remember that salad you made on our river trip?"

Our experience with spices and condiments is matched by explorers who participated in one of history's most unique 'camping trips' — a 96-day spaceflight aboard Salyut-6 in 1978. As James Oberg describes in *Red Star In Orbit*, Russian cosmonauts Grechko and Romaneko found their diet adequate but boring and developed "insatiable cravings for items they hadn't even thought about on earth."

Having underestimated the importance of varied flavors in the spacemen's diet, Soviet Ground Control attempted to correct the problem: "The presence of a second docking port on Salyut-6 enabled visitors to come calling in orbit. Some of these spacecraft brought special food treats to the cosmonauts, with both dietary and psychological benefits...fresh fruit, fresh bread and additional spices, such as mustard and horseradish — Grechko and Romanenko having gone through their three month supply of spices in five weeks."

After Lorena and I completed a 68-day ocean kayak voyage an acquaintance asked us to describe our most important food. Lorena didn't hesitate: "Garlic!" We had taken garlic powder, dried minced garlic, whole dried cloves and garlic salt—as well as fresh heads, too. Every food

inventory began with, "We've got enough garlic to last until..." Salt could be licked and scraped from rocks above high tide line but garlic had to be carefully rationed.

The Spice Rack: My biggest complaint with spices is that they are difficult to pack. By the end of a hiking trip I often find myself sweeping spices from the inside of my pack and praying there's more flavor there than lint. Lorena's solution is simple and very practical: she sewed small cloth pockets onto a large bandanna and filled these with tiny Zip-Loc bags of spices, all carefully labelled. This ingenious 'spice rack' can be rolled and tied into a very compact bundle that protects the spices from spilling and casual damage. On the beach we lay the spice bandanna out on a convenient rock or log; in the woods and desert it hangs from the nearest branch or cactus. (These 'shelves' can be made to organize your other foods, beverages and utensils.)

Plastic 35mm film cannisters are very useful as spice containers, though I've yet to find a reliable and durable method of labeling them. By the second day I'm reduced to my standard practice of opening each can and sniffing the contents. There's nothing quite like a snort of chile powder when you're looking for parsley for the morning omelette.

On long trips and for food caches, extra spices can be packed inside a plastic bag, then sealed in a second 'Seal A Meal' type bag. Because spices tend to be handled frequently, it pays to carry extra containers to replace those that are damaged or lost.

One of our worst camp kitchen disasters came when a raccoon-like creature raided our kitchen one night and made off with the Chinese mustard, chile peppers and soy sauce. We had carefully stowed away our staple foods and had no idea that precious condiments would be attractive to a wild animal. "It shows a well-developed palate," I said to Lorena.

But we lost more than condiments—three screw top plastic jars. This posed an apparently insoluble problem (we had more condiments in our reserve food bags but no extra containers) until a long beachcombing foray turned up a sun-and-seawater-faded plastic pill jar. I eventually found other pill containers, evidently tossed from passing ships. Though I often cursed the adult-proof tops, they made excellent spice containers. Ask for some at your local pharmacy.

Buy your spices at a bulk foods store or health food shop. They'll be cheaper than already packaged spices and you'll be able to buy the exact quantities that you need. (Dried herbs and spices should be replaced each year.) Spices that go unused waste both money and space. On tough hikes you'll resent that unneeded extra half teaspoon of tarragon as if it were a lead brick.

Vegetables: Dried

At first glance dried vegetables seem to be almost perfect for camp cooking: lightweight, durable, colorful and fairly nutritious. My complaint, however, is that dried vegetables often don't taste very good.

To top it off, most cooks use a heavy hand when adding vegetables, especially 'vegetable mix' (which runs heavily to peas and carrots). This imparts an all-too familiar institutional flavor that I associate with crowded basement cafeterias rather than a wilderness meadow.

The solution, as usual, is a compromise between flavor, weight and convenience. We carry fresh, strong flavored vegetables that keep well (onions, garlic, cucumber, parsley) and use them sparingly. We pack dried vegetables individually, rarely in a mix. 'Mix' becomes a single mixed flavor I call 'gray' or 'monoflavor', similar to mixing brightly tinted paints to produce a dead dull brown.

Our personal dried vegetable preferences are celery, green and red sweet peppers, chiles (milder varieties), garlic, mushrooms and potatoes. Lorena likes dried onions but I don't unless they're sautéed or baked into a casserole.

If you are preparing for a long expedition I strongly suggest that you buy samples of dried vegetables from various sources and give each a careful taste test. Flavor and price can vary considerably.

Use dried vegetables as 'bulky spices' rather than as vegetables to avoid overwhelming your taste buds. You'll also stretch money and food supplies. A dish of fried rice, for example, will look and taste fine even if every bite isn't half vegetables. People who live in less prosperous areas of the world know from necessity and long practice that vegetables and other delicacies (meat, poultry, cheese) go a long way when used as garnishes rather than as main dishes. If your recipe calls for half a cup of dried onions try reducing it to a heaping tablespoonful. Add a pinch of garlic to give a little boost and I doubt that you'll have many complaints.

Drying your own vegetables isn't half as complicated as you might think. (See *Recipes: Drying Fruits & Vegetables*.)

Vegetables: Fresh

Campers who face strict limitations on weight and bulk often make the mistake of asuming there's no room for fresh vegetables in their larder. Unless you'll be climbing (as in mountains) or doing some sort of fanatical sprint-hike, there's no reason to limit yourself to dried foods. The trick is to avoid taking too much fresh produce or produce that is easily squashed, bulky or difficult to prepare.

Because strong flavors are always appreciated in camp, we take onions, garlic, cucumber, carrots and perhaps cabbage. These vegetables are all 'nomadic staples': in some parts of the world, people who live and travel on a very basic level have found them to be reliable, useful foods. They can be eaten raw or cooked, in main dishes, salads or by themselves. Radishes, celery, green pepper and tender squashes such as zucchini are also good for camping.

Select your vegetables carefully. If the trip will be short, don't buy a huge cucumber if a smaller one will satisfy your needs. Small onions are better than large since few meals require an entire big onion. Cutting a large vegetable into halves or quarters allows it to dry out and lose flavor before it is used up.

While van and boat camping, we carry small cabbages with dense, tightly formed leaves. Rather than slicing into the cabbage, peel away enough outer leaves to make the meal. This leaves a smaller ball of cabbage, intact and relatively impervious to damage. Cut surfaces also hasten spoilage and increase waste, since dried out and often dirty edges will be trimmed away.

If the trip will be short, however, or the vegetables intended for immediate use, by all means give them a reasonable 'processing'. I trim away everything that I don't intend to eat and select only the most tender and tasty parts of the vegetable. Some food value may be lost but I'm prepared to accept that on a short trip.

Seal vegetables in separate plastic bags to avoid mixing flavors and then seal the smaller bags inside a larger one. If the weather is warm you'll want to keep a close eye on the vegetables and use up any that show signs of spoiling. If possible, rinse the vegetables and bags in fresh water once a day.

A good quality plastic vegetable container will keep your produce fresh and crisp for days. It will also prevent crushing, a problem if you're lucky enough to have lettuce or leafy greens with you. We use our vegetable container as a general mixing/kitchen bowl when the vegetables have been used up.

On long trips and full-scale expeditions it is possible to enjoy fresh produce of certain types if you're willing to go to a bit of extra work in preparation and handling. See *Cooking Tips & Techniques: Preventing Spoilage.*

Chapter 3

Foraging

Foraging for food is a term that never fails to spark my imagination. Suddenly I am gliding through the cool, green, dark forest, my moccasins treading with deadly silence as I reach into my quiver for a flint tipped arrow.... Later, as I stagger under my burden of fresh venison, I will come upon Lorena squatting beside our campfire, stirring an aromatic stew of savory wild mushrooms, delicate fern tips and roasted acorns. Lorena will, of course, pass on the barbecued loin and feast instead on dark strips of smoked trout, washed down with cups of steaming pine needle tea. Sated, I will whittle on my totem pole or perhaps beat out a few legends on my new skin and sinew drum.

   The reality of foraging for food while camping often turns into a re-hash of a C-grade Mountain Man movie, with desperate campers snorting through the brush like enraged grizzlies in search of anything edible: hiking boots, belts, candy bar wrappers... The skill, attention and plain hard work required to actually forage for satisfying food in the wilds is beyond most of our abilities. Even those who are good at foraging will often admit, though reluctantly, that much of what they've grubbed out of the forests and jungles isn't all that tasty. To palates that have grown accustomed to Dinty Moore stew and Cheerios, a plate of roast skunk cabbage hearts, no matter how lovingly prepared, leaves something to be desired.

This doesn't mean, however, that foraging is a waste of time. To enjoy foraging and to be successful at it you should first determine what type suits you best. I generally break foraging into two main categories: casual foraging, which provides fun and entertainment (and, if you become hooked on fishing, inner peace, spiritual fulfillment, or maybe even Enlightenment) and serious survival foraging. The latter category includes eating grubs, worms, roots, shoots and other ground-level delicacies. It helps to have strong teeth and an even stronger stomach.

The Army manual, *Survival, Evasion and Escape*, sums up serious foraging quite well with these words of advice on fishing: "A hand grenade exploded in a school of fish will supply food for days." I once had the opportunity to test this method, using what a friend called 'Mexican bait', sticks of dynamite lobbed into a shaded pool near the mouth of a jungle lagoon. The people of rural Mexico take foraging quite seriously and though my friend and his neighbors bombarded the pool with enough dynamite to clear forty acres of stumps, all we got for our barrage was half a bucket of pulverized minnows — which were carefully divided among the group and presumably eaten.

Recreational foraging is much more to my liking: fishing, clam digging, picking mushrooms and berries, hopping a fence to grab an apple or two.... (I do not include hunting because of the intense degree of regulation and very limited seasons. From a food standpoint, the most practical target for a hunter is the common robin or song bird, and the best weapon a BB gun or pellet rifle. Enjoying what a friend calls "a nice mess of robins" never fails, however, to outrage other campers and the Law.)

Casual foraging can provide the motivation for a variety of interesting camping trips, many of them off the beaten track. On a recent hike in the Cascade Mountains, for example, Lorena and I were disappointed at the number of people using what we had expected would be a deserted trail to a mountain lake. Later I met a fellow who had hiked nearby on a less popular trail, searching the higher ridges for blueberries. "We didn't see another soul for two days," he said, "and got gallons of berries to boot."

Berry picking is a great activity for children; it not only keeps their hands out of their noses, but rewards them immediately for work with something good to eat. A hint: give the kids a fairly small container for their berries. There's nothing more depressing to a youngster (I recall vividly) than staring into a trashcan-sized bucket with only a few mashed blackberries in the bottom.

Mushrooms are another favorite of foragers. In the Pacific Northwest we have been cursed with an incredible variety of 'rooms' and fungi. I say 'cursed' because my mind is boggled every time I set off into the dark, dank woods in search of mushrooms that I am confident are safe to eat. Deadly impostors seem to crop up near every suspected 'good' mushroom and as the search goes on my self-confidence wears as thin as my patience. I can't seem to match mushrooms from one so-called guidebook to the next. Though these books assure us that positive identification can be made through spore prints, I haven't trusted spores since watching *The Invasion of the Body Snatchers.* By the time I get my mushrooms home, jumbled together in old plastic bread sacks, they look so unappetizing that I immediately bury them deep in the compost pile.

Of all the many types of foraging none compares, in my opinion, to fishing and general seafood scavenging. Have you ever seen a skinny seagull? With very basic equipment even novices can take more fish than they can eat (a continuing problem that will solve itself when the fish are finally gone).

Fishing is almost synonymous to me with camping; I would gladly walk many miles for a trout or drive thousands of miles to surf fish for a big jack crevalle.

One of our finest outdoor trips came as a result of a personal disaster: after a long Spring and slow Summer, Lorena happened to balance out our checkbook.

"We're broke," she announced, switching off the battery powered calculator in a symbolic act of economy and self-denial.

"So what else is new?" The word 'broke' is as familiar to most free-lance writers as 'rejected'.

"I mean *really broke,*" Lorena said, emphasizing the *really* in the same tone that our friend Steve says "really hungry" when on the verge of a rampage through the cupboards and refrigerator.

"You mean so broke we don't have any money?" She nodded solemnly, confirming my worst fears. "Too broke to go sailing?" I continued desperately, thinking of several months' work and resources lovingly poured into our thirty-year-old wooden sloop. Other than dry rot in the mast and evil spirits in the engine the boat was ready to go, freshly painted and straining eagerly at her mooring lines. Puget Sound and its many secret coves and waterways lay just beyond our...budget?

"We have about seventy-five dollars to last us the next two months." This, as the old joke goes, was the good news. "*If* we turn off our water and lights and phone, don't use any gas in the van or buy *Time* magazines." I flinched involuntarily; abject poverty was one thing, but life without *Time*? Pressing world problems left in the bungling hands of career amateurs?

"There is a possible solution," Lorena's voice promised faster relief than a Rolaids commercial.

"Just so it isn't a suicide pact," I answered. "At the price of lumber these days we could only afford a small pine box."

She ignored my attempt at humor. "I was thinking we could just load the garden into the Osprey and sail away. Go north and see what happens."

She waved vaguely toward the Pole. "We've got enough fresh produce to keep us going for quite a while, especially if we pack it up carefully. There must be some place up there with lots of fish and seafood to scrounge. Didn't someone tell us that British Columbia has abandoned homesteads? Maybe we could find some orchards?"

We sailed away five days later, like refugees from the American Dream, the bilges of the Osprey packed with boxes of green tomatoes, potatoes, cabbage, carrots, onions, squash and the contents of our kitchen cabinets. Two-thirds of our money had been earmarked for a Canadian fishing license, the remainder would eventually go for gasoline, laundry soap, charts and matches.

The plan was simple: sail north, using the engine only when absolutely necessary, and search out those overlooked inlets and anchorages where clams were still to be dug at low tide and rock fish schooled near kelp-choked reefs.

Our constant need to forage, especially for seafood, began to influence and eventually dominated our itinerary. During a heavy rainstorm in the lower Gulf Islands we learned everything we ever wanted to know about catching, cooking and eating Dungeness crabs. On the third day, "Crab Bay" began to stick in our throats and in spite of the foul weather we gladly made a rough passage to an area of salmon and cod, wild huckleberries and butter clams. The wilder and more remote the country, the more abundant and varied the free food.

The days and weeks slide by easily when you've got nothing more to worry about than the weather and your next meal. At the end of the first month, in an almost totally protected harbor on a rarely visited island, Lorena completed the fantasy.

I had spent the morning taking advantage of a low tide by gathering a bucket of oysters. Baking on top of an oil-fueled 'Gypsy' stove aboard a sailboat is always difficult, but I had increased the challenge by adding oysters to the bread dough. 'Fisherman's Pot Pie' would either be a sublime success or a slimy mess; it was all a matter of timing and fanatical adjustment of the fuel drip valve. When Lorena came aboard, announced by the thump of the skiff against the hull, I barely took notice. Until I heard her chew.

"What're you eating?" I asked, keeping a close eye on the cast iron Dutch oven. Constant foraging has side effects, one of which is an increased awareness of all things edible: odor, texture, size, heft, ripeness, availability. Lorena was chewing, therefore Lorena had found something to eat. I wanted some. As I turned to face her she reached into a bulging jacket pocket and produced, magically, no mirrors, a fresh bright red apple!

"Abandoned homestead?" I asked around a crunchy mouthful. "Old orchard?"

Lorena smiled, nodding her head. Apples put a whole new face on things. With an adequate supply of apples we'd have little to fear: apple pie, applesauce, apple...jack?

Boxes of wormy, gnarled apples filled the gaps in the larder. It was just a short leap in logic to barter our treasure to other fruit-impoverished boaters. What sailor in their right mind could resist the temptation of a fresh baked apple pie?

A final suggestion on foraging, inspired by our friend Fred Feibel. Fred, better known as Monoped, lost a leg in Vietnam while mixing a rum and coke. This left him so traumatized, he says, that he has never been able to cook or do dishes again. He can sail, skin dive and even dance, but the very sight of a skillet sends Fred reeling toward the nearest comfortable chair. To avoid starving while camping and beyond the range of restaurants, Fred has developed a unique foraging technique called "Whining & Dining."

"Sure smells good. What is it?" is his standard opener, followed immediately by, "Anything I can do to help? Oh! My leg!" To take the edge off this type of sting, Fred will go to great lengths to praise the cook and if all else fails, he will even provide the groceries and a kitchen (cleverly built into his van). Unsuspecting hitchhikers and fellow campers by the dozen have fallen for his wide grin and casual "Hey, sure is getting hungry around here!"

Steve was leading on the narrow trail, laboring up the pine-covered mountainside with enough gasps and deep wheezing breaths to soundtrack a dozen X-rated movies.

"Aah! Look!" At his cry I turned to admire the view. Several hundred square miles of Colorado lay spread out beyond us, forests of dark green conifers splashed with the rust and gold of autumn-bright aspens.

Lorena came up behind me, cheeks flushed with the exertion and altitude. High country hiking takes a heavy toll on lowlanders.

We admired the spectacular view with cries of "Wow! Incredible!" and "Fantastic!" that seemed more appropriate to a Buck Rogers comic strip than the wilderness Southwest.

"Where ... *puff* ... is Steve?" Lorena motioned inquiringly toward the steep section of trail ahead. Steve had taken the lead half an hour earlier, determined, he said, to make camp before his heart burst from over-use. The logic was slippery but familiar, similar to his habit of driving faster when the gas gauge on his van is low, in order to reach a service station sooner.

The trail was now empty.

"That's odd," I said. He was standing right there just a few seconds ago. Maybe he..."

"Ohhh *WOW!*" The sudden bellow was followed by heavy crashing in the dense underbrush on the slope below us. Small trees quivered and branches snapped. "Hundreds!" Steve's excited voice echoed in the clear mountain air. "Maybe even *thousands!* I can't... oh! *More!*" I caught a quick glimpse of Steve's dark tangled hair as he scrambled on hands and knees behind a clump of bushes. His backpack snagged for a second on a low limb but tore free as a headlong rush took him downhill and finally out of sight.

"What's he doing?" Lorena shrugged off the heavy pack and quickly assumed Position A: prone, eyes half-closed, long legs crossed at the ankles. Steve's behavior might be bizarre, but by his standards it wasn't unusual enough to cause real concern.

I pulled out my pocket watch. Like arctic explorers racing a fatal chill, I knew that if Lorena didn't start moving within three minutes, it would take heroic measures to stir her blood and get her back on her feet again. On the thickly wooded slope below, Steve's rampage continued. I listened curiously.

"Can't get 'em all into... don't want to crush... incredible bonanza!!"

I realized that he must be onto the scent of food. Like a truffle-hunting boar Steve had gone to ground, foraging up some low-level delicacy that other, less observant hikers had overlooked.

He reappeared on the trail a few minutes later, eyes bright with excitement. Stumbling heavily on a tangle of small vines that clung to the eyelets of his hiking boots, Steve rushed up to us, hands outstretched and overflowing with "...*Mushrooms!*" His beard trembled with excitement. "Look at these mushrooms, would'ya! I got a huge bag of them! Look at this one!"

He thrust a moist meaty-orange blob at me, then just as suddenly snatched it back. "That one's a little bit smashed. Still good of course but I did step on a few. Just need a rinse!" His hand plunged into a bulging pants pocket. "Look at these!" Badly crushed mushrooms were mixed with assorted keys and small change. "Hardly a worm in them! More than enough here to make a really great spaghetti sauce! Guess that takes care of dinner, huh?" The relief in his voice was proof that Steve's concern over his immediate health was based as much on the condition of his stomach as his straining heart and lungs.

I hesitated, then blurted, "But Steve, how do you know if these mushrooms are... what if they're...?" The unspoken word hung between us.

"*Poisonous?*" Lorena obligingly filled in the blank.

"POISONOUS?" Steve's outrage echoed off distant mountain sides. I glanced uneasily toward the sky, expecting dark clouds and angry thunderbolts to answer our blasphemies. "Poisonous?" Steve repeated, his voice now but a sad and disillusioned whisper. With eyes turned dramatically heavenward, he cast off his sixty pound backpack as if it were an empty paper bag. Freed from this annoying burden, he began running the palms of his open hands over the bulging expanse of his red-checked

wool shirt. Like the pawing of an enraged brown bear, this belly stroking signalled an impending charge. I braced for the worst.

"What do *you* know about mushrooms, anyway?" Steve's voice was thick with bitterness and sarcasm. "Who around here flunked botany?" He gave me a hard stare, then adroitly cut off a protest from Lorena by sneering, "Maybe you'd rather fix a few fried mice?"

I felt the stirring of tired blood. "Just one minute!" I shouted. "How do you suddenly know so much about mushrooms?"

Steve looked away, thinking hard.

"What kind are they? Can you identify them?"

He shrugged angrily, dismissing my question with a disgusted wave of his hand. As his left thumb idly stroked the side of a glistening mushroom Steve said hesitantly, "Morels?" He looked again at the heavy squat mushroom. "Chanterelles? Chicken of the Woods? Maybe they're..."

"Fly Amanitas? Death Angels?" I hissed, exhausting my entire knowledge of mushrooms and fungi in one last attempt.

Steve's head snapped up. "They're *definitely not* Amanitas!" His head shook an emphatic *no*. "Actually they look more to me like a cross between morels and chanterelles."

"A cross? Isn't that unlikely? They could be something really weird, don't you think? After all there's hundreds and hundreds of different mushrooms." I paused, adding, "Many quite *deadly*." in my best Vincent Price voice.

Steve's face clouded with frustration. A university degree in zoology and professional scientific training were butting heads with an awesome appetite. "Morels! Chanterelles! Toad stools!" he shouted. "What's the big difference? They're all basically good!" He threw his arms apart, embracing all mushrooms in a common bond of compassion and edibility.

"Couldn't we just wait and have somebody identify them?" I gave him a hopeful, conciliatory smile. "We can always buy some real mushrooms at the Safeway?" Steve snorted impatiently.

"Is this good enough for you?" His hand darted to his mouth, teeth baring for a quick nip. A slow, tentative chewing gradually became a triumphant, somewhat weak grin. Steve gulped dryly, then gasped, "Tastes great!" as he proudly displayed a bagel-sized mushroom with a tiny portion bitten from the edge. "Don't worry! Relax!" Steve said expansively, "I'm going to fix a spaghetti sauce you'll never forget!"

"Oh Lord, I feel beat!" Steve lay sprawled on his back, one hand seemingly thrust into the flames of the cookfire as he stirred his beloved spaghetti sauce. "That last few miles was a killer, wasn't it?" Smoke plumed lazily across the cool evening sky. "Sometimes I think we ought to take up a sport that's a little easier on the old body: overweight and over forty, but not quite over the hill!" He choked with laughter, then gave a startled howl of pain as a hot ember leaped into the thatched hair surrounding his belly button.

I nudged the fine focus on my binoculars, indulging in a harmless session of spying on our nearest neighbors. As Steve's cry carried across the remote valley I saw startled heads turned anxiously skyward.

"What are they up to now?" Steve asked, idly chopping at a few mushrooms left over from his earlier cooking frenzy.

They seem to have the fire under control," I said, "and now they're either putting up a complicated tent or erecting some sort of distress signal. Whatever it is, it's very colorful."

"Maybe they'll stop by," Steve said wistfully, "and have a plate of spaghetti." We both knew this was unlikely. Our neighbors had passed us on the trail earlier, looking askance at our battered gear, faded clothing and unkempt hair and beards. Even Lorena's cheery smile had failed to ease the suspicion on their well-scrubbed faces as they edged around us with a polite but nervous, "Have a good day?" Steve summed it up quite well when he complained, "No matter how much stuff I order from L.L. Bean, I still end up looking like the Wild Man of Borneo."

"Guess we're in for a big siege of leftovers," Steve said sadly, stirring the sauce with the blade of his huge pocket knife. He licked the razor-sharp blade clean as casually as if it were a spoon. Leftovers rate very low in Steve's culinary hierarchy, falling somewhere above what he calls "McFodder" and below bologna omelettes. Leftovers are a useless byproduct, a barely recyclable waste material that delays the next portion of 'real' food.

"Nother drink?" Steve offered, waving the plastic jug of tequila toward me.

"Later," I said. "The altitude is giving me a headache."

He smiled sympathetically. "I know what you mean," he said. "That's why I like drinking above 7,000 feet. The stuff hits you like a freight train." Steve wrapped his rubbery lips around the mouth of the jug, sucking deeply.

"Especially on an empty stomach!" he choked. "So it goes a lot farther. Saves weight."

"Just a little bit more," Steve urged, forcing another huge spoonful of sauce onto my noodles.

I snatched the bowl away as he tried to add yet another portion.

"Geez!" He snorted disgustedly. "What is this, some kind of hunger strike?"

Retiring to the shadows, I sat crosslegged on the ground, took up my bowl and probed hesitantly at a spongy dark mass, coated thickly with tomato sauce and herbs. Offering up a silent non-denominational prayer, I closed my eyes and slowly opened my mouth...

I woke slowly, crawling toward consciousness across an endless, blistering plain of soft sand, my throat raw with thirst. On the horizon, shimmering refrigerators stacked with frosty bottles of root beer and orange juice lured me on. I tore the tops off, desperately guzzling the freezing liquid...another...and another...

"Carl! Carl! Wake up, would'ya?"

I jerked up, confused by the cold darkness. Steve's prone bulk was barely visible on the other side of our dying camp fire. I heard the crackle of twigs as he fed a small limb into the glowing embers.

"You...okay?"

I smacked my lips together, groping for the canteen. "I've got a killer thirst," I yawned, unscrewing the cap and pouring the cold water into my mouth. Steve has a well-known reputation for using garlic and cayenne in industrial quantities. His mushroom spaghetti sauce would have scoured the bottom paint off a Coast Guard icebreaker.

"Not feeling...sick or anything?"

Drowsy, I ignored the anxiety in his voice. "Feel fine," I answered. "Though I'm dry as an old bone." I ran my hand over my stomach. "Gut burns a little. Probably ate too much. Indigestion."

At the word "indigestion" Steve let out a piercing cry of agony that reverberated through the dark woods like the screech of a dying rabbit.

"What's wrong!" I yelled, horrified by his contortions inside the narrow sleeping bag.

"Carl!" he gasped, "I...I...*ohmygod!* Ahh! Ahhhhh!" The twigs gave off a sudden flare. Steve's eyes were wide and glazed with fright; his face a ghastly pale even in the warm fire light. Sweat beaded his forehead and with each yelp, his knees moved closer to his chest, straining the seams on his Army surplus mummy bag.

"Those mushrooms!" he choked, tears squeezing from his eyes as another spasm rocked his body. "Poisoned! I'm *poisoned!*" He rolled suddenly to his knees, shuffling away from the fire with a strange humping motion, the sleeping bag tangled around his legs and waist.

I felt the bile rising in my throat. Poisoned? If Steve was...then that meant that we...

"Whazzit? 'Smatter?" Lorena had finally awakened. "What's happening?" she demanded, reaching automatically for her water bottle and Vitamin C powder. In Lorena's world, all problems respond to Vitamin C, preferably in massive, throat and stomach searing doses.

"We're dying!" Steve wheezed, rolling onto his back at the edge of the bushes. He took a long ragged breath. "Oh Lord!" he cried, "Please don't let this be one of those nerve toxins that turns you into a vegetable!"

My stomach has somehow calmed itself. I couldn't resist. "Like a mushroom? You are what you eat, right?"

Steve rolled heavily onto his side, facing me across the fire. His eyes filled with hurt. "Very, *very* funny!" he groaned. "Maybe you can carve that on my gravestone!" His snarl turned to yelps of pain as he lapsed into another attack.

I crawled quickly to Lorena's side. "Feel okay?" I whispered anxiously. She hesitated for only a moment.

"Sure. Little queasy, maybe, from all those spices."

"*Carl?*" Steve's call was weak, yet perfectly pitched to reach the most distant listener. His hand clawed feebly in the air, beckoning me to him.

"Doing any better?" I asked, kneeling on the ground beside him.

"Bad. Real bad!" He wiped at his forehead with the back of a trembling hand. His lower jaw went slack, then snapped closed as he suppressed a tremendous shuddering belch.

"Gas?"

"No! No! No!" Steve gasped. "This isn't gas, it's..." he pawed skyward, as though warding off the Black Angel, "it's *poison!*"

"Well, your pupils look good," I said, wondering to myself just what *bad* pupils even meant, "and your pulse seems strong." I squeezed his wrist, shocked to feel a throb as heavy and wild as a runaway voodoo drum. "Feel any...uh..." I racked my memory for an appropriate medical term, "any mental anguish or feelings of, say, *impending doom?*"

Steve's eyes widened horribly, then snapped shut. Tears trickled from the corners of his eyes.

"How about shortness of breath?" He began panting like a marathon runner.

"Involuntary muscle cramps?" His legs drew up with a gasp of pain.

"Uncontrollable salivation?" His jaw worked slowly, like a kid preparing a particularly awful spitball.

"Itching between your toes?" His eyes opened thoughtfully.

"You rotten son of a...!" Steve hissed, "You think this is funny, don'tcha?" He turned away, drawing the sleeping bag over his head. "You can laugh all you want at the funeral, you turkey!" The words were muffled, punctuated by little gasps of pain. Shivering, I went back to my own bed.

"Carl?" Steve's voice was unnaturally calm and controlled, very bad signs, indeed.

"Yeah, Steve?"

"Could you do me a favor?"

"Sure, I suppose. What?"

"Give all my cooking stuff to John Kibbons." There was a tremor in his voice. "My knives and things. You know."

"Sure, no trouble."

"And you and Lorena...can have the van."

"Really?" I cringed, stuffing my wrist into my mouth to keep from laughing.

"Why not?" His voice blended resentment, fatalism, self-pity and resignation with the skill of a Renaissance painter mixing oils on a palette. "*I* certainly won't be needing it," he added.

"Steve?"

"Yes?" The response came as a weak sigh. The End was near.

"Do you happen to have the title with you?"

"To the *van?*" He was up on elbows now, peering suspiciously across the fire.

"Yeah," I answered, "It would really cut down on paperwork and red tape if you signed the van over to me now, rather than, you know, having to get it from the estate."

"WHY YOU UNGRATEFUL...!" Steve was on his feet, kicking angrily at his sleeping bag. "I spend six hours fixing dinner and this is the kind of appreciation I get! You make me..."

"Sick?" I regretted the taunt as Steve dropped heavily to his knees, clutching his belly with a truly agonized moan. A sudden burning rumble in my own stomach quickly wiped the smile from my face. Grabbing a flashlight and plastic trowel I hurried into the bushes, tripped, stumbled, and sprawled head-long to the ground.

"What is *this?*" I yelled, angrily untangling the wire handle of our largest stewpot from around my ankle. I lifted the pot and caught a strong whiff of garlic.

"OH, that?" Steve answered with elaborate casualness, "That's the mushroom sauce pot. I put it out there in case any creatures came by and wanted to lick it out." Steve's dishwashing methods are not *Good Housekeeping* approved.

"Well, where's the leftover sauce?" I grumbled, getting back to my feet and fumbling in the darkness for my roll of toilet paper. "I thought you said we had gallons left?"

"Oh, well..." his voice was too controlled, "you know how it is...hassling with...well, I, uh, sort of polished them off. No one else seemed to care so I guess it was up to me, *as usual!*" He ended on an indignant note of self-righteousness. After all, how many camp cooks would choose martyrdom with mushroom spaghetti sauce over the shame of leftovers?

"Well, that answers the poisoning question." I dropped the empty pot next to the fire. Lorena shook her head in silent amazement.

"If Lorena and I got indigestion from one serving, I think we can safely assume that eating three quarts of the stuff would..."

"Carl?"

"Yeah, Steve?"

He snuggled deep inside his sleeping bag, "Do you think you could just sort of *shut up for a while?* We could all use some sleep. I want to get up really early tomorrow. I think there may be another patch or two of mushrooms back down the trail that I missed." He gave a deep contented yawn. "Doesn't a mushroom omelette sound tempting...?"

Chapter 4
The Complete Camp Kitchen

The selection of specific equipment and utensils for your camp kitchen depends on the type of trip—from desert hiking to motor home vagabonding—your personal cooking style, food preferences and your budget.

If you will be camping from a large vehicle, assembling a kitchen may be as simple as dumping the contents of a few cupboards and drawers into boxes and loading them aboard your pickup or motor home. Friends solved the camp stove problem by disconnecting their home gas range and installing it in a converted schoolbus. Those going on foot, by small car, canoe, animal back or a raft will have to pay much closer attention to what gear they take—and don't take.

Select kitchen equipment that is compatible to your personal cooking and eating style. A friend who is a fanatical wok cook took one hiking instead of a frying pan. He soon discovered, however, that the wok would not sit securely on top of his backpacking stove (fires were restricted) and had to be watched constantly to avoid a disastrous fall.

Another friend bought a beautiful stainless steel pressure cooker for car and canoe camping. After a number of rather bland, overcooked meals, she realized that none of her favorite recipes benefited from pressure cooking.

Some outfitting mistakes can be much more serious: did you know that propane and natural gas stoves often won't work at low temperatures? Since hot food and water from melted snow are vital for winter and high altitude camping, a good reliable stove is more than a convenience, it is an essential survival tool.

Other examples aren't quite so dramatic but deserve consideration: we took one small can of minced green chiles as a special treat on a backpacking trip. Because neither of us happened to have a pocket knife with a can opener at the time, we had to carry a full-sized opener. Lugging a four-ounce can opener for ten miles in order to eat two ounces of chiles seemed more ridiculous by the mile.

If, at this point, you feel a sense of impending confusion and hysteria overtaking you, take heart! A few Words-of-Wisdom are in order; words that I stumbled upon on a camping trip long-ago. I stumbled because I was carrying a small iron skillet in my pack. The words were engraved on the stone I tripped over. They read: *"Keep It Simple!"*

Unfortunately, simplicity isn't always the goal of outdoor equipment designers and manufacturers, some of whom are doing their best to increase profits while making simple camping a thing of the past. I have to admit to feeling like a slow learner when confronted by the complexity and sophistication of new camping gear.

Recently, I went to a fancy wilderness outfitter's shop in search of a stove...

"May I help you, sir?" The salesman approaches with the casual movements of a hunting shark. One false move and I'll leave the store wearing snow shoes and carrying a Himalayan Bivouac Pack stuffed with freeze-dried lobster tails.

"Uh, what kind of camp stoves have you got?"

"Well, just exactly what are your *requirements?*" He flashes me a knowing smile. Last weekend he clung to the summit of Mount Endurance with his fingernails and boiled Russian Tea on a cloud top. He is very knowledgeable.

"Well, er, beans...making some coffee, frying fish. You know."

Barely suppressing a groan he leads me across the thickly carpeted shop to an oak and plate glass display case. "Gas, pellets, solid, liquid, disposable, rechargeable or multi-use? Kerosene, butane, gasoline, naptha, alcohol or special blend?"

"Brass," I answer, licking my lips as my eyes roam nervously over the bewildering assortment of stoves that crowd the shelves.

"Brass? Did you say *brass?*" He repeats the word several times, peering at me as though through a dangerous winter white-out.

"Yeah, brass," I answer, plunging ahead. "I like shiny brass things. What have you got?"

The groan is no longer suppressed; I am off the Final Assault Team, obviously not summit material, just another low-level load humper and gear hauler. He impatiently opens the display case and points at a stove. His description flows as quickly as a drawn-out yawn: "This is Model ZR Nine-oh-five-seven with twenty-four-point-two ounces dry weight, fuel capacity point-nine liters, giving you an average boiling time at five thousand meters of three hundred and twenty seconds and total burn time of..." his eyebrows raise significantly, "just over two-point-six hours!"

Before I can register the proper degree of amazement he continues to reel off information. "Stability factor is a bit low when compared to the XR Seven or the older DX Ten...but then they've been out of production for seven years...anyway, it's highly rated for ease of operation, compactness, durability and subzero — Celsius, of course — operation. What do you make of it?"

"It's pretty. Got a nice polish."

He stares at the stove for several seconds. His lower jaw is working back and forth as though clearing his ears at high altitude. His shoulders flex in the manner of a climber shifting the weight of an enormous backpack. "Yes," he sighs, a well manicured thumb idly polishing the sleek surface of the stove's fuel tank.

I impulsively make the momentous decision to buy the stove. The salesman's interest perks up as he equips me with spare parts and vital accessories: filter, funnel, spare 0 rings, wire orifice cleaners, a nifty vaporizer for improved fuel economy (my new burn time is hard to beat), windscreen, eyedropper, spare fuel flask and emergency priming pellets ("Once on Deadman Pass..." he tells me).

"That ought to wrap it up!" he laughs, steering me toward the front door. Another customer is inquiring about the loft factor of a cross-block, baffle bivvy bag and it is nearly closing time.

"Just one more thing!" I say, ignoring the ice-axe grip on my left elbow. He stops, eyeing me suspiciously. (What will it be this time — a canvas wall tent for twelve?)

"Yes?"

"Do you have a small can of Brasso?"

The hazards of over-equipping, buying useless or novelty gear and impractical 'conveniences' are especially obvious when outfitting a camp kitchen. Take, for example, the portable plastic kitchen sink. This isn't a bad joke but an actual piece of 'camping' gear available in many large sporting goods stores. Whenever I spot a label proclaiming that a piece of equipment is designed 'especially for camping' I immediately suspect it of being useless or unnecessary — or both.

Equipment that is truly useful and versatile isn't always the most attractive, ingenious, compact or lightweight. It is, however, often the best bargain, the easiest to use and the most durable. Consider the humble bucket. When filled with hot soapy water it makes an excellent kitchen sink, as well as laundry tub, foot bath or personal bathing 'sink'. Although a folding plastic bucket will tuck into a small space when not in use, it cannot be used for heating water.

A metal bucket, however, can be used for dipping and heating water or snow, makes an excellent container for hauling truly heavy loads of clams, rocks or what-have-you (for some reason I seem to haul a lot of mud and sand on certain camping trips), and can even be used for cooking (if it's not painted or galvanized).

Improvised Cooking Gear

One of my first camp cooking outfits wasn't much more than a set of mismatched tin cans I'd scrounged from my mother's kitchen trash. I screwed on clumsy handles out of six inch sections of an old broomstick, and fashioned lids from aluminum foil. This Hobo Special wasn't much to look at but it cooked quite a few low-budget meals on several camping and fishing trips. Tin can pots work so well, in fact, that I still use them from time to time. What they lack in beauty is more than made up for in their low cost.

To prevent food from sticking to the bare can, try this: wipe the inside with cooking oil and place it in a 250° oven for an hour. We have a wood cook stove at home, so I 'season' my tin cans on top, taking care not to overheat and scorch the oil. Repeat this seasoning process after every trip. When washing the cans-pots, try to avoid deep scrubbing that will scour away the protective coating.

A FEW USES FOR THE
UNGALVANIZED METAL BUCKET

Tin cans make good baking pans and double boilers. Place one can inside another, and add water to the outer, larger can so that it insulates the inner can. A few small stones under the bottom of the smaller can will allow water to flow under it and help prevent sticking and scorching. The double boiler method is ideal for slow cooked meals. (Use stiff coat hanger wire handles for better nesting or buy a 'pot grabber'.)

Junk stores and garage sales are wonderful sources of inexpensive cooking gear. A frying pan might not have the latest space age non-stick coating, but if the price is low enough — and I've found good pans for as little as 25 cents — you'll feel more patient with sticky spots.

If a used utensil isn't quite right for camp cooking, consider a modification. Sauce pans with long, heavy handles can be converted into sauce pans with short handles, or even no handles, with a few careful swipes of a hacksaw. Missing lids can be improvised from foil or matched up from other pots and pans. Large knobs can be replaced by lightweight wing nuts or wire loops.

Aluminum coffee pots with missing 'guts' are a dime a dozen in thrift shops and junk stores. They make excellent cook pots and are obviously well-suited for heating tea and coffee water. I especially like them for soup; the strainer spout makes it easy to get an equitable division of the goodies at the bottom of the pot.

Outdoor Shops and Alternatives

Outdoor specialty stores have a reputation for high mark-ups on camping gear. Labeling a plastic bottle as a 'Backpacker's Flask' somehow justifies doubling the price. To avoid paying too much, leave the outdoor shops for the last resort.

Dime stores, supermarkets, discount stores and hardware stores can supply much of your gear at just about the lowest retail price.

In a dime store we bought plastic bottles sold as glue dispensers and used them for soy sauce, cooking oil, liquid soap and other liquids. They've held up as well as expensive bottles we bought in backpacking shops.

Similar bargains on an amazing variety of plastic food containers, plates, bowls, cups and very lightweight pots and pans can be found in discount stores and large supermarkets.

Buying camping equipment by mail is tricky. A significant difference in price can often be found from one company to another. At the same time, one catalog may offer a real deal on a popular item (known in supermarket jargon as a 'loss leader' to attract customers) but overprice other gear. Quality control may be sloppy; check their return policy and allow enough time to send defective gear back for replacement or refund. A number of mail order supply houses are listed in the *Appendices* of this book.

Once you've exhausted the alternatives and must shop in a specialty store to complete your equipment, here are some final hints:

- Ask a poor but knowledgeable friend to accompany you, someone who will wince at every price tag.
- Be rested and cheerful; weariness leads to "Ah, what the hell?" spending.
- Take a list of what you *need*, not what you want.
- Examine the most pared-down models available. Once you determine that it fulfills your requirements, stop there; more elaborate and expensive versions aren't necessary.
- Look for slightly damaged goods or 'seconds'. Competition also creates good deals: ask for last year's models at substantially reduced prices.
- Watch for sales, especially end-of-season (late summer and fall), inventory (after Christmas and New Year) and pre-season (early spring).
- Don't sacrifice quality, however, just to save a few bucks. Careful shopping also means buying gear that will survive the rigors of a long camping trip.

Camp Kitchens

After thousands of camping meals we have divided our kitchen gear into three basic categories: the Backpacker Kitchen, the Suitcase Kitchen and the Colonizer's Kitchen (or, if you prefer, the Expedition Kitchen). The type of trip we plan to make determines which kitchen we'll use. We also make liberal adjustments. The Backpacker Kitchen, for example, is also our Kayaking Kitchen with a few additions and changes. Because driftwood is plentiful on remote beaches in Puget Sound we don't need our small stove when kayaking and camping there. If firewood is not available at a particular camp we should have enough food on hand that can be eaten raw or unheated to tide us over.

The Backpacker's Kitchen is a compact and lightweight setup that also forms the heart of the Suitcase Kitchen.

As the name implies, the Suitcase Kitchen is designed to fit into a small suitcase or sturdy box. We use it on short van trips, or longer car and boat camping expeditions where space and weight are important considerations.

The Colonizer's Kitchen is an expanded version of the Suitcase Kitchen. We take it on extended vehicle trips and when cruising by sailboat. It is ideal for expeditions that have no definite goal or timetable, and for trips where eating is a major entertainment.

A detailed discussion of specific gear follows the kitchen lists.

Backpacker's Kitchen

This kitchen is for two people but with it we've fed as many as six for short periods of time. With the addition of another cup, an extra spoon and a bowl, it served three of us quite well on a seven-week kayaking voyage.

We sometimes had to use hats for salad bowls, but otherwise we had few problems.

The equipment listed is of backpacking weight, that is, as light as reasonably possible. When you're travelling in a vehicle or boat, you can substitute standard kitchen items for many things without overloading.

Stove
Grate
2 Fuel Bottles (1 liter)
Stove Primer (if needed)
2 Pots (nesting)
2 Pot Grabbers (I lose one)
Frying Pan (8-10 inch, Teflon)
Spatula (plastic or wooden)
4 Dish Towels/Bandannas
Frisbee (optional)
Teapot (metal, 4-cup)
Zip-Loc Bags (assorted)
Aluminum Foil (several yards)
Pot Scrubber (plastic)
Lighter, Matches

Knife (We carry Lorena's small filet knife and a vegetable knife)
Pocket Steel
Can and Bottle Opener (optional)
2 Cups (metal)
2 Bowls (plastic with lids)
2 Plates (metal, optional)
2 Spoons, Chopsticks
Jars and Bottles (plastic, assorted)
Storage Bags (for Kitchen)
Purifying Pills or Liquid
    (See *Camp Kitchen Skills: Staying Healthy*)
Soap
Comal (tortilla griddle)

The Suitcase Kitchen

Imagine the looks of amazement and envy on the faces of other campers when you wheel your Mini Motor into the camp area, leap briskly to the trunk, whip out what appears to be an ordinary suitcase, pop it open on the hood of the car and lo-and-behold, reveal a complete kitchen! Their mouths will drop open, especially when you add the master touch of conjuring up a five-course meal that sends them drooling to their own camps to heat another can of hash.

The Suitcase Kitchen should fit onto the back of a motorcycle, under a canoe seat or in the trunk of even the smallest car. We try to keep ours stocked with a basic assortment of non-perishable foods. The Suitcase sits at home in a corner, waiting to be grabbed for spur-of-the-moment camping trips. A quick stop at the local supermarket should fill out the list of fresh foods you'll want for a weekend trip or even longer.

This list is *in addition* to the Backpacker's Kitchen:

Forks

Paper Plates

Salt Shaker

Cutting Board (thin plywood)

Egg Container

Grater

Vegetable Peeler

Mixing Whisk

Small Strainer

Drinking Water (1 quart)

Rice (½ pound)

Noodles (½ pound)

Cooking Oil (1 pint)

Honey (1 pint)

Dried Milk

Cheese (2 pounds)

Vegetables (onions, tomatoes, etc.)

Eggs (1 dozen)

Herbs and Spices

Coffee, Tea

Dried Fruit (1 pound)

Cereal (½ pound)

Here's how to put it all together. Assemble everything on your living room floor. Put the foodstuffs into their containers, or if you haven't got the containers yet, use bags and small boxes. The idea is to calculate how much space it will all take, without putting it together into a tight, interlocking Chinese Puzzle. If things aren't easy to get at and put away again, confusion will quickly become chaos.

Okay, now pack it all into a cardboard box. Use a shallow box, roughly the dimensions of a suitcase or small foot locker. Does it fit without piling too many things on top of each other? If so, head for the Goodwill or discount store and find a suitcase that will hold everything. Ours is a small, cheap, tin and cardboard suitcase we bought in Mexico. After many years of use, it is rusty but still serviceable.

The best kitchen will be in one suitcase or box, but two or even three containers are fine, just as long as each has its own internal order and logic (condiments and spices in one, food in another, utensils and stove in another, etc.).

Dividers inside the suitcase or box will improve the organization. Use stiff cardboard, thin plywood, masonite, pegboard, thin aluminum or plastic. Discount stores are great places to find 'organizer' containers used for kitchens, workshops and offices. Attach a piece of pegboard inside the lid and use clips, lengths of elastic and strong magnets to hold knives, spatulas and other utensils.

I love to use our Suitcase Kitchen in hotels. By cooking our own meals we can justify paying a little more for a room. Just go easy on the garlic or you'll have curious guests and hotel employees lined up outside your door.

The Colonizer's Kitchen

If you take eating as seriously as we do, the Colonizer's Kitchen should satisfy your needs, both for long camping trips and short bouts of complex gluttony. This kitchen is based on the Suitcase Kitchen and will fit into a medium-sized footlocker with careful packing and luck. The complete version isn't really lightweight, so if it flattens the springs on your Ford you'd better do without a few items.

Pressure Cooker

Blender

Electric Skillet

Large and Medium Kettles

Dutch Oven or Covered Skillet

Food Mill

Plastic Funnel

Measuring Cup, Spoons

Vacuum Bottle

Apron

Folding Oven

Baking Pan

Bucket or Dishpan

Butcher Knife

Bean and Potato Masher

Casserole Dish

Salad Bowl

Wooden Utensils

Fire Fan

Shopping Bags

Baskets

Mortar and Pestle

Rolling Pin

Large Fire Grate

Towels and Rags

The Bare Bones Kitchen

One other type of camp kitchen deserves mention: the Bare Bones or No-Kitchen-At-All. I used this in my younger days, when all I'd take on a week-long trout fishing trip was a roll of aluminum foil and a salt shaker. On overnight visits to the beach, I'd expand this basic outfit with a geoduck clam shell. These huge shells are tough enough to boil up a generous serving of Tide Flat Stew: anything edible that can be scraped off the beach and boiled.

The Bare Bones Kitchen listed here represents just about the minimum for actual cooking while camping. The typical Bare Bones menu runs heavily to soups, stews and true one-pot concoctions. It is very easy to assemble and to clean up after. Using the Bare Bones Kitchen might seem like a cruel and unusual punishment, but once you've mastered simple cooking techniques I think you'll be pleasantly surprised at how well it works. The sense of accomplishment and satisfaction will make up for some inconvenience. For two or even three campers:

Cook Pot or Tin Can (1 quart with lid)   Aluminum Foil
Pot Grabber   Matches
2 Cups (metal, not too small)   Carrying Sack
Knife (with can opener)   Pot Scrubber (optional)
2 Spoons

The cups serve double-use as bowls and plates; the sack might also hold staple and fresh foods.

Kitchen Equipment Discussion: Take It or Leave It?

Go through this list and discussion before making any final gear decisions; if you're like me, reading about frying pans can spark a good idea about hot pads.

Aluminum Foil   Dish Towels and Bandannas
Apron   Electrical Appliances
Bowls   Flashlights
Canteens and Water Jugs   Food Mill
Containers: Frisbee
  Plastic Containers   Frying Pan (See *Pots*)
  Plastic Bags, Zip-Loc Griddles, Tortilla *Comal*
  Cargo and River Bags Grills
  Stuff Sacks   Hot Pads
Cooking Kits   Ice Chest and Refrigerators
Cups

Knives
Lights (See *Stoves and Lanterns*)
Ovens: Folding and Reflector
Plates: Paper Plates and Towels
Pots, Pans and Frying Pans
Pot Grabbers
Pressure Cooker
Spoons
Stoves and Lanterns
   Choosing a Camp Stove
   Backpacking Stove
   Fuel Containers

Stuff Sacks (See *Containers*)
Tables and Cutting Boards
Vacuum Bottles
Water Tanks and Containers
Zip-Loc Bags (See *Containers*)
Portable Herb and Salad Garden

RV, Truck, Van and Car Kitchens
Storage Containers and Cabinets
   The Drift
Furniture
Awnings
Ventilation

Aluminum Foil

Foil is obviously handy for wrapping and baking fresh vegetables, fish, fruit and even casseroles, but heavy foil can also be folded into improvised bowls, cups, plates and cooking pots. Heavy foil makes a good windscreen for stoves, open fires and improvised smokers. Foil will also reflect and direct the miserly heat of small stoves and camp fires when attempting to thaw out chilled fingers and toes.

We often improvise mini-reflector ovens from aluminum foil to heat sandwiches, tortillas and leftovers. Fold a two foot long section of foil in half, with the shiny side facing in. Lay this next to your fire and prop open the upper half of the folded foil with twigs or metal tent pegs. Place the food to be heated on the bottom side of the foil 'V'. This is a good method for cooking tiny bits of meat, fish and seafood that won't stay on a grill.

Heavy duty foil can survive a great deal of use and re-use. We carry ours in a bag to prevent it from sooting up other gear and loose clothing.

The most ingenious use of aluminum foil I've seen was a homemade fishing lure created by a ten-year-old Mexican boy. He wrapped foil around a hand-carved wooden 'plug', attached hook and line and trolled it behind his father's dugout canoe with amazing success.

Apron

I hooted in disbelief when Lorena produced an apron on a hiking trip. Later, after I'd used her apron innumerable times — to wipe my hands, to protect the camera from sun and dust, to dry myself after swimming, to cover my improvised pillow and to protect myself while cooking—I reluctantly admitted that an apron is useful around camp. (Think of an apron as a towel with strings attached and it's easier to justify.)

Bowls

Plastic bowls with tight-fitting lids sold for leftovers and freezer containers make excellent general-use soup and salad bowls. I like a high-quality, slightly flexible plastic bowl. It will be crack resistant and more impervious to stains and odors than cheaper models. Tupperware is famous for high-quality plastic containers. Though relatively expensive, they withstand a great deal of abuse.

Lightweight stainless steel mixing bowls are very nice, but weigh more than plastic. We use them while car and boat camping. They are easy to scrub in sand, serve well for heating foods and can be boiled clean when accumulated grease and camp grime become distasteful.

We find bowls to be generally more useful for camping than plates. Including two bowls per person allows you to mix up salads, batters, desserts, soups and other runny concoctions. Two or three course meals can easily be served in bowls and cups. Bowls with lids are nice and in a pinch the lid can be used as a small plate.

Canteens and Water Jugs

A strong, leak-proof water container will be one of your most valuable pieces of equipment. Boaters and hikers will want to be very sure that their water supply is safe, especially when travelling in areas where replenishment is uncertain or difficult. Many trips we've made were limited by our ability to carry water. Water containers can be improvised (such as plastic bags filled with water and carefully carried inside cardboard boxes, stuff sacks or towels), but I'd be very leery of trusting my safety to them.

Buy the best quality water containers to carry your basic supply (survival minimum is two quarts per day per person). Several one-quart jugs are easier to stow in a pack than a single large container. Extend your supply with cheaper containers and always keep your jugs topped off. A simple pratfall in the desert can become a disaster if one or more containers rupture.

Keep an eye peeled for metal canteens when visiting flea markets and junk stores. Most need nothing but a good rinse and new gasket material inside the cap to be perfectly useable.

Collapsible water jugs, which we call 'elephant bladders', are one of the most useful items of modern camping gear I've encountered. They are durable, lightweight and stow easily in canoes, backpacks, vehicles and saddle bags. When empty they can be inflated for emergency floats or used as buoys.

We carry at least one elephant bladder each while backpacking (one gallon or larger). When water holes get few and farther between we fill a bladder or two. By carrying extra containers and working like donkeys, Lorena and I were able to spend four days and nights camped on a barren volcano. When travelling by van, an extra ten or fifteen gallons of fresh water can save long and tedious backroad trips to the nearest faucet.

When shopping for water containers I always subject them to a few tests: Look for thin spots in the plastic, cuts, cracks, pinholes, etc. Remove the cap and blow into the jug. Feel any air leaking? If the store manager gripes about your mouth on the merchandise, fill the jug with air, close the cap tightly and discreetly give it a tremendous squeeze. Jugs that hiss or explode should be set aside.

If your jugs start leaking while you're out, they can be repaired using duct tape and a gluey stuff called 'Sportman's Goop'.

REI Co-op sells a collapsible water jug that is very useful for all types of camping. It is a simple and durable cloth bag with a replaceable plastic liner. The 'water sack' has a cloth strap handle and a squeeze type spout. It can be carried by hand or hung up on a branch, nail or rear view mirror. It gives an economical stream of water and we've used ours as a crude but effective shower. (A shower head attachment is also available.)

The advantages of this type of container are its durability, light weight and compactness. An empty two gallon bag will literally stuff into your pocket. When filled, they stow beautifully in the bottom of small boats. In the van, we carry our water sacks in cardboard boxes. I recommend them highly.

Our only complaint is with the spout: on a long kayak trip, four out of five water sack spouts eventually turned into 'droolers'. We made jury-rigged gaskets from a spare plastic bag to seal the leaky spouts.

Containers

I seem to go through phases when I become convinced that a certain type of bag or box is the latest ultimate solution to the problem of how to pack things up. Once, the answer was lightweight aluminum boxes that fit neatly together like the halves of a clam shell. Unless, of course, you sat on them, dropped a heavy boot on them or otherwise subjected them to the type of pressures commonly found around our camps. My final use for my lovely aluminum boxes was to hold spare change and flashlight batteries. By some electrolytic coincidence, I created an awful corroded mess that threatened to eat the frame of my backpack.

From there I went to plastic: wide mouth jars, bottles, screw top lids, freezer boxes, self-sealing salad bowls; even a Mexican contraption designed to keep tortillas warm that seemed ideal for making yogurt *as we hiked*. Do you know how long it takes to wipe a quart of yogurt from a backpack?

Plastic Containers: Jars made of Nalgene, a supposedly inert plastic that resists stains and odors, seemed the answer to our prayers when preparing for a recent kayaking expedition. After all, they were unbreakable, watertight, translucent (so we could identify the mysterious contents) and came in convenient sizes and shapes.

I'll never forget the thrill it gave me to see those neat rows of plastic jars and bottles arrayed in military precision across the kitchen floor. It transformed a run-down room into Expedition Headquarters and sent a shiver of anticipation up my spine.

"There's just one problem," Lorena said, running her pencil down the lengthy list of foods we intended to take with us.

"What's that?" I asked, thinking she might object to these containers on some obscure aesthetic grounds — too pale in color, tops should twist to the left instead of the right, etc.

"They won't fit into the kayak."

"Won't FIT!" I jumped from the stool, setting off a domino-like collapse along a file of quart-sized bottles. "What do you mean, won't fit? We worked this out *weeks* ago! Let me have that list!" I grabbed for the clipboard but Lorena snatched it away.

"I didn't say the food wouldn't fit," She answered. "I said the jars that the food is in won't fit into the kayak. They're too bulky. You didn't take into account the size of the food containers themselves. This stuff would fill a truck."

I didn't bother to tell her that it *had* filled a truck; even the UPS driver had blinked with amazement when I'd mentioned that the contents of the boxes would eventually be stowed into a kayak. "Gosh!" he'd said. "I always thought kayaks were, well, sort of cramped."

"Plastic bags are the answer," Lorena said quickly, anticipating my animal-like howls of frustration. "They're compact, flexible, relatively strong, transparent and better yet, cheap!"

I flinched at this last. Our beautiful plastic jars and bottles had added up to quite an investment, one that we'd rationalized over the long term.

I agreed, though reluctantly, to a test of Zip-Loc plastic bags. The evidence was dramatic: the food-filled bags not only fit nicely into nooks and crannies but as the food was used up, the empty bags could be folded and stowed away as spares.

The plastic jars and bottles we did use on that trip were often only partially filled, though they still took up an irreducible amount of space. Our main complaint was that many of the screw top lids did not seal completely. (We bought our containers mail order, a desperation measure. Always try to test each container before buying. See *Canteens & Water Jugs.*)

The best uses of rigid food containers are in RVs, larger boats and rafts, and kayaks or backpacks on short outings, when space is not at a high premium.

Plastic Bags, Zip-Loc: I now reluctantly consider Zip-Loc plastic bags to be the most practical and versatile container for food and small camping gear. Reluctantly, because I inevitably tear rather than un-Zip-Loc most of the bags I take camping, usually in a frenzy to get at a desperately needed snack or fishing lure.

Ordinary plastic bags sealed with wire twists or rubber bands are also quite useful.

Unfortunately, the plastic bag is a fragile container. They have a way of falling to pieces for no apparent reason, probably because most are designed for one-time use rather than hard travel. Get heavy gauge bags (such as freezer bags) if your trip will be for more than a few days.

We taped many tears and holes and even chopped up some bags to glue over large breaks on others. This worked temporarily, but after months of steady use some bags simply disintegrated, as though they'd been passed through a paper shredder.

While boating, we were reduced to panhandling from passing yachts. "Say, you folks couldn't spare a few plastic sacks, could you?" The looks of amazement on the faces of these sailors when we paddled out from a hidden sea cave to beg more bags was almost worth the indignity.

Cargo and River Bags: Heavy gauge vinyl plastic cargo bags with watertight closures (snaps or 'slide') are almost essential for boaters who face inevitable dunkings, splashings and rain squalls. We use two types: clear plastic bags by Phoenix with metal twist-lock closures and solid, colored, non-transparent bags by Voyageur with rigid plastic slide closures.

The latter model is faster to open and close than the Phoenix bag, but the stiff plastic closure does not stow well into narrow or confined spaces. For that reason, we reserve Voyageur bags for the camera and accessories.

The transparent Phoenix bag has the additional advantage of allowing you to more-or-less identify the contents of the bag without opening it. Both the bags have an air valve and can be inflated—or, more importantly, if you're trying to jam the thing into the bow of a kayak, the bag can be compressed and excess air bled off. This also reduces condensation inside the bag, a serious problem in hot weather.

On the long kayak trip, most of the Zip-Loc food bags were kept inside Phoenix bags. These cargo bags were placed inside lightweight cloth bags sewn from rip-stop tent material to protect the plastic from abrasion. Strap handles on the cloth bags allowed the food to be easily portaged or suspended from rocks and branches. This system extends the life of your cargo bags and simplifies loading and unloading.

Cargo bags can be repaired with kits available from the manufacturer. On long trips test your bag regularly for pinhole leaks by emptying the bag, then sealing and inflating it. Allow the bag to sit undisturbed for several hours; if it goes soft, you've got a leak. In cool weather, however, some softening can be expected as the air inside the bag condenses.

As a bonus, these bags can be filled with hot water and used for warming your sleeping bag or feet. Don't use too much water or you'll risk popping the bag. I like to jury-rig a hot water bottle when the strains of kayaking stiffen my back muscles.

Garbage bags make inexpensive, temporary substitutes for the more expensive cargo bags. Try this: put three of the sturdiest garbage bags you can find inside each other. As they wear out and are punctured, exchange the outer bag for an inner one. Duct tape will also delay the inevitable final destruction. I wouldn't depend on garbage bags, even in layers, for longer than a week or two.

Plastic containers have a common disadvantage: in sunny weather they absorb the sun's heat like miniature greenhouses. In the desert our food bags and jars almost melted when left in the direct sun. This can ruin your food and reduces the life of the plastic. Dark garbage bags also heat up. The solution is obvious: cover your plastic containers at all times.

If plastic containers overheat, moisture released from the food will condense inside the container. This quickly leads to mold and spoilage. Open or empty the containers and air dry their contents regularly.

Stuff Sacks: To reduce confusion in our camp kitchen we carry our utensils, spices, condiments and other culinary odds and ends in a confusing assortment of convenient stuff sacks. The sacks are coded in a confusion of colors.

"Where's the garlic?" A note of panic creeps into Lorena's voice as she rummages through the many pockets and flaps of her backpack. The beloved 'stinking rose' is the keystone for many of our favorite camping dishes.

"Don't panic," I say, tossing her a small red stuff sack. "It's right here."

She takes a close peek and then bounces the sack off my shoulder with a disgusted, "Those are your dirty socks!"

"That's odd," I answer. "I thought I put the garlic in the red bag because garlic is a rose. Get it?"

Silence, broken only by the sound of butter sizzling furiously in the skillet.

"Here, try this one." I toss her a bright blue stuff sack. Lorena plunges her hand into the bag, gives a quick shriek and pulls out a finger adorned with needle-sharp fish hooks.

"Now that's really odd," I mutter. "I could swear I put those hooks in the tan colored bag. Tan for trout." I pass her a forest green bag.

"Dried potatoes!" Her eyes are wide and rolling.

"Oh, yeah? I guess I forgot. That's green for hash browns." Lorena stares, unblinking, awaiting an explanation. "It's really fairly obvious," I say. "H is for hash browns but there's no H-color so I went to G, the closest letter. I thought about silver for spuds, you know, S, but I couldn't find a sack that color."

"Wouldn't green for garlic have been easier?" Lorena sucks at a bloody hook mark in her finger.

"Maybe, but..." I retreat into a protective mumble while pawing through the remaining bags. "Black...yellow...white...just a second, here it is. Grape!"

"Grape?" Lorena's voice is high and strangled. "That looks purple to me!"

I give her my most patient and understanding sigh. "It could have been P for purple if we'd put the potatoes in it, but I made it grape for garlic; a G, just for convenience. Next time we'll put...."

"Lorena?"

As she disappears into the forest I snatch the scorching butter from the fire and begin peeling garlic. Now which of these bags did I put that onion in?

The best stuff sacks are of waterproof nylon. This protects the contents from water, grease and dirt.

On one hike we used a stuff sack as a bucket: by lashing sticks across the opening of the sack we were able to lower it into a deep well. It wouldn't hold much water but it was far better than nothing and eventually dipped enough to fill our empty canteens.

While kayaking long distances on the ocean we carried bags of very odorous smoked fish and squid lashed to the deck. These stuff sacks endured weeks of rough treatment, including continual soakings in salt water. Our only problem came later: convincing customs officials at the U.S. border that the smelly and stained bags were actually bags and not some ghastly form of sea life that we'd caught and dried.

Good containers not only keep your food under control, but protect it from the elements and hungry creatures that live in the outdoors. Boaters must be careful to keep their provisions dry and mold-free. Backpackers are especially vulnerable to raids from ants, porcupines and bears. RVers don't have to contend with as many storage problems, but mice and crawling insects love to stow away and seem to thrive while travelling. The curtain shelf described near the end of this chapter in *RV, Truck and Car Kitchens: Storage Containers* makes a good food and utensil organizer, even without a vehicle. See *Shopping and Provisioning: Spices* for Lorena's Spice Rack. (See *Stoves and Lanterns* for *Fuel Containers*)

Remember:

- All empty containers will be filled to capacity, and then over-filled.
- Small containers hold small amounts; large containers hold too much.
- Whatever fits cleverly into a small space will, when unpacked, refuse to be crammed back into the same space.
- The most needed items are packed in the most inconvenient places.
- Containers are indestructible only until destroyed, waterproof until they leak, airtight until they hiss and crushproof until crumpled or flattened.

Cooking Kits

The classic Scout mess kit is probably the most widely available basic cooking setup. Generations of Scouts have seared their hands on bare metal handles and sobbed in frustration as scorched tomato soup, liberally mixed with cinders, spilled into the fire.

Expanded, sophisticated versions of these kits now flood the market. The sight of a large cardboard box loudly advertising "97 Piece Cook Kit for 12 Campers!" nevers fails to strike terror in my heart. Tiny plastic cups that sag when filled with hot coffee; huge aluminum kettles so thin that food scorches into a scrubber-resistant layer previously found only on used Mercury space capsules, and a pathetic assortment of plastic forks and plates that cry out to be chucked in the nearest Goodwill donation box.

As you may have guessed, I do not like cook kits. Practicality is sacrificed for compactness. For example, the six person kit provides a 7" skillet barely large enough to fry two portions of eggs. There is always one pot that doesn't seem large enough to make soup in or small enough to drink tea out of.

The solution is simple: continue reading through this discussion (especially *Pots, Pans and Frying Pans*) and then assemble a kit that truly reflects your needs and personal cooking style. In most cases you'll get a better bargain and higher quality utensils.

For those who must have a ready-made cook kit, I strongly suggest that you buy the best you can find. Cookware that isn't easy to use will make every meal an ordeal rather than a pleasure.

Cups

Metal cups are definitely more practical and versatile than plastic. We use our cups for food and drink as well as melting butter, mixing up sauces and even steam-cooking small portions of vegetables (with foil lid). Your cup may be scarred by such hard use, but it will enhance your image as a rugged individualist.

I much prefer enamel coated metal cups (the medium-large 12 ounce size) over the popular bare steel Sierra cup. Enamel insulates the cup and prevents scorching of the lips. Take care, however, when cooking in an enameled cup to avoid overheating and popping off the enamel coating. My cup was made in Mexico and has a dancing pig painted on the side.

Aluminum cups are too thin and heat-conductive to serve as a 'first line' cup, but we have a couple kicking around our van kitchen. They weigh almost nothing and make good guest cups and small mixing containers.

Dish Towels and Bandannas

Small, lightweight dish towels and large colorful bandannas have many uses in the camp kitchen. We use ours as mini-tablecloths, especially when camped on sand, as hot pads, wash cloths, food wrappers, spoon wipers and even for drying dishes and blowing noses. The battle against creeping grime will turn in your favor if you use a cloth to wipe things down every few days.

Electrical Appliances: Blender, Skillet, Crockpot, Hot Plate

These are indeed luxury items for camp cooks, but if you'll be using a vehicle as a camp or base, such 'mod-cons' aren't at all frivolous. Trailer parks usually provide electricity, and a long extension cord can tap into a friend's garage outlet. On long cross-country car and van trips I like to take an electric skillet for motel room cooking. I paid two bucks for my skillet at the local Salvation Army. It has saved us a considerable amount of money over the years by easing the temptation to eat in restaurants.

Backpackers, as well as motor campers who are travelling light, would probably prefer a small coil-type water heater to a heavy hot plate. These tiny heaters are very cheap and can be used to make instant coffee, tea and soups.

A simple 110 volt light cord with a bulb socket weighs only a few ounces and makes a very handy light. Use a soft glow bulb. When you set up your tent in a friend's backyard this light will save your candles or portable lantern fuel for nights when you really need them.

Flashlights

We always keep a small flashlight on hand for those inevitable situations when the lights go out in the middle of a meal. Mallory makes a pocket-sized light that jams nicely into the mouth, effectively cutting off the cook's curses while illuminating the dark inside of a cook pot or frying pan. Battery powered headlamps are also useful and allow full freedom for the hands and mouth while cooking and eating.

Food Mill

A food mill is really a hand-powered blender. Very useful for soups and purees.

Frisbee

This isn't a joke; we use our Frisbee for a plate, lid, soup and mixing bowl, cutting board, sand shovel, fire fan, serving dish, emergency kayak paddle, hat (drill two holes, lash to head with shoelace), and even a toy.

Griddles, Tortilla *Comal*

One of the most useful pieces of cookware in our camping kitchen is nothing more than a 12" diameter piece of tin. We use this for cooking and reheating tortillas (round clay and tin griddles are known in Mexico as a *comal*), making toast and as a flimsy sort of stovetop for keeping coffee cups hot. The *comal* is never oiled; authentic tortillas are cooked on plain metal, even if it's rusted. For this reason the *comal* isn't good for pancakes or frying meat or fish. (To prevent toast from sticking, sprinkle salt onto the hot metal.)

Unless you eat a great many pancakes I wouldn't bother with an iron or aluminum griddle. A frying pan works almost as well and is much more versatile. There's something very attractive about griddles, however, and though I don't eat pancakes often, I own two griddles. Like large enamelled coffee pots and Dutch ovens, a fire-blackened iron griddle seems an integral part of the complete romantic camp kitchen.

Grills

Most grills sold for outdoor cooking won't support anything heavier than a hamburger or half a dozen weinies. Stewpots and cast iron skillets sag toward the coals, waiting until you've turned your back to spill into the fire. Fancy grills, with clever folding legs, also tend to fold when I least expect them to, usually an instant before I can snatch the food to safety.

The easiest solution to the camp grill dilemma and certainly the most economical, is to use a regular oven grill. Which is why our oven at home doesn't have one; I can never remember to return it after a camping trip. Oven grills are very cheap at junk stores.

The best camp grill I've used was made by welding together lengths of steel 'rebar'. This grill would support *anything*. It was heavy enough, however, to give most camp cooks a hernia and needed a very stout support.

For those concerned about weight I recommend an ultra-light grill sold by REI Co-op. It is small but holds an amazing amount of weight. After years of hard use, including many dunkings in salt water, our grill shows no ill effects.

The big disadvantages of the backpacker's grill I've just described is that it makes a lousy surface for barbecuing. Foods tend to fall through, especially when tender and limp.

Our solution is simple and inexpensive: in a discount store I bought an entire home barbecue kit, including a flimsy aluminum charcoal pan, several meat skewers and a large but very lightweight grill. The grill was made of closely spaced wire rods, ideal for tender fish and vegetables. I reduced it to the size I needed with a hacksaw. The rest of the set went to the Goodwill, adding a good deed to a bargain.

Carry your grill in a tough cloth sack to prevent dirtying other equipment. Wash the sack every couple of years.

Warning: Some refrigerator grills are said to contain dangerous substances that can contaminate food when the metal is heated. Never use a refrigerator grill for cooking. Most of them don't withstand heat well, anyway.

Hot Pads

I consider hot pads to be a vital part of the camp kitchen, a classic example of simple gear that can literally take the pain out of cooking. The importance of hot pads was impressed on me at a Boy Scout camp. I was approaching our communal cook fire after an outing in the woods when a friend called, "Hey Carl! Hand me that pan, would ya?"

A large iron skillet sat several feet from the fire. Without thinking I grabbed the handle and ... let out a bloodcurdling scream as the hot metal seared my tender young palm. My cries brought sadistic laughter from my fellow Scouts — it was all a healthy outdoor joke. They had heated the pan in the red hot coals, then dragged it away to await an innocent victim. I picked up a blistered hand and a fanatical love for hot pads.

Bandannas and dish towels make versatile hot pads.

Ice Chests and Refrigerators

Ice is not only useful for preventing food spoilage but a few chunks of the stuff in your favorite beverage can be the final luxurious touch to a day in the wilds. What can be done, however, to avoid the dreaded Meltdown of a precious block of ice or bag of cubes? Here are some suggestions to delay the inevitable:

• Blocks are cheaper than cubes and last much longer. An icepick will chip pieces off for drinks in the blink of an eye — and put a hole in your ice chest just as fast, if you aren't careful.

• Use extra space in your home freezer for plastic jugs or milk cartons of fresh water. This gives a free source of ice for camping, extra drinking water if you should need it and will keep your home freezer cold longer if the power goes out. When you return from camping, dump the melted water and refill the containers. Ice water tastes better if it hasn't been frozen and thawed twenty times.

• To make a larger block line a cardboard box with a plastic garbage bag (check for leaks first) and fill with water.

• Remember: water expands as it freezes. Don't use glass or hard plastic containers that can shatter.

• Chill your entire ice chest, contents and all.

• Some fancy ice chests with hinged lids can be used either lying down or standing up. If possible, don't use it in a standing position. Opening the door spills heavier, cold air and greatly speeds up melting. Lay the chest flat so the top opens upward.

• Don't drain melted ice water until it threatens to submerge the butter; It is keeping things cold too.

• Pre-cool things before putting them in the ice chest. A bottle of beer or a watermelon, for example, will be much cooler in the morning or after a few hours in the Drip Cooler (see *Camp Kitchen Skills*). Think of food and drink as lumps of heat.

• Put ice cubes in a plastic bag and keep it tightly sealed. This slows melting and protects the cubes from dirty water or unwashed food. By wiping off bottles and food before storing them in the ice chest, you'll reduce messes and health hazards.

• Keep your ice chest shaded at all times. We wrap ours in a sleeping bag or cover it with a foil-backed blanket. If your chest doesn't have a tightly securing lid, keep something heavy on top. Make sure the lid seals well and if it doesn't, use a plastic sack for a gasket.

• Bury your ice chest, even if it's only a few inches into the sand or dirt. The deeper you go, the longer the ice will last. A chest kept buried to the lid, in the shade and with additional insulation over the top (blankets, sleeping bag, palm fronds, branches, etc.), will keep ice up to three times longer. (See *Camp Kitchen Skills*; *Sleeping Bag Ice Chest*.)

Refrigerators must be the ultimate camp kitchen luxury. I alternate between denouncing them as degenerate and morally corrupt and lying awake nights wishing I had one. The final decision, however, is usually based on your checkbook. Camp refrigerators are expensive. (A new breed of portable refrigerators that use 12 volt DC and 110 volt AC current are less expensive than other built-in gas and electric refrigerators, but I have yet to try one out under rigorous camping conditions.)

Unless you'll be doing a great deal of hot weather travelling and camping or plan an open-ended odyssey, the cost, bulk, weight and maintenance of a refrigerator probably aren't worth a few ice cubes and cold sodas. An ice chest will do just as well, especially on short trips. A 'reefer' comes into its own when food spoilage is a continuing problem and when the refrigerator's capacity is large enough to allow stockpiling of fresh and frozen foods.

Knives

Although a simple pocket knife or paring knife will serve your needs while cooking outdoors, knife cultists will want to carry something more impressive. I once met a Danish hiker who swore that he couldn't get by in the wilderness without a military saber at his side. Others will feel the need for a Bowie knife or so-called 'hunting' knife.

There are several reasons to leave these blades at home, not the least of which is that you'll be chopping onions, not moose haunches, and the closest most of us come to wildlife while camping is the occasional dead rabbit or coyote squashed on the side of the highway. Large knives, especially in the hands of excited children, are usually used to scar the nearest tree trunk or to self-inflict a nasty wound.

Although I confess to being a 'knife freak' myself — and have the scars to prove it — I rarely go outdoors with anything other than an aging but versatile Scout pocket knife. On trips to the beach I also take a filet knife and a short, strong bladed utility knife for opening oysters. Lorena carries a very small filet knife or a paring knife.

I insist on keeping my knives very sharp since a dull knife is hazardous and no fun at all to use. I hone my knife daily with a ceramic sharpening rod. Steel rods tend to rust, especially around salt water, and are heavier than ceramic types. Mine is slightly smaller than a pencil and with care I've used it to fine tune the blade of a machete.

Many campers sport expensive sheath knives that fold up and have one or two locking blades. These knives are heavy and, though strong, the tips of the blades will not withstand constant use as can-openers. The blade locking device, however, is a fine feature and makes these knives much safer than the average folding pocket knife. I learned this the hard way, on a remote Alaskan beach.

My companions had gone off in our skiff for the day and I was left alone to tend the fire. Out of boredom and mild hunger I decided to cook a trout without using a frying pan. I caught a fat 18-inch Dolly Varden and, with my Scout knife, began to drill holes in the side of a driftwood log. After cutting small pegs from green alder I would 'nail' the fish to the log and build a small fire a few inches away.

It was a nice idea, but as I bored the second hole I pressed too hard on the knife and it folded up in the blink of an eye. On my index finger. To the bone. I clawed at the knife with my left hand but it had scissored right into the knuckle and jammed. Both hands were quickly covered with blood, making it almost impossible to grip the knife.

I fainted for a few seconds, then had the sense to plunge my hands into the chilly sea, rinsing away the blood and coincidentally slowing the bleeding. By the time I'd removed the knife, warmed my frozen fingers and wrapped my right hand in my t-shirt, I looked and felt as though I'd tangled hand-to-paw with a brown bear.

When my friends returned that evening, they looked incredulously at my blood-soaked clothing and mangled finger. "You did that, all by *yourself*? With a Boy Scout knife?"

Folding and Reflector Ovens

Coleman makes a popular folding oven that fits nicely on top of larger camp stoves and over open fires. It is too heavy for backpacking but might be considered for vehicles and canoes. The oven is small but comes complete with an inside grate and door thermometer. We use ours on van trips. Because our recipes tend toward stove-top and open fire cooking, however, the oven is a luxury item rather than a basic piece of gear.

Reflector ovens are lighter than the Coleman type but take much more attention and skill to use properly. You'll also need a hot open fire. Lorena and I improvised a reflector oven by covering pieces of cardboard with heavy aluminum foil and propping them like a shiny house-of-cards next to a fire. It worked fine and we enjoyed baking bread as a change from tortillas. But because baking requires pans and preparations that are not a regular part of our outdoor cooking style, we soon drifted away from reflector ovens. (See *Camp Kitchen Skills*: *Tin Can Oven*.)

Plates

We sometimes use small and very battered aluminum plates scavenged from some long-lost cook kit. They are easy to scrub clean in sand and unlike plastic plates do not attract odors. Metal plates can also be boiled clean, a precaution against health problems that too many people tend to overlook. My favorite plates are as large as the hubcaps on an old Studebaker, with blue enamelling and a slightly recessed center. They are heavy but these plates have an authentic Gold Rush look I can't resist.

Paper Plates and Towels: The use of paper plates and towels in the Great Outdoors is at the heart of a controversy that has raged between campers for many years now. My own position lies somewhere between the battle lines: I use paper plates and towels on occasion but I don't like them. On short trips paper plates can eliminate a good deal of dish washing and, if fires are permitted, serve as soggy kindling after a meal.

When car camping we reserve paper plates for guests and times when we're too tired to wash up. The argument and logic become even fuzzier if you buy high quality paper plates and *wash them* after use. It is amazing how many meals and miles a good paper plate will survive. Carry a set of paperclips and a line for drying.

Partially burned paper plates and wads of used towels are an all-too familiar sight in campgrounds and wilderness areas. If you use them at all, dispose of your paper products carefully. Pack them out rather than leaving a mess (and ashes are a mess, too, unless fire pits are allowed).

Pots, Pans and Frying Pans

We use aluminum 'nesting billies' with wire handles and tight-fitting lids. We call the larger pot (about a three-quart) 'Bill' and the smaller one 'Billy'. Billy fits inside Bill. Bill is perfect for boiling potatoes, stews, clams and noodles. Billy is just right for making coffee, rice and sauces.

Bill and Billy travel inside the Billy Bag, a light, waterproof sack with a zipper along one side. The bag can be attached to the outside of a backpack, a saddle or canoe thwart. The Billy Bag also holds the pot scrubber, pot grabbers, matches, bowls and small odds and ends.

On trips to the beach, especially by boat or vehicle, we also include an anonymous six quart aluminum pot with lid for steaming clams, crabs, lobster and other treats. It adds the luxury of being able to heat large amounts of water for bathing, laundry and dishes.

Frying Pans: Whenever I set out to buy a new piece of cooking gear I always subject the item, be it a simple spoon or nifty folding oven, to a ruthless series of Acid Tests. These tests include cost, versatility, weight, bulk, durability and even appearance. No one likes to use ugly cookware.

"Hey, Lorena. Check this out." I held up a ten inch coated skillet for her to admire.

"Not for backpacking," she said simply, moving on to pans designed for self-starving dieters, the skinny and the undernourished.

"What do you mean?" I protested, turning the pan to catch the overhead light. I gave it a thoughtful heft. "It doesn't weigh much more than any other pan I see around here." I reached into the box for the lid, a beautifully curved dome that fit with a good tight seal. The knob was large without being ridiculous and somehow *felt right* in my hand. Yes, this pan had definite camping possibilities. I could fry a large Oriental-style rice dish in here or steam cook an entire Dungeness crab or make a big batch of vegetable stew...

"Are you getting serious about that thing?" Lorena replaced the ridiculous mini-pan she'd been admiring and gave my new-found treasure a hard look. "Have you subjected it to your famous *Tests*?" There was a tone to her voice that I chose not to respond to, offering her instead a seductive peek at the pan's slick inner coating. "What does it weigh, in grams and ounces?" She persisted. "What are its exact dimensions, including volume? Can you paddle a canoe with it? Will it cook waffles and eggplant at the same time? Will it double as a snow shovel or a..."

"All right! All right!" I said disgustedly, moving on down the aisle. Sure, the pan was on the hefty side, but even Lorena would have to admit that it looked good, in fact, *very good*, and would fit perfectly into any idyllic camp cooking scene. Isn't there more to life than hard logic?

I reached absentmindedly for a large stainless steel coffee pot. "Make a good shrimp steamer, don't you think?"

Lorena sighed.

"Or even a stew pot. If you clean the coffee grounds in the morning, or for baking..."

Because our cooking style tends toward one pot meals with simple side dishes and pan breads or tortillas, the ten-inch covered skillet I just described became our all-time favorite. It serves four people, or two with planned leftovers.

The slight extravagance in overall bulk and weight is more than justified, in my opinion (and I have to carry it), in the pan's versatility and ease of use. There is nothing more maddening, for example, than trying to fry rice and vegetables in a skillet no larger than the palm of your hand.

Our pan's high sides and high tight fitting lid makes it good for soups and stews, steaming and slow cooking (including pan breads and cakes). The inner coating cuts down on the use of oil (and waste) and makes clean-up much easier.

When I compared this aluminum pan to a 'heavy duty' nine-inch skillet (without lid) designed for camping, I could feel little difference in weight. Even lighter weight pans with lids are available in discount stores. I found one on sale for $3.00 that would be ideal for camping and backpacking, though it too was bulkier than a 'camper's' fry pan.

Pot Grabbers

The most useful piece of special camping gear ever invented. A metal pot grabber turns a tin can into a cooking pot. Watch your pot grabbers around sand; they will sink and disappear in an instant. Drill a small hole in the handle and tie on a piece of brightly colored string or yarn. Bent-nosed pliers also make good pot grabbers but they're heavy.

Pressure Cooker

A pressure cooker greatly reduces cooking time, as well as conserving fuel and water. This makes it possible to cook foods such as beans, brown rice and tough beef without exasperating waits. A pressure cooker will also speed up the sterilization of drinking water (See *Camp Kitchen Skills: Staying Healthy*).

My complaint with pressure cookers is that too many cooks use them to overcook food. Mushy beans and gummy rice aren't worth the savings in time and fuel. Pressure cooked stews and soups also have a tendency to become bland and boring since it is easier to add all ingredients at once and cook them until the toughest is done — or overdone. Tender foods just melt away. Avoid this by following the directions in a pressure cooker instruction book.

Spoons

Forks are unnecessary, though useful for mixing and poking as you cook. Wilderness etiquette allows soup slurping directly from the bowl or cook pot as well as the liberal use of twigs and fingers for dredging up special morsels.

We like enamelled spoons, but if weight is a consideration plastic is probably your best choice. Fortunately, the days of the droopy plastic spoon have passed. Space age plastic tableware designed for campers really is durable.

Stoves and Lanterns

Stoves and lanterns are a natural combination. No matter how often or how sincerely I vow to cook dinner before the sun sets, I inevitably find myself groping in the dark, usually armed with a razor-sharp knife, tripping over tent pegs, tree roots and misplaced pots and pans.

Stoves and lanterns have one vital thing in common: fuel. By using the same fuel in both appliances you'll avoid the usual scene of running out of propane (in the lamp) the day after you've topped off the white gas (in the stove) or vice versa. You'll need fewer fuel containers and will have similar spare fittings and gaskets. You'll also be able to juggle between stove and lantern when the fuel does begin to run out. Shall we read *Valley of the Dolls* tonight or eat popcorn in the dark?

Although stoves are required in many wilderness areas, it is ironic that the closer to civilization you get the more desirable a stove usually becomes. Firewood is scarce outside of forests and the temptation to stop at a cafe is difficult to resist if the alternative is a cold or raw meal.

However, you may not need a special 'camp stove' or lantern to get by. We've cooked over newspapers, briquets, cow chips, brush in a tin can stove (check local fire regulations) and once, chokingly, over a discarded Mexican truck tire. Light can be provided by flashlights, headlamps, candles or a tin can lantern. This is basic camping but it works. (See *Camp Kitchen Skills* for ideas on making a *Tin Can Stove* and *Tin Can Lantern*.)

Choosing a Camp Stove: To simplify this discussion I will briefly summarize our own preferences. First, while camping from a vehicle, whether it's a VW Bug or some lavish Highway Yacht, I recommend a stove fueled by propane. Not the expensive disposable cartridge type but a stove with a refillable tank or cylinder, preferably of five or more gallons. This should give weeks of intense cooking. Propane is clean burning, economical, doesn't stink and handles nicely (without annoying fuel cans that inevitably leak). Propane also burns hot and fast without priming, pumping or the other tedious rituals normally associated with camp stoves.

Our second choice, while camping from a vehicle, is the all-American standby, the Coleman two-burner white gas stove. The fuel is expensive but the stove itself is relatively cheap, especially if you pick one up at a garage sale or junk store. Used Colemans are a true bargain and even a stove in apparently poor condition can usually be repaired quite easily. If you can't afford to feed it white gas, try unleaded automobile gas. It won't burn as clean as white gas (sometimes called naptha), but unleaded automobile gas does work. Impurities will clog the stove's generator, though this can be remedied by regular cleanings. (See *Camp Kitchen Skills: Coleman Stoves: Care and Cleaning*).

Warning: Never use leaded or regular automobile gas in a white gas fueled stove or lantern. The lead given off by burning gasoline is dangerous — it may be inhaled or eaten, risking lead poisoning. It also gives a terrible flame so there's not much point in even trying.

If you don't have the money to buy a propane setup but are leery of a Coleman consider this: the white gasoline-fueled Coleman stove can be converted to propane by using standard fittings and adapters. Then just hook up a propane bottle to your Coleman and you're all set. This not only saves money, but the stove body is easily replaced when the present one rusts out or gets beyond cleaning.

The Coleman propane conversion has another advantage: it will burn hotter than any other camp stove I've seen. When turned up full blast, it is ideal for Oriental stir fry cooking, quick pots of coffee and melting lead to cast your own fishing sinkers. Ask your local Coleman dealer for advice on these conversions.

Backpacking Stoves: For those concerned about bulk and weight I recommend a kerosene fueled backpacker's stove. I've used the Optimus 00 for several years. It is reliable, inexpensive to fuel and repair, surprisingly clean burning, hot, stable and takes a helluva shine. It also has classic styling.

Kerosene is a much safer fuel than gasoline and far cheaper than disposable propane cartridges. If your travels will take you to foreign countries, especially in the Third World, kerosene is definitely your best bet.

When travelling and camping with a vehicle I always keep the Optimus close at hand, in a small wooden box. It serves as a back-up for lavish meals and in cold weather, with adequate ventilation, has been used as an economical heater. (When heating the van, we cook a pot of beans or stew to kill two birds with one stove.)

Coleman offers a white gas fueled backpacker's stove called the Peak 1. I haven't tried one yet but it has been highly recommended by friends. The Peak 1 is heavier than average, but performance is said to be excellent and the cost is reasonable.

Propane cartridge stoves are popular with weekend and mild weather campers. The convenience of cartridge fuel often balances out the cost and a vague sense of guilt at using a disposable container. The main disadvantage of cartridge fuel, however, is that it won't burn well — and sometimes not at all — at low temperatures. Cartridge fuels are not readily available in any but the most industrialized countries of the world, making them a poor choice for globe-trotting campers.

Mountain Safety Research (MSR) makes a highly sophisticated and very lightweight stove that burns several fuels. These stoves are expensive, however, and have a reputation for crankiness. Borrow one from a friend, give it a good field test, and then compare its performance against your personal requirements and budget. Stoves are very tempting attractions, but their cost demands careful appraisal before buying.

Small gasoline stoves, especially the Svea 123, are cheap to fuel and parts are easily available in the U.S. For world travellers, gasoline is a good second choice, after kerosene.

Fuel Containers: A high quality fuel container is very important. I once bought three one-liter aluminum fuel bottles that were inexpensive copies of the well-known and reliable Sigg bottle. All three of these bottles failed on their first trip. The tops stripped out and leaked, and the sides dented as easily as aluminum beer cans. This not only created a serious fire hazard — in my backpack — but saturated my food, clothing and gear with kerosene.

Never carry fuel in plastic containers, especially when camping where the sun is warm or hot. The jug will heat up, expand, soften and often rupture. At best, it will be weakened and have to be replaced before it breaks. Buy metal containers, the best you can find.

Tables and Cutting Boards

Lorena once remarked that our camp kitchen was equipped with "all the modern discomforts." This wisecrack came as she attempted to mince celery on top of a very round rock. I immediately set out to solve this problem and now, several years later, I can unveil the Backpacker's Table:

an ordinary aluminum clipboard that cost me five bucks in a large stationary store. (Cheaper clipboards of wood-like material work too, but give off fine shavings.) The aluminum clipboard has travelled thousands of miles and served us well while van camping, boating and hiking. We use the board for journal keeping and map reading, rolling out tortillas, as a very small 'dining' table, for fire fanning and as an all-purpose chopping block and cutting board.

The most ingenious cutting board I've used was made of narrow strips of wood glued to a cloth backing. This cutting board actually rolled up into a compact tube. When properly supported it looked and acted like any laminated board. Unfortunately, when lifted, the board went completely limp, spilling everything to the ground. Back to the drawing board...

Tables: Recreational vehicle equipment suppliers offer a mind-boggling and budget-sapping array of camp gear, including many types of tables. One of the slickest actually rolls up and could be used by boaters. Folding tables are an excellent addition to full-scale camp kitchens, but they're not always cheap. The best bargain I've found on a lightweight aluminum folding table is from Sears. As a second choice we use a square piece of plywood placed on top of an apple crate. Crude but convenient. (See *RV, Truck, Van and Car Kitchens: Furniture* later in this chapter.)

Vacuum Bottle

I like coffee while on the road, and by making my own at rest stops I can save a considerable amount of money during a long trip. A wide-mouthed bottle for soups is also nice: make soup in the morning for quick lunches and snacks later in the day.

RV, Truck, Van & Car Kitchens

A fellow camper once joked that our camp kitchen was the first he'd seen that included wheels, engine and a double bed. Because we spend so much time on the road, either travelling from one camping area to another or just vagabonding, with no specific schedule or destination, a complete kitchen is an essential part of our vehicle. We've made extended camping trips (from month-long to a two-and-a-half year odyssey) in a variety of vehicles, including an open pickup truck, a Datsun sedan, an old station wagon and assorted vans, mainly VWs.

Organizing living quarters and kitchens in these vehicles has often strained our creativity and patience to the limit. Car and van camping have much in common with long-range boat cruising: although space and weight are severely limited a reliable and satisfying diet must be maintained, even when conditions are rough and uncomfortable.

In the Northwest, we have to cope with persistent rainfall. When it isn't raining, it's clouding up. This means that our kitchen has to be usable inside the vehicle, often with the doors and most windows closed. You haven't lived until you've cooked a spaghetti dinner in the back seat of a Datsun. (The secret is to set up your Suitcase Kitchen on the rear seat while cooking from the front seats.)

Your vehicle may be equipped with a factory-built kitchen or you might be shopping for a complete motorhome or other type of RV. If so, read this section carefully; it could well save you frustration and money. A

The Portable Herb & Salad Garden

When Lorena and I set sail for British Columbia in our aging wooden sloop, I could barely restrain a Captain Bligh attack of outrage when she revealed a wooden box stuffed with potted lettuce, green onions, parsley, chives, basil and even celery. We would be the laughingstock of the Inland Passage! My ranting failed to impress her, however, and for the next two months we enjoyed an amazingly steady and prolific harvest of salad makings from that simple crate garden stowed on top of the cabin.

It seemed natural to pack up another portable garden while travelling and camping in our station wagon, and later, in a van. These not only survived the most varied and amazing hardships but actually seemed to thrive on quick changes in temperature and altitude. Unfortunately, salad gardens are viewed with great suspicion at international borders. Our sea-borne salad was confiscated by U.S. Customs agents as we returned from Canada and our southern van salad was nabbed when we later returned from Mexico.

Give your garden plenty of fresh air but avoid too much sun. Most salad plants do very well in the shade. Protect your garden from cigarette smoke and cooking fumes. A frequent misting of fresh water keeps the plants cool, clean and content. Don't be afraid to prune them; a healthy lettuce plant will spring up again even if trimmed almost to the roots.

disturbing number of factory-made camp kitchens are kitchens in name only. Modern conveniences that have been shrunken to doll house sizes are rarely convenient while camping.

Tiny stainless steel sinks look marvelous when your RV is on the showroom floor but how about after two weeks on the road, when you realize that the sink will only hold three dirty coffee cups and one small plate? You'll probably discover, as so many other campers have before you, that a large bucket makes a much better sink.

The importance of good ventilation can't be stressed enough. In hot weather it is quite common to see campers sitting outside in the shade, sipping cool drinks, while inside the van or motorhome some unfortunate person is being baked and steamed alive over the galley stove. Experienced travellers try to live outside and around their vehicles, rather than inside. Who wants to be cooped up when there's a fine breeze and magnificent view?

Your camper is best used as a mobile bedroom and warehouse, with normal daily activities, including cooking and eating, centering around, but outside, the vehicle. When travelling by car or van we often include a large tent for lounging and sleeping and reserve the vehicle for side trips and storage.

Living around your camper or car means that removable storage containers, cupboards, trunks, ice chests, water jugs, stoves, chairs, lights and tables are much more practical than permanently built-in ones. This is where a do-it-yourself project or two can save a great deal of money. In fact, do-it-yourself camper kitchens are often more practical and efficient than flashy factory-made models. Whether you use your camper for short trips

near home or extended journeys, you'll soon discover that simplicity and versatility pay off in more ways than one.

• *A reassuring note for the unhandy:* Do-it-yourself projects often require special tools and skills. I have few of either, and the following suggestions take the easy way out while still creating a good practical camp kitchen. Take heart; Lorena and I have camped from our present VW van for four years. It is completely equipped from ready-made and 'found' objects, with minor modifications requiring only a hammer, saw, hand drill and lots of baling wire.

• *A note of caution for the handy:* I've seen do-it-yourself campers and owner-improved RVs that would boggle the mind of a Swiss watchmaker. One fellow specialized in hidden conveniences: the front passenger seat of his VW van actually concealed a two burner propane stove and fully stocked knife and utensil cupboard. Another RV had extra lights, fans and fold-down tables everywhere. So many tables, in fact, that when they were all folded down only a very agile person could wend their way to the stove.

Go easy on improvements until you've tested what you already have under actual camping conditions. A complicated, ingeniously built kitchen may well be less convenient in the long run than a much simpler arrangement.

Storage Containers and Cabinets

Our present van kitchen is packed into two medium sized footlockers, the cheap cardboard and tin types sold in discount stores. They don't serve well as seats, which is why the tops are cracked and split, but the lockers are lightweight, portable, of reasonable dimensions and will be easy to replace when worn out.

Building your own storage containers, in my opinion, is a last resort. Good quality cabinets are very difficult to put together, especially if you want them to be lightweight and attractive.

Unfortunately, factory-installed cabinets in many RVs just don't make the grade. Some are literally stapled together and plastic and pressboard are used instead of plywood. Pressboard is fine for home use, but it doesn't withstand vibration well. Screws will eventually pull loose, particularly in humid, damp climates. Door and cabinet knobs and hinges may loosen or fall off after a few weeks of hard bouncing on dirt roads. This type of camper is designed for freeways and well-groomed campgrounds, not the rigors of off-road and back country travel.

Inspect your cabinets and lockers carefully. Reinforce any weak spots and carry a good supply of screws, fasteners, clamps and strong glue. Aluminum makes a good repair material; it comes in a variety of shapes and sizes and can be worked easily with hand tools, much like wood.

Wooden fruit crates and wine bottle boxes make fine storage containers. They are lightweight, surprisingly sturdy and inexpensive, if not free. By adding wood screws here and there, lashings of wire and twine and the odd nail or two, a crate will give years of service. With a quick sanding, a splash of varnish or paint and a lining of colored cardboard, you'll make *Sunset* magazine.

Plastic milk bottle crates have become so popular among RV campers that some camp supply stores now carry them.

A lightweight lid and seat top can be made from a piece of thin plywood. Just drill a few holes along one edge and wire or tie it loosely to the box.

Plastic buckets with tight fitting lids are another popular and practical storage container. Get some that have held food. No matter how clean a bucket might look, I wouldn't trust it for food storage if it previously held a chemical, paint or potentially poisonous substance.

We use strong plastic buckets with lids for food and dishes, as well as for small gear and loose odds and ends. A round pillow or cushion makes a nice seat top.

The sealing lid is a good example of how an apparently insignificant feature makes a piece of gear much more useful and versatile. Food can be stored for long periods of time, protected from mice and moisture, and the buckets can be used as back-up drinking water containers, as improvised toilets (we use one in our van), as laundry and dish washing 'machines' (see *Camp Kitchen Skills: Washing Dishes*), for salting fish and meat, pickling, wine making, etc., etc.

Baskets are excellent portable kitchen containers, both for food and utensils. Import shops and many supermarkets now offer a bewildering selection, including some large enough to hold an entire kitchen. We use baskets as organizer containers inside our kitchen footlockers: a tall basket once filled with Mexican strawberries for utensils, a rectangular Chinese basket for spice containers, and so on. Fresh fruit and vegetables are kept in a set of nesting wire baskets that can be suspended from the ceiling of the van, a tree branch or tarp pole.

When your baskets get dirty or stained, don't be afraid to scrub them with warm soapy water. Dry them well afterward and line the bottoms with paper or thin towels.

We live in the midst of a phenomena called The Drift. You have probably experienced this yourself, either at home or while camping. The Drift picks up small objects, from pencils to potato peelers, and mysteriously moves them away or hides them for a time. "I wondered where that went!" is the standard exclamation when the Drift finally releases something and you stumble upon it in a logical but unexpected place. I find fishing lures in the ice chest, pencils in the fruit basket, garlic in my toolbox...

To reduce confusion and control the Drift, surround yourself with a handy assortment of bags, small boxes and baskets, organizer containers and empty coffee cans. The sanity and order this will bring to your kitchen are worth the effort.

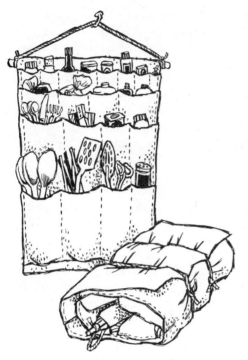

If needle and thread don't intimidate you, try this: an ordinary curtain, bath towel or length of strong cloth can be made into the perfect kitchen organizer and storage 'shelf'. Just sew pockets onto the cloth and hem a length of wooden dowel or a coathanger into the top so it can be used as a curtain or moved about the kitchen. I like towels the best; in a pinch the pockets can be emptied and the towel used for drying things. We have a cloth 'shelf curtain' for spices, another for small utensils and yet another for tea, coffee, beverages and condiments. The curtains can be rolled up, tied and stuffed into a corner.

A safety tip: We try to keep a penlight, backpacker's flashlight and/or candle and matches in one pocket of each major curtain in the van (a curtain near the bed holds eyeglasses, pocket novels, pencil, etc.). If the lights go out or you need to see in the dark, fast, you'll be able to grope for these curtains in an instant.

Organization in the kitchen can be carried one step further by color coding. 'The Old Yellow Box' immediately conjures up an image of a beloved wooden chest that held our spices and condiments for years. If I hadn't run over Old Yellow with a pickup truck it would still be with us today...Color code everything from bags and boxes to your shelf curtains. If the colors become confusing, call it interior decorating.

Once you've got your basic cupboards and containers, don't overpack them. By overpacking I not only mean overstuffing, but also excessively neat arrangements that won't survive the first bump or hasty rummaging. If it takes fifteen minutes to get your kitchen gear into a box, you can bet it will take four times that long to repack at the end of the first hard day of travelling. Camping gear has an irrepressible tendency to fluff up, pour out, and sprout unpackable corners once you're on the road.

Furniture

A certain amount of furniture can make cooking and eating much easier. The instant I relax on top of one of our kitchen footlockers, Lorena finds it absolutely urgent to get at something inside. This problem is easily avoided by carrying a couple of aluminum stools or lawn chairs. When pared down to the bone on space and bulk, the plastic bucket with lid and pillow serves as our only chair.

Cooking without a table is about as enjoyable as eating corn on the cob without dentures. The iron rule around our camp is that the cook gets preference on the table, even if it means busting up a hot poker game.

Folding tables attached to interior walls and side doors are quite nice. A door shelf, for example, allows you to swing the stove in or out, depending on the weather. Many folding tables I've used—especially those I built myself—had an unfortunate tendency to become collapsing tables, at the worst possible moment.

There's nothing quite as depressing as cooking a full-scale meal under adverse camp conditions and then having the whole thing, stove, stew pot, coffee and dessert, crash into a steaming heap at your feet. Support your folding tables well and don't overload them. A safety chain of some sort is the easiest solution; props can always be kicked out or sink into the ground.

There are reasonable limits (somewhere) to equipping a camp kitchen but I see nothing wrong with a few small end tables. Ours are squares of lightweight plywood, masonite, pegboard or whatever else comes to hand. These are placed on top of boxes, buckets and baskets, covered with a large colorful bandanna and arranged around the camp fire or stove. End tables keep utensils out of the dirt and away from crabs and ants. They also give our camp kitchen a deceptive air of orderliness that impresses visitors.

Water Tanks and Containers

Built-in water tanks were a status symbol in early RV days, but like most status equipment they lack a certain practicality under actual camping conditions. When a hose for filling built-in tanks isn't available, or worse yet, stops a few feet short of reaching the filler spout, you'll be back to the tried-and-true bucket brigade method.

In areas where water is precious, such as remote deserts, the bulk of your supply should be close at hand and easily inspected. A leak in a built-in tank will be quite annoying, but in the desert it could be fatal. Keep at least a few gallons in sturdy jugs (see *Canteens and Water Jugs* earlier in this chapter).

If your kitchen is outside your RV, a portable water jug will be much more convenient than an inside tap. We have a 'kitchen jug' of fresh water near the stove and a smaller jug or water sack at the edge of camp for rinsing hands and utensils. (The rinsing bag holds sea water if we're near the ocean.) This system reduces traffic in and out of the vehicle.

Awnings

Cooking and eating outside are much more comfortable with some sort of protection from the sun and rain. Without shade, desert camping can be an ordeal for the cook. A simple awning extends and expands your living area.

If you're camping from a small car or truck this additional room is invaluable. Crowding leads to attacks of RV Fever, when the great outdoors suddenly seems as confining as a closet.

Our tarp is of lightweight rip-stop material. It is fairly large (11' x 14') and shades a good portion of the van as well as the outside kitchen area. The tarp is attached to the van with a confusing array of lines and shock cords, and supported by adjustable aluminum poles and pieces of bamboo. Camping neighbors have compared our tarp arrangements to free-form modern sculpture executed by crazed chimpanzees. I disagree, though not too loudly.

Tie strips of colorful yarn or cloth to the tarp lines. When you trip over the lines or snag your sunglasses on them, these markers will remind you to watch your step.

Avoid rigging a tarp too low over the stove or lantern. Both give off a column of rising heat that can melt a tarp or send it up in a terrifying sheet of flame.

Lights

Cooking in the dark is a cruel and unbearable punishment. The standard camping solution is to jam a flashlight halfway back to your tonsils and then grope and mumble around the kitchen for an hour, trying to get dinner prepared as the batteries die down to a feeble yellow glow. Vehicle campers should take the trouble to install lights that work, when and where they'll be needed.

Lights are available in auto junkyards, discount stores, auto supply stores and, if you can afford the high markups, trailer and RV supply outlets. I prefer portable, rather than permanently attached lights; they are more versatile and easier to install. Buy the type that plugs into the car's cigarette lighter. Spotlight models use a lot more juice than bulb types, but also give considerably more light.

Our van is a non-smoker model so I clipped the plug off the portable light's cord, stripped the insulation from the two ends and crimped (soldered is better) alligator clips to the bare wire ends. The light doesn't have a switch, so turning it on is a matter of attaching the alligator clips to two connections

on the van's fuse panel. Clip one to any fuse holder and then touch the other alligator to any bare piece of metal on the vehicle that makes a good ground. (You can also bare part of a 'hot' wire for one clip and connect the other on any good ground. There is a risk, however, of an accidental short circuit should something later touch the bared spot, but you can't have everything.)

Our light has a magnet built into the case. It almost sticks to the van's body. Magnets can also be glued to cabinets or strategic points that aren't metal.

A friend who burned down his 'fireproof' van, complete with his cookbooks, spatulas, coffee grinder and other worldly goods, suggests that candles be used with extreme caution. The votive type, in reusable glasses, can be held in metal devices sold as drink caddies. Candle lanterns are far safer than open candles; look in your local camp supply store.

Ventilation

I was visiting friends in a large motorhome recently while dinner was being prepared. After fifteen minutes of conversation, the woman looked at me and said, "Am I boring you?"

"No," I answered. "You're cremating me! How can you bear the heat in here?" Not only was the stove going, four burners and an oven, but a huge Aladdin lamp was putting out enough BTUs to smelt iron, not six inches from my nose. My distracted look was caused by impending heat prostration.

Ventilation might seem obvious but I've yet to see a factory built RV that gave more than half-hearted attention to the problem. Good ventilators, including windows that open, cost money. They also have an annoying tendency to leak, especially after a year or two of tough roads and harsh weather.

Neither factor, however, is reasonable justification for inadequate ventilation. Without good ventilation, your camper will be uncomfortable: stuffy and airless in warm weather and damp when it rains. More important, however, is the very real hazard of carbon monoxide poisoning caused by an inadequate flow of fresh air in spaces that are heated by cookstoves, heaters and even lanterns. A dismaying number of people seal themselves up in their campers at night and succumb to monoxide poisoning. Don't take chances: use your ventilators and if you don't have any or you need more, install them as soon as you can.

Chapter 5
Camp Kitchen Skills

The sun's rays kneaded my bare shoulders like the fingers of a skilled masseuse probing toward the edge of pain. I raised my kayak paddle wearily, squinting into the fierce afternoon glare.

"How about that spot?" Steve's voice boomed across the water, startling a flock of dozing pelicans. A shrill whistle blast signaled the boats to gather for an at-sea conference. Steve and Tina edged their long kayak close to ours as my brother circled restlessly, Rob's sleek boat seeming to mock our heavier two-place craft.

"Looks good," I said, sweeping the binoculars over a long expanse of deserted sand beach washed by gentle waves. When calm, the Sea of Cortez is an inviting area for the small boater. After three days of steady paddling, however, our initial excitement had been tempered by a great deal of plain hard work. We had yet to experience the darker side of the Sea's moods but caution, common sense and a growing fatigue told us to land early, while daylight would make camp chores just a bit easier.

Steve pointed a dripping paddle toward a spot between us and the beach, a darkening of the otherwise clear blue water. "Should be some fish on that reef for dinner." He pointed at the beach. "Firewood, too." His paddle traced the outline of a low shadowed bluff. "Great spot for a kitchen. Out of the wind and sun." Like an expert artillery observer who sees all terrain in terms of fields of fire and strategic trajectories, Steve's world view is colored by his appetite, interpreting everything in terms of food, fuel and kitchens. A good place to cook was a good place to camp. Who could argue?

"Got any urgent thoughts on dinner yet?"

I looked up, brushing the back of a sunburned hand at a rivulet of sweat that stung my eyes, then heaved again on the bow of the kayak. At the stern, knee-deep in waves, Lorena struggled for a grip as we dragged the heavy boat onto sticky sand. Steve waited patiently for an answer, eyes locked on the reef shadow.

"Forget it!" I gasped, sinking to my knees for a brief rest. "Don't we have some leftover beans and tortillas?"

"Behind my seat," Lorena added, "in a big plastic bag." She dabbed cautiously at oily gobs of sunscreen ointment that coated her glowing red nose.

At the mention of leftovers, Steve's brow furrowed in unspoken disgust. "I was thinking along the lines of something really *substantial*." His hands moved at his sides in a curious flapping motion, a familiar signal of deep inner turmoil. "After all," he said, "we've been out here for ages. It's about time for a treat."

I quickly translated these remarks into plain English: "out for ages" meant he'd read his crumpled Time magazine from cover to cover and back again; "treat" meant a no-holds-barred taste-bud extravaganza without regard for rationing or economy; and "substantial," a key buzz word in Steve's vocabulary, was nothing less than a full-scale sit-down meal with at least one plate and bowl per person, not to mention appetizers, soup, salad, dessert and strong beverage.

Most of us experience Steve's version of a substantial meal once or twice a year on major holidays. He finds this interval quite unbearable.

"I'm just not up for it, Steve," I said, flopping backwards onto the hot sand. "I'm too beat to go diving and too tired for much else. Why don't we have leftovers and save a big meal for tomorrow?"

Steve seemed deeply puzzled. "Tomorrow?"

"Yeah," Lorena said. "We can steam some rice and mix in the left-over beans."

Steve shuddered in spite of the heat. One-pot meals, he'd often said, were as unsatisfying as one-handed poker, solo sex and checkers by mail. But a one-pot meal of *leftovers*...?

"If we all pitched in..." he turned to look up the beach. Tina was struggling to erect their tarp against an increasingly strong northwesterly breeze and Rob had disappeared on a shell collecting expedition. Steve gave a melodramatic sigh. "This is worse than Weight Watchers!" He began a slow trudge toward his kayak. "I guess I'll have to go out *all alone!*" He looked back quickly, hoping to shame us into cooperation. I waved him away.

Steve burst from the shallows like a bizarre impostor of King Neptune, thick strands of golden sargasso weed tangled in snorkel and beard, a long pole spear clutched in one hand and a bulging red nylon dive bag in the other. His garish green and orange Hawaiian-print bathing shorts sagged precariously below his broad belly. Spitting out the snorkel's mouthpiece, Steve took a deep breath and yelled, "Hey you guys! Come over and see what I got!" He waved the dive bag, hoping to entice us from the restful shade of the tarps.

"We'd better take a look," Rob sighed, setting aside the necklace of delicate shells he'd been threading onto a short length of fishing line. Tina marked her paperback novel with a small man o' war feather and led us to the water's edge.

"Feast your eyes on this!" Steve said, gleefully dumping the contents of the dive bag at our feet.

"Gaaaah!" Rob leaped backward, toes curling away from the touch of a squirming three foot long moray eel.

Steve gave an expansive laugh. "Bet you can't wait to bite into that, huh?"

Rob answered with a rude comment, then bent to examine the remainder of the booty. A dozen spiny sea urchins, a small pile of assorted sea snails, a few limpets and a medium-sized lobster; Steve's foraging takes up where Sherman's scorched earth policy left off. This march from the sea included anything even marginally edible.

"Is that a fish?" Tina poked gingerly at a rubbery blue ball with pouting lips and dazed eyes. "It has *eyelids!*" She blurted an incredulous, "What *is it?*" in a tone that quickly put Steve on the defensive.

"Why that's a ... well ... it's an Aunt Betty fish, one of many species of Gumballs." He flashed me a conspiratorial wink. Steve is, in his own words, "a reformed marine biologist," and has a heretical fondness for renaming sea creatures after their more distinctive physical characteristics.

In the case of Gumballs, however, his humorous name had a purpose some people felt to be sinister: to disguise the fact that these were puffer fish and contained a deadly toxin capable of fatally poisoning the unlucky diner. Although puffer fish are prized delicacies in Japan, a special training program and license is required for anyone who wishes to prepare them. Steve had acquired his 'training' by reading a description of the fish's dangerous innards in an obscure magazine found in the waiting room of the Portland, Oregon Greyhound bus depot.

"We call them Aunt Bettys," Steve hurried on, "because they have those polka dots and ... uh, blue skin. Like my Aunt Betty's favorite dress." Tina pursed her lips thoughtfully and gave him a penetrating look.

"This one's a Suitcase, also known as a Samsonite or Trunk Fish." He probed at a large and curiously rectangular fish with the tip of his spear. "All it needs is a couple of hinges and a handle and you could pack your clothes in it." Tina nodded slowly.

"Now *this* is a real delicacy. A Football, isn't it, Carl?" I looked at the fish's strangely familiar face.

"That's a Mortimer Snerd," I said, recalling the famous puppet's pathetically homely features.

"Are you planning on *eating* these?" Rob's outspoken doubts erased Steve's smile instantly.

"Of course!" he answered. "They're all perfectly good!" He gave me a quick warning look. "Uh, if you know just how to fix them. Like this one." His big toe nudged an especially grotesque combination of fins, spots, awkward angles and bulging eyes. "This is your basic Coffin Fish. I clean these real carefully, believe me. They taste just like chicken."

"I never was that fond of chicken," Tina muttered, turning her attention to the lobster. "How about this?"

Steve brightened. "Oh, let me see... maybe a nice lobster bisque or a cold seafood salad or combine it with this other stuff into a big paella-type rice or..."

"Hey Carl! Could you give me a hand for a second?" I raised my head warily. Steve's tone of carefully contrived nonchalance was all too familiar, like a friendly neighbor calling over the fence on Saturday morning, "How about helping for a few minutes while I drop the transmission on my Edsel?"

"What is it?" I stalled, relishing the opportunity to lie back on the hot sand and stretch cramped neck and shoulder muscles. Rob had summed it up earlier when he said, "I didn't realize that kayaking was so *painful!*"

"Don't panic," Steve said dryly. "I just want a simple suggestion on dinner. I'll do the work." When either sarcasm or butter are called for, he invariably doubles the measure.

"Come on!" he urged. "What do you recommend for this crazy Suitcase?" Steve is not only a compulsive cook but belongs to that eccentric cadre of food-aficionados who actually enjoy cleaning fish and washing dishes. The least I could offer was an opinion.

"Apply Cardio-Pulmonary Resuscitation and throw the poor thing back."

"You're sure helpful!" Steve shouted. "I'll keep that in mind when I dish out the pudding!"

I raised up on one elbow, suddenly alert. "The *what?*"

"Oh, the butterscotch pudding." He yawned elaborately. "No use carrying it around forever. Besides, I feel the need for a jolt of preservatives."

"Why don't you filet and skin the Suitcase, dredge it in a light batter and then fry it in about half an inch of oil with a lot of garlic?"

"Great idea!" Steve said quickly. "You can make the batter. Lorena, would you peel these?" He reached into the pocket of his tattered shorts and produced a thick wad of loose garlic cloves. Lorena's hand opened automatically.

"Seen Rob around?" Steve was eager to press-gang another victim into his seaside galley. "Tina's going to make up a nice batch of cole slaw. With fresh onions and raisins."

I got the hint: finger Rob or forget the cole slaw. Would I turn in my own brother for a few mouthfuls of shredded cabbage?

"He's behind those dunes," I said. "Looking for shells again."

The cook fire is the traditional centerpiece of the outdoor camp. In Steve's mind, however, this vital flame is an altar upon which he performs esoteric religious devotions with a fervor capable of rocking both Heaven and Earth. Adhering to the tenets of gastronomy with a fundamentalist's disdain for the so-called physical laws of science, Steve knows in his soul that: *oil and water do mix*, especially in Italian salad dressings; *fire does not burn* but sautees, simmers, bakes and broils; and *time is not relative* when baking potatoes.

Like other high priests, Steve surrounds himself with religious trappings and sacred objects: apron, spatula, garlic press, wire whisk and paring knife. And at times, like a chaplain called upon to offer the reassurance of faith to weary troops, Steve finds himself cooking on bended knees while the wind flings sparks into his beard. He takes these discomforts and inconveniences in his stride. Or sort of...

"This is impossible! I HAVE TO HAVE THOSE DRIED ONIONS!"

"But *why?*" Rob argued, his shoulders sagging toward inevitable defeat. "What's so important about...?"

"Because," Steve snarled. "Because it is impossible...*impossible*...to make..." he choked with frustration, "onion gravy without onions! Even you should be able to understand that!" He banged the pan onto the sand but Rob remained obstinate. Rob makes no bones about a fondness for microwave-heated sandwiches, processed cheese and frozen dinners. Steve was up against a hard case.

"If *you* don't get the dried onions," Steve threatened, "then I guess I'll have to."

Rob yielded immediately. The packet of dried onions had been tucked into the very bow of his kayak when we'd divided up the food bags. The kayak, of course, was now fully and tediously loaded. It is a basic rule of camp cooking that the most urgently needed item of food is also the most inaccessible. If Steve made good his threat it would take Rob several hours to sort and re-stow the load exactly as he'd arranged it earlier. Muttering, he headed down the hot beach to the boats.

Steve now plunged his thumb into the bowl of batter I'd prepared, transferred it to his mouth and began smacking his lips noisily.

"Needs an egg," he announced.

"We only have half a dozen left," Lorena protested. "Shouldn't we..."

"Use 'em up!" Steve waved aside the suggestion of rationing as if it were an annoying wasp. "I'm not out here to lose weight. We're suffering enough as it is. Where are those onions?"

Rob appeared as if on command, his face streaked with sweat. Steve snatched the small bag with an impatient "thanks!" and turned to the gravy pan. "Better stoke up another fire, Carl, if you're going to fry those fish." Before I could protest, he added. "You too, Lorena, or the tortillas won't be done until it's too late. Timing is critical!"

"Three cookfires?" I thought guiltily. "What if the Sierra Club finds out about this?"

"Come on, what's the delay?" Steve prodded, reading my mind. "There's enough wood here for at least a week." He waved toward a waist-high windrow of driftwood stretching for hundreds of yards, the tangled debris of a recent hurricane.

As I moved away, stooping to pick up choice pieces of hardwood, I heard Steve call, "Hey Tina! Build a fire to steam that lobster on, would'ya? I want everything to be done at the same time, not in relays."

The sun moved steadily toward the horizon, a relentless solar kitchen timer winding down toward darkness. When the lights went out, the complex cooking tasks Steve had set up would become even more difficult. Spice containers sink unnoticed into the sand, precious spoons and knives hide in deep shadows and stumbling feet court disaster at every turn. Worst of all, good food should be seen to be fully appreciated. Steve fervently believes that eating in the dark is a punishment properly reserved for ill-mannered children and political prisoners.

"Hurry it up!" he urged, stalking restlessly around the circle of cook fires like a general commanding a battle on several fronts. "The birds are going home. There isn't much time!" Offshore an undulating flight of pelicans swooped and dipped over the sea as they returned from a long day of diving for fish.

Lorena scowled, brushing her hair from her eyes, then said rebelliously, "I can't mix this corn bread in my lap! Let's just have tortillas. I'll need a bowl or a pan or..."

"Stay calm!" Steve consoled. "We'll just have to improvise." He looked left and right, sighed heavily, then stared heavenward, thinking hard. "Granola!"

"Thank you," Rob answered, mimicking a sneeze. Steve was oblivious to the joke.

"Empty the granola jar and use it for mixing up the cornbread," he suggested, giving us the benefit of a smug grin.

Lorena hesitated, "But what about the granola?"

Steve looked over at Rob, grinned again and said, "Put it in Rob's hat for now. Sun's almost down, anyway," he added, stifling Rob's protest.

"Hey!" Tina called from across camp. "Bring something to put this cole slaw in!" Steve's smile dissolved into a puzzled frown as he bent to stoke the fire under the soup.

"I forgot the salad," he said distractedly, giving the cook pot a fond pat on the lid. Rising slowly to his feet, Steve said, "Keep an eye on this," and set off in the direction of the kayaks.

Although our camp was well situated for an outdoor kitchen, it left much to be desired as a landing place for relatively fragile kayaks. As in other camps it had been necessary to beach the boats where the best conditions of surf, rocks, reefs and smooth sand could be found. This spot was separated from the kitchen and sleeping area by a hundred yards of soft sand. Tina and Rob had already tramped a distinct trail between kitchen and kayaks, obeying Steve's urgent requests for desperately needed spices, utensils, condiments and containers. That Steve would himself embark on a search for a salad bowl and leave the kitchen in the hands of heathens was ample testimony to the gravity of the situation.

Scant minutes later a bright orange object flashed over our heads and buried itself in the sand at Tina's feet. She gave an indignant shout, flinging her arms protectively over the grated cabbage.

"A flying salad bowl!" Steve laughed, dismissing Tina's angry complaint about sand in the cole slaw with a casual shrug. "I knew that Frisbee had to be good for something." In the excitement of planning our expedition this toy had been included as an amusing diversion for lazy days. So far, however, none of us had found time to unpack the Frisbee, much less the energy to actually lift our paddle-weary arms and toss it into the air.

Steve's attention now shifted to the lobster.

"This deserves a good chowder," he said, turning the spiny lobster from side to side, admiring its savory qualities as if it were a rare gemstone, "but there isn't really enough to go around..."

Rob looked up from the wood pile. Steve had insisted that he inspect every piece of wood, no matter how small, for tiny gobs of a sticky black tar-like substance that could quickly ruin a barbecued fish with evil-tasting soot. This tar, from distant oil spills and the bilges of passing ships, could be found on even the most remote beaches.

Wood that had been inspected and certified 'kosher' was carefully segregated from the general pile.

"Why not chuck the lobster into the rice with everything else?" Rob now suggested.

Steve grimaced. The thought of 'chucking' a lobster into anything was hardly worthy of that wonderful crustacean's dining potential. The idea did not merit a response.

"I had a dream a few nights ago about dipping lobster tails in drawn butter," Steve sighed, his voice trailing off as his thoughts suddenly focused into a Good Idea. "Mayonnaise!" he shouted. "That's it! We've got fresh eggs! We've got oil! We've got limes! Lobster dipped in real mayonnaise!" His bare belly shook with emotion.

"I need a bowl!" Steve announced, moving quickly to the table, a crude arrangement of beachcombed boards placed side-by-side on the sand.

"Forget it," Lorena said. "We are completely out of bowls. We don't even have plates to eat off of. You've got them all tied up in the cooking!"

Steve stopped short, absentmindedly dropping the lobster onto the table. He right hand crawled up his neck and onto the top of his head, tugging and pulling at his black tangled hair as if to coax forth a solution to the bowl problem. It was a familiar and fascinating ritual. No good ideas hiding up there, so his hand moved downward, idly stroking his hairy belly.

Now his left hand was called in, moving up to tug insistently at a thick earlobe, then across and into the beard, fingers splayed out like a garden rake, combing at bits of driftwood and seaweed in hopes of revealing hidden treasure. Frustrated, his hands met at his nose, the heel of the right grinding into rubbery cheeks, the left pushing aside his sunglasses as the knuckles vigorously massaged his tightly closed eyes.

We waited expectantly as a look of great peace and contentment gradually settled over Steve's troubled features. Returning to his belly, his hands clasped themselves together in Buddha-like repose.

"The rice is almost done so I can use the lid of the skillet to whip up the mayonnaise in." Steve's voice was soft, almost a chant. "I'll separate the egg yolks from the whites in plastic bags." Only one problem remained. "We'll serve the mayonnaise and Chinese mustard in clam shells. Individual settings, of course. How is that cornbread, Lorena?" Without a backward glance he plunged once again into the fray.

"Okay, how do we stand?" Steve's voice had lost its fine edge of excitement as he moved with a noticeable sag toward a grill crowded with fish. There was no response to his query as we stumbled through our chores with the enthusiasm of sunburned zombies. A good camp cook, however, is also a practicing psychologist. Sensing a mood of resentment that could turn our meal into an angry free-for-all, Steve immediately laid a firmer hand on the reins.

"Rob, be ready to light that next fire when it gets dark. I don't want to eat by flashlight." Rob answered with a crisp mocking salute. He had spent the final minutes before sunset busily gathering a huge pile of 'sockwood'. This dry, very light driftwood burned with a bright flame and the choking odor of smouldering gym socks. It was no more annoying, however, than sunburn, scorpions, moray eels, burrs, stinging jellyfish, wind squalls, ants, cactus spines, dust storms, giant manta rays, brackish drinking water, tide rips, blisters, heat stroke and other hard facts of kayaking life we'd been exposed to.

"Cornbread's done and cooling," Steve continued, cataloging the afternoon's accomplishments. "But how about the tortillas? Lorena?"

Lorena lay flat on her back, seemingly steamrollered into the sand. Her eyelids barely flickered; otherwise she registered no Vital Life Signs.

"Tortillas?" Steve repeated, his voice rising impatiently.

Lorena's hands twitched, then rose slowly into the air to display long fingers coated with monster-like incrustations of flour and dried dough. Steve nodded approvingly.

"Well, then!" Steve crowed, rubbing his hands together. "Tina's got a salad and Carl's got fried fish. That just leaves me with the paella, the grilled fish, the pudding, the soup and mayonnaise for the lobster. Am I forgetting anything?" He arched his eyebrows expectantly, like an understanding schoolteacher who has fed the correct answers to an unusually dull class.

"The smoker!" Steve's irritating heartiness broke the silence. "We've got a full load with that moray eel and the extra Coffin fish. Plenty of fish for lunch tomorrow, don't you think?" He turned quickly to the next challenge.

"Here, Rob, hold this." Rob took the large skillet lid by the knob, giving Steve a wary look. "Turn it over," Steve said patiently. "Haven't you ever made mayonnaise?"

Rob shook his head slowly. Back home in the real world, mayonnaise always came in nice jars, never in skillet lids...

Steve let out the first in a long series of patient sighs. After wiping a fork carefully on the seat of his well-travelled shorts, he said, "After I pour the egg yolk I've got in this sack here into the lid and add the lime juice, I want you to whip it with the fork."

Rob took the fork as though he'd never seen this tool in his life.

"Whatever you do," Steve instructed, *"Don't stop!"* A plastic squeeze bottle of cooking oil appeared magically in Steve's left hand. "Go!" he cried, aiming a thin stream of oil into the lid as Rob obediently took up the beat.

"Tina! Turn that fish! No, no! The middle one with the crinkly fins! Right!" Without interrupting the flow of oil into the lid, Steve continued to direct Tina at the distant barbecue fire, giving Rob an occasional quick word of encouragement. Rob's right arm moved in a blur as he whipped the oil and egg mixture.

Steve's attention now wandered from one cook fire to another, anywhere but on the growing puddle that Rob held cross-legged in his lap. "Hey, look!" Steve cried, distracted by a swooping man o' war bird.

"Watch it!" Rob yelled, flinching as cooking oil spattered over his bare thigh and down the side of his chest.

"Keep whipping!" Steve retorted, giving the bottle another squeeze.

"Didn't I see this scene in the Exorcist?" Rob panted, eyes widening in astonishment as the mixture began to take on a distinctly creamy texture. Before he could utter another word, Steve's arm twisted the oil bottle away. Turning now to actually look into the lid for the first time since the operation had begun, Steve said blandly, "Mayonnaise," and moved on to another chore.

Night had come, and with it a cool steady breeze that stirred the ashes of the dying cookfires. Steve lay on his side like a beached whale, glazed eyes fixed on some distant and unreachable horizon.

"Pretty good dinner, after all, wouldn't you say?" He probed his molars with a wicked driftwood splinter, eyeglasses askew as his head drooped onto the sand. Steve's capacity for compliments is as vast as his appetite. "I thought there'd be enough juice in that lime to get a good *do* on the mayonnaise," he said, "but it wasn't until I actually began squeezing that..."

His voice droned on, recounting a blow-by-blow instant replay of the afternoon's creative cooking frenzy with an intensity and eye for detail that would shame Howard Cosell. At pointed pauses in this monologue we injected the obligatory "Sure was good!" and "Oh, really?" as we retreated deeper into warm sleeping bags.

"I really liked those tortillas," Steve continued dreamily. "They were so... so *yeasty* and so flexible." He smacked his lips appreciatively, laying the groundwork for his next cooking extravaganza with all the cunning of a professional politician. "That cole slaw was just right, Tina. Not too tart or too sweet. I like the way you shredded the cabbage, too."

"Thanks. I hoped you'd notice." Tina's sarcasm went by unnoticed as Steve turned his attention to Rob's contribution. "Good job on the firewood. Think you could make mayonnaise yourself now?" His answer came in the form of an unusually descriptive obscenity involving a Frisbee. Steve sidestepped adroitly. "Carl, what did you think of the meal in general?"

I paused for a second, then began reciting my part in the traditional review that follows Steve's major cooking efforts. Like a novelist or playwright, his creative works merited analysis and formal recognition, though in this case it would be from a captive critic.

"That soup was wonderful," I said. "I like the way you added dried parsley at the last moment. And those toasted sesame seeds with the Chinese mustard. That was a very nice touch." My mouth watered involuntarily; the rich crusty batter had trapped the juices from the fish in a golden wrapper, releasing them with each bite to blend with the sharp tangy mustard. No wonder the Japanese risked life and limb for such sensations...

And the lobster: steamed to perfection, then sliced into delicate rosy sections and dunked into creamy homemade mayonnaise lightly flavored with herbs, sprinkled with coarse black pepper.

The cornbread, moist and steaming, smothered in melted honey... My stomach rumbled at the memory. Pudding with fat raisins, swimming in warm milk laced with vanilla and rum; the seafood paella, the gravy!

No doubt about it, there was something to be said for the seven pot camping meal.

The Moveable Feast

It is no exaggeration to say that our camps are planned around the kitchen. If a large flat rock would make a convenient table that's where the heart of our camp will be. Never mind that there's a spectacular view site fifty yards to the south; it's much easier to stroll over for a few minutes of quiet reflection than to chop onions at ground level.

When camping with a vehicle we try to park so that the kitchen area, and stove in particular, are shaded and protected from the wind. "This is just too much hassle; let's break out the munchies!" is a typical response when a poorly planned camp kitchen makes cooking a total chore.

Some campers go all the way and set up Model Kitchens. I look upon these outdoor arrangements with mixed envy and amazement, well aware that our own kitchens represent the more chaotic side of human nature. It isn't that we don't try to keep our act together ... it's just that our act is too complicated. Like stand-up comics we usually find ourselves ad-libbing rather than working from a well planned script/menu.

On a recent boating-camping trip my brother and I went to elaborate pains to keep our kitchen gear neat, clean and orderly. The firewood was cut into one-foot sections and stacked upwind of the fire."

"Short pieces are more economical," I explained to Rob, "and easier to handle. They're also a good size for adjusting the temperature of the fire while you're cooking. And they look neat, stacked up like that." Rob nodded absentmindedly, staring up the beach.

"Wind's shifting, isn't it?" he said.

Five minutes later we were madly scrambling to catch loose gear and clothing that had been caught by the squall. While Rob flattened out the tent and weighted it with rocks I hurried to pack away our fresh vegetables and fruit. Flying sand can work its way like magic right under the leaves of a cabbage.

"*Fire!*" Rob yelled. I turned to find our woodpile fully engulfed in flames as the newly shifted breeze fanned the fire white-hot. A well-aimed bucket of seawater took care of that, though it would be another month before the wood dried out enough to burn again. There was no choice but to move the cook fire to a more sheltered spot. We had to eat and the wind was obviously out of our control.

"It's at least a hundred yards to the nearest good rocks," Rob complained. I surveyed the beach, unable to find a closer place not exposed to wind or tide. Reluctantly we packed up the entire kitchen, from food and water to pots, pans and kindling, and lugged it over the slippery rocks. An hour later, as I began cooking dinner, the wind shifted again and worse yet, intensified.

"We can't move back to Kitchen A," Rob said. "It's just as exposed now as Kitchen B." We took the only course open, moving kit and caboodle two hundred yards down the beach, to a snug hole in a jumble of high boulders. This was Kitchen C.

"I feel like I'm on a merry-go-round," Rob laughed bitterly, dropping another armload of firewood onto the sand. "I've gathered half a cord of driftwood and we still don't have a fire going. I wonder what's next?"

"Next" came in the morning, as the wind shifted back to its original direction and only Kitchen A was sheltered. As we stumbled along the beach from Kitchen C, arms filled with a jumble of provisions and utensils, I struck upon an idea.

"It's too windy and rough for boating and if the weather behaves the same, we can count on more wind shifts, right?" Rob agreed, though with obvious reluctance. "So, why don't we spread our gear and food out, leave some at Kitchen A and B and some at Kitchen C. Chances are we'll have dinner at C and breakfast at A or B."

Rob fumbled with a sooty tin pot as he slipped on a sand covered rock. "Sounds okay to me," he answered. "Perfectly obvious, really. Who ever said camping was a lot of work? *Look at us!*" His voice rose, dangerously high and strangled, "We're working out your basic ABC's of camp cooking!"

The wind howled in appreciation.

Cooking & Camping

For many campers, outdoor camping isn't a pleasure but a chore, a daily 'ordeal by fire'. To ease the burden, these reluctant cooks search out alternatives and E-Z conveniences: packaged and freeze-dried foods, camp kitchen gadgetry, newer and niftier utensils and yet another cookbook that swears it will make cooking as simple as falling out of bed.

There is a popular myth that good campers were either born that way or had an authentic Mountain Man in the family, training them from early childhood to master the challenge of outdoor life. In actual practice, however, comfortable and enjoyable camping doesn't require an encyclopedic knowledge of woodcraft and arcane survival skills, nor is it necessary to own ultra-lightweight tents and portable kitchen sinks.

Learning to camp and to cook well while camping involves paying attention to what you really need and *don't need* in the outdoors. I need a clean, sand-and-dirt-free surface to spread my utensils on and something to support the garlic as it's chopped. A square of cloth satifies the first requirement, and a table, board, clipboard or rock takes care of the second problem. Next: find good wood or fuel up the stove.

Simple routines such as these soon become automatic. When this stage is reached, you'll find that cooking and camping give more pleasure and satisfaction. Be patient; it takes a little time to learn any new skill.

I vividly recall many camping trips that began with a 'klutz period' when nothing went quite as easily as I'd expected it to. I'd cut myself with the saw, over-inflate my air mattress, kick sand into the frying pan and generally fumble through every minor kitchen and camp-keeping chore. By the end of the trip all these irritations would be under control and forgotten... until the beginning of the next adventure.

Some of the projects and ideas discussed here go beyond the kitchen limits. The reason is simple: we can't separate cooking from camping. The easier and more comfortable camp life is, the more relaxing and enjoyable the cooking will be.

Here's what's ahead:

Kitchen Improvements
Quick and Easy Tricks
Washing Dishes
Garbage and Litter
Sleeping Bag Ice Chest
Drip Cooler
Cook Fires
  Gathering Wood
  The Fire Pit
  Building the Fire
  Using the Fire
  Dousing the Fire
Tin Can Stoves and Ovens
  Solid Fuel Stove
  Liquid Fuel Stove
  Large Tin Can Stove

Tin Can Oven
Tin Can Lantern
Stoves: Care and Feeding
Coleman Stoves: Care and Cleaning

Staying Healthy Outdoors
Purifying Water
Diarrhea, Dysentery and Food
 Poisoning
  Diarrhea
  Diarrhea Cocktail
  Food Poisoning
  Dysentery
Cramps: Stomach, Muscle, Menstrual
Burns
Infections and Wounds
  Puncture Wounds

Kitchen Improvements

Quick and Easy Tricks

Do your best to keep things off the ground. This helps prevent dirtying, stops or delays insect and predator raids on food and gives the camp a Scout-like appearance.

• Drive a forked stick or branch into the ground next to the cookfire and use it to hold cups, utensils and cook pots.

• Stretch strong cord and use powerful clothes pins or wire clamps to hang things from: clothes, dish rags, small food and utensil bags, the coffee pot, etc.

• Tie small loops in a length of cord and tie it around a tree trunk. Hang utensils in these loops, handles down. Bend large S hooks from stiff wire and hook these onto the cord. Now hang odds and ends from the S hooks. Shower curtain and drapery hooks work, too.

• When hiking I try to tie my backpack to a tree trunk at about shoulder level or, if there are bears or climbing critters in the area, suspend it from a high branch. Pack all food into the backback when not in use. Even innocent looking insects can wreak havoc on your larder. In a desert canyon, a small army of crickets chewed holes in every plastic bag. *Crickets?* That's right . . . crickets.

• Hang fresh produce in a light mesh bag. This retards spoilage and helps keep the food in sight. Where did I put that avocado last week? Oh, here it is, in a puddle under the spuds.

• Store dry foods in closed containers, preferably well sealed. Suspend the containers, and if crawling insects are a problem, paint the rope or cord with kerosene every day or two. Rodent guards can be fashioned from the ends of tin cans (if you have a pair of metal snips on hand) and slipped over the rope.

• Lash the ends of three sticks together (three feet or longer) so that they stand as a tripod. Hang a basket, bag, box or kettle from the top of the tripod. This makes a portable 'caddy' for the kitchen. It can also be used to suspend pots over an open fire.

• While car camping, we carry a lightweight lawn rake. When other campers see what a ten minute sweep does to improve a site, they invariably quit sneering and ask to borrow the rake. Thorns, broken glass, bottle caps, burrs, cigarette butts and carelessly strewn but all-too-common litter is quickly gathered up with the rake. A daily raking also keeps down flies and bugs that come to dine on tiny bits of spilled food.

Washing Dishes

By an unfortunate coincidence Lorena and I both hate to wash dishes. We whine, wheedle, argue and finally barter off other chores in a desperate attempt to escape this chore. Like the search for perpetual motion and the perfect mouse trap, we constantly seek easier ways to do the dishes. Our latest methods include the following: when water is plentiful (fresh or seawater) we use the bucket brigade method.

Line up three buckets or two buckets and a hanging plastic shower bag. (We use plastic buckets that fit nicely inside each other.) Put a tablespoon or so of liquid soap into the first bucket. (Ivory Liquid seems to work best in salt water.) The second and third buckets are for rinsing, though you may want to add a quarter cup or more of plain household bleach to the second bucket. A mild bleach solution helps disinfect dishes. We take this precaution when camped with large groups and in prolonged warm weather. The risk of hepatitis is reduced by careful attention to washing.

When buckets aren't available, dishwashing sinks can be

improvised. Line a box or basket with a plastic tarp or garbage bag. An inflated inner tube can also be used to form the sink sides. Or dig sink-sized holes in the ground and line them with plastic sheets or bags.

Fill the sink with water and begin washing. To be even fancier, cover the water-filled sinks with another sheet of plastic and allow the sun's rays to heat the dishwater. This method also works quite well for laundry and personal bathing.

A portable dishwasher for unbreakable dishes can be improvised from any good-sized watertight container. We use a five gallon plastic bucket with sealing lid. My brother prefers an ice chest and a friend uses a surplus ammo can. Whatever your choice, add dirty dishes, soap and water, seal, and then drive around the countryside with the 'washing machine' in your trunk. We used this method on our sailboat; the rougher the weather, the cleaner the dishes. Works nicely on clothes, too.

When near the beach, dishes can be scrubbed thoroughly with sand and rinsed with salt water. To prevent the build-up of grease, particularly on frying pans, soak all dishes and utensils in boiling hot soapy seawater every couple of days. Grease inevitably leads to diarrhea and upset stomachs.

Before washing greasy things, rub them vigorously with dry table salt. A skillet or cup will look and feel cleaner than you would have believed possible. After the salt rub, wash with soapy water and rinse well.

Dishwashing becomes much more of a problem when water is scarce. It's tempting to say *What the heck?* and do a sloppy job — or not wash up at all. Don't take the easy way out; it not only leaves the dishes in a disgusting condition but can create very serious health hazards. The following suggestions have served us well on many extended camping expeditions where water was severely rationed.

When there is no wash water, dishes can be cleaned fairly well in dry sand (or salt). Wipe the dishes with a rag or scraper, then rub them with clean sand. Now, if you can afford it, heat a cup of your drinking water. Add a few drops of soap — not too much; most people use more soap than necessary. Scrub the dishes with a rag dipped in the hot soapy water. To rinse, repeat the process with another cup of clean hot water and a clean rag.

Dishes can also be washed and rinsed over a pan, to collect run-off water. This water shouldn't be too dirty if you previously cleaned the dishes with clean sand, salt or a rag. It can be used again for washing.

After rinsing, wipe the dishes dry to remove any soap you might have missed.

All washing and rinsing should be done well away from running or standing water: streams, springs, lakes, etc. Your soap may be biodegradable but it still doesn't belong in the local water, especially if others use it for drinking.

Suggestions for purifying water can be found under *Staying Healthy*, later in this chapter.

Garbage and Litter

Garbage is a pain in the neck while camping, especially if you are hiking or boating. *"Pack It Out!"* is an excellent motto, but too many people still balk when faced with a gooey mess of used paper towels, greasy sardine cans and tomato sauce smeared paper plates. This sort of garbage is all too often stuffed under a rock or buried in a shallow grave. Like a bad penny, refuse will turn up again after the first big rain storm or a visit from a scavenging creature. A little bit of garbage makes a hell of a big eyesore.

The easiest way to reduce garbage is not to take any with you when you go outdoors. As you pack up, remove useless wrappers, bags and boxes and transfer their contents to reuseable containers. This goes for everything from cigarettes to candy bars. Don't worry: few things will go stale or spoil if you handle them properly.

Paper can be burned in camp but don't leave lumps of charred foil and plastic behind — gather them up, stuff them into a strong plastic bag and carry them out. Garbage bags should be in every pack and RV, canoe and raft. Buy the toughest bags you can find and if they'll get heavy use, double them up.

Burying garbage is a last resort, especially in heavily used areas designated 'wilderness'. If every camper digs one hole, the wilderness will soon look like a golf course invaded by moles. Holes settle and sink. They damage fragile mosses, roots and burrows.

If garbage must be buried, do it well beyond the highest tide, spring flood and storm-wash line or it will be coughed up one day. Dirt makes a much more permanent grave for garbage than sand.

When camped on the beach, we sometimes bury cans at sea, well offshore (in situations where packing it out is impossible) and cremate so-called 'organic' garbage (fish skins, onion peels, etc.). If you burn it, however, keep the garbage in a very hot fire for half an hour or more or you'll just cook it. We chop our garbage into small pieces and burn it a bit at a time, whenever more wood is added to the fire.

Some campers clean up and dispose of garbage that others have left behind, often at the cost of backpacking out large quantities of litter when they could have come out empty and light. I've heard these good samaritans scoffed at as 'do-gooders' and 'ecology nuts'. Well, it takes all types, but from those of us who think garbage belongs in the city dump rather than behind the tent and under the picnic table — Thanks and keep up the good work.

Sleeping Bag Ice Chest

On a kayaking trip in Mexico, Lorena and I were camped on a hot and very remote beach. We received a surprise visit from a friendly American couple on a passing boat. They took one look at our sunburned faces and parched lips and generously offered us a large block of ice. Ice! It was too good to believe; even though we had nothing to cool but instant tea mixed

with brackish water, we felt as though we'd been given a genuine treasure. To keep the ice from melting instantly we improvised this 'ice chest':

Put your block of ice or bag of cubes into at least one and preferably two, heavy-duty plastic bags. If bags aren't available, a large sheet of plastic can be used. Just be sure it's large enough to wrap around everything without dribbling out the sides.

Spread out your sleeping bag or jacket and place the ice bag in the center. Wrap the sleeping bag snugly around the ice bag. If you're using a jacket, zip it up, turn it upsidedown, slide the ice bag inside and tie the jacket arms together.

A foil-backed blanket can also be wrapped around the ice bag before it is placed in the sleeping bag or jacket. Put the foil side facing in toward the ice.

We've used this type of cooler with great success while staying in hotels, on the beach and camping from a small car. The 'cooler' can also be partially buried for additional insulation. Lay a sheet of plastic in the hole before spreading the sleeping bag to protect it from dirt. The person who donates the sleeping bag is always given the first and last cold beers.

Drip Cooler

Don't laugh at this until you've tried it; it really works. Put a thick layer of cloth in the bottom of a basket or bag (one with a handle is best). If you don't have cloth, use your extra clothes, grass, newspapers or whatever. Soak with fresh or salt water. Place whatever you want cooled onto this wet layer and cover it with more wet material.

Now hang the basket in the shade, preferably exposed to the wind. Drape another wet cloth over the basket; the thicker the better. Keep the cloth damp and within a few hours the food or beverages will be chilled. They won't be so cold that they make your teeth hurt, but they'll definitely be cooler than the outside air. This type of rustic refrigeration can prevent seafood and leftovers from spoiling for a full day beyond their normal 'shelf life'.

For an even simpler variation, put whatever you want cooled into a woven plastic, cloth or burlap bag, dip it into water and hang it up. When it dries give it another dunk.

Model Campers may prefer to rig a drip bottle over the cooler to provide a slow but steady source of water for evaporation. A plastic sack with a tiny hole also works. To build a luxury model Drip Cooler, replace the basket with a well ventilated box.

Those who doubt the principle of the Drip Cooler should try this: dip a T-shirt in warm water and put it on. Now run as fast as you can. The wind you feel against your chest will get colder and colder, even on a hot day. That's the wonder of evaporative cooling.

Cook Fires

I hate to burn trees but I love to build fires. A campfire warms the spirit, sparks the imagination and gives a romantic flavor to the outdoor experience that no stove can begin to match. We all know, however, that fires are very hazardous and are prohibited in many areas to protect and

preserve the wilderness. I assume that you'll use a stove and lantern unless you're camping where fires are allowed.

Gathering Wood: Many camping books suggest that dead wood be used rather than green, living wood. This protects healthy trees. Unfortunately, dead wood — especially both fallen and standing dead trees — is an important habitat for nesting birds, squirrels and other small creatures. I hate to camp where others have scoured the ground for every dry twig and branch; it just doesn't look right. Bare ground is also bare of birds and animals, who need the underbrush for protection. If you want to spy on small wildlife near camp, don't raze the dead wood to the ground. Use dead trees only as a last resort.

My wood gathering starts as far from camp as possible. Pick your wood here and there, not all in one spot. Small wood is easy to handle and doesn't require Paul Bunyan routines with axe or saw. Small wood makes an efficient small fire; big wood becomes a big, wasteful fire. Apparently nit-picking conservation measures such as these do make a difference, especially when practised by thousands of campers.

A word on tools: saws, axes and (heaven forbid) chainsaws have little use in the average camp. If there's enough wood around for a fire you should be able to scrounge dead stuff from the ground. In some cases, however, the careful use of a small folding saw may be recommended. Breaking dead and dying limbs from a living tree, for example, can damage the tree, especially the bark. By careful sawing you'll minimize injury or eliminate it entirely. Cutting wood into small pieces, especially tough hardwoods, also makes it easier to build and maintain a small fire.

When gathering firewood, remember that hard, dense wood burns hotter, cleaner, longer, and gives nicer coals than light, soft wood.

The Fire Pit: The actual site of the fire is very important. It should be *at least* fifteen or twenty feet from the nearest flammable object. Sparks, spitting coals and popping rocks can travel amazing distances. We once had a rock explode under a cook fire, showering flaming embers into our camp with all the force and drama of an eruption of Mount St. Helens. It was almost funny — until I found a chunk of burning wood inside our kayak.

If there's a breeze, place the fire pit downwind of your tent or vehicle.

What is the ground like? Hard and dry, or soft and porous? Fires built on top of decayed leaves and root masses can spread underground and burst into flame well beyond the pit. I found this hard to believe until we spent most of a long night digging up smouldering roots from a steep tree-covered mountainside. I'd built the fire on ground filled with roots that I assumed were too damp and well protected by dirt to burn. I was wrong.

A thick layer of sand or dirt may be your only protection from exploding stones. For some reason smooth rocks seem to pop and explode more than rough rocks. River and beach stones are especially hazardous. We've camped on beaches where even the smallest gravel exploded.

In one memorable instance, Lorena and I were forced to skin dive for sand to build a foundation for the cook fire. The beach was entirely rocky and isolated by deep water and high cliffs. Every attempt to build a fire resulted in a steady barrage of exploding rocks. After dredging up enough sand to make a thick base about eighteen inches in diameter for the fire we were finally able to get dinner simmering.

There are many clever fire pit designs, but after years of experience we prefer the traditional 3-stone method, still in use in rural Mexico and other parts of the world. Find three rocks of more-or-less similar shape and size. I like stones as big as grapefruits; larger rocks put the cook pots too high above the fire, smaller will tend to crowd the wood.

Arrange the stones in a triangle, eqully spaced about six inches apart or less. You now have a universal fire pit that can be fed from three directions and will even support round-bottomed pots. Once the wind direction has been established, you can fill two open sides of the pit with other stones, though this tends to reduce the fire's area and efficiency. The beauty of the 3-stone arrangement is that long branches can be fed into the fire at an angle that does not interfere with the cook's activities.

The 3-stone pit has drawbacks, however. Pans can be crowded close to the open sides of the fire, but the heat is focused upward, on one pot. If you want to fry rice and fish at the same time, you'll need a second fire.

If stones are not available the fire can be placed in a shallow hole. Don't go too deep or the fire won't be able to draw enough air and will turn into a smoke hole. Because digging disturbs the soil, avoid this method in fragile wilderness areas. Fire scars are visible for many years and even fire-blackened stones should be concealed after use, though if you're camped where others will surely follow I would leave the fire pit intact. There is no benefit if a series of campers all prepare different fire pits in the same general area. A single pit will serve everyone with minimal damage.

Keyhole fires are made by arranging stones in the shape of a keyhole. The narrow portion of the hole, a slot, is for cooking; the larger, rounded area is for heat, light and a constant source of coals. The coals are dragged, scraped or even spooned into the cooking slot as needed. This is a neat arrangement but if stones and fuel are scarce, it isn't as practical or efficient as two small and separate fires.

3- STONE FIRE RING

A small fire used for illumination can be fed small bits of very dry wood. This gives off quite a bit of light and a brief surge of heat. In the keyhole arrangement, a large bed of coals will consume this dry wood in a flash — and sear the eyebrows off the cook or scorch one side of the cook pot. The two-fire arrangement sounds extravagant but in actual practice it can stretch fuel while still providing light.

KEYHOLE FIRE RING

Building the Fire: I like to shave wood chips and build elaborate arrangements of dry twigs to get my fires going. However, some of my fires fail in spite of the most careful attention and preparation. I am then forced to tear the cover off a good novel or melt a candle into the kindling.

Use patience and imagination to start your fires rather than gasoline or other explosives. Gas stinks up the camp and is far too dangerous for any but the most desperate situations. If, however, you are in such a desperate fix right now, don't waste your gas by pouring it over the wood. Soak this book in about half a cup of gasoline, taking care not to drip any on your clothing.

Arrange the kindling over the book and light it—holding the match at full arm's length or pinched in the split end of a long stick. This book should burn slowly, with little risk of flaring or exploding.

Campers in the rainy Northwest often develop a cynical attitude about fire starting, mainly because wet wood makes lousy fuel. I carry newspaper or cheaply printed magazines, even while hiking, and use pages for kindling after I've read them. Fire starting pellets, jellies and other concoctions are also useful and much, much safer than gasoline. If you must use a liquid, carry kerosene or charcoal briquet starter fluid. Neither, with proper handling and use, is as explosive as gasoline.

Using the Fire: Some people are quite literally addicted to large fires. My brother is a classic example; when his eyes glaze over and his hand twitches toward the bow saw, I immediately begin my pre-recorded lecture on firewood conservation, the ethics of wood cutting, the immorality of bonfires, etc., etc.

When all else fails I gather up expendable odds and ends of flammable material—food wrappers, books, maps, paper plates, and sacrifice them for a brief pillar of soul-satisfying flame.

The cook tends the cook fire and woe to any camper who carelessly stirs the coals or adds more fuel without the cook's permission. When camped with people you don't know well, a simple public service announcement should get the point across: "OK, folks, I'm going to cook now so if anyone throws anything on the fire ... I'll break their arm!"

Another simple rule: if the area of the coals or flame is larger than your cook pot, the fire is probably too large. Compare your fire to an electric burner or backpacking stove. A small fire gives a steady temperature when tended closely. Some campers build huge blazes and then have to go to ridiculous lengths to support a grill three feet over the coals to avoid melting the coffee pot.

Build your fire, and while it burns down to a bed of coals—usually 20 to 30 minutes—drag out the kitchen gear and begin preparing the meal. Add small wood from time to time and feed larger pieces into the edges of the fire. Very dry wood is nice if you'd like to sear or brown the food first and then reduce the heat to that given off by the hard coals.

Many cooks underestimate the heat of an open fire. Thin, lightweight cookware contributes to the problem by conducting heat almost instantly.

When a twig flares or a friend tosses a wad of tissue into the fire, this sudden burst of heat can turn well simmered eggs into slightly scorched ones.

The solution is to find the proper balance between the size and temperature of the fire and the distance above the fire for the cookpots and grill. When barbecuing, for example, hold your hand over the coals, palm down. If you can't count slowly to three the spot is too hot. Withdraw hand with a yelp and repeat the procedure a few inches higher. The proper distance above the fire for barbecuing is also about right for light cookware and gentle cooking.

When you finally get it just right, you'll probably discover that the coals have somehow gotten even hotter and the grill needs to go higher. Try this: lay a small piece of aluminum foil (shiny side down) on the grill and place your pan over it. This will reflect away some heat.

Or fill your mouth with water, take in a deep slow breath through your nose, purse lips and exhale a cooling atomized spray onto the coals. Don't get too close or steam and ashes will burst up into your face. A safer method is to remove coals or add green wood to the fire. This traps heat but it also produces smoke. You can't have everything...

Dousing the fire: It takes an amazing amount of water to douse a good sized fire, to drown it to the point where it *definitely* is not capable of smouldering into flame once again. I once had the opportunity to measure how much water is takes — when a fire that began to grow on its own had to be killed with our precious drinking water, quart by quart. The loss of this water caused a major detour in a week-long hike through tinder dry mountains.

Break your fire up as soon as you can, well before your intended departure from the camp site. This allows coals to turn to ashes and smouldering sticks to die out on their own. If they don't, dunk them into water (the most effective method) or drown them with repeated showers. A fine spray directed back and forth across the fire will cool it much more effectively than a big slop from a bucket (the worst method).

Stir the wet fire with a shovel or stick. If water is scarce, take turns peeing into the remains. This leaves an odor that the next party will not appreciate but it's preferable to a forest or brush fire. Cover the dead fire with a thin layer of dirt.

In areas where wood is very scarce or the fire hazard is high, plan your meals for a minimum of fire use. Cook enough at dinner, for example, to have cold leftovers at breakfast. The fewer fires the better.

Caution: In deserts and jungles, dead wood is a popular hideout for scorpions and other stinging creatures. Biting ants love dead wood and here in the Northwest wasps may nest in rotten logs and stumps. Gather wood carefully and don't heap it up near sleeping bags or tents. In scorpion country keep the woodpile at least ten yards from camp. Many cooks are stung by scorpions escaping the fire. Minimize the risk by putting small chunks well into the coals.

Tin Can Stoves and Ovens

Some call these modern appliances hobo stoves, but I prefer the more romantic name Gypsy Stove or Vagabond Stove. These stoves, in spite of a rather seedy appearance, can do a remarkably good economical job of cooking food. The so-called 'solid-fuel model' makes an excellent mini-barbecue. I have to admit to a perverse sense of pleasure whenever I fire up my tin can stove in some neatly regimented campground or trailer park.

Solid Fuel Stove: A one-gallon can or three-pound coffee can is ideal for this stove. Begin by removing the top of the can. If your can didn't come with a reusable lid, make one out of something fireproof — a piece of foil, tin or even a slightly larger can that will fit over the stove. The lid will be used to snuff out the fire and to keep its dirty insides from spilling out into your trunk or van. (A carrying container for this stove is a very good idea: use a larger can, a tough bag or build it a nice box.)

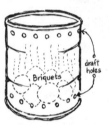

SOLID·FUEL·STOVE

After the top is off, punch a row of holes about an inch from the bottom of the can. Ice pick or pencil-sized to start with, larger holes later if you need them. This gives an air draft; without holes the fire will be lower in temperature, smokey and more easily snuffed. If you use charcoal briquets, however, this may be an advantage.

I sometimes put a row of holes near the top of the can. The upper holes prevent a pan from sealing the can and snuffing out the fire. Fool around with various arrangements and you'll soon find one that suits you and your particular fuel best.

Put a double layer of briquets, or kindling and wood in the bottom of the can. A 'starting fluid' can be used, but don't slop it on too heavily. In this small, enclosed space, it won't take much to get the fuel going. Briquets may take longer to become white hot than you're used to with an open barbecue, but the reward is how much longer they'll last — I snuff mine out after cooking, then use them again.

Pots and frying pans can be placed directly on the tin can stove or it can be used with a grate, as a barbecue. This is a one-steak-at-a-time arrangement.

If space is limited, carry your briquets in a bag stuffed inside the stove. One gallon of briquets will cook many meals; the total weight and cost of this arrangement are quite reasonable. When compared to the cost of white gas, for example, the Gypsy Stove suddenly looks much more respectable.

Liquid Fuel Stove: This universal stove is especially favored by refugees and retreating armies. It will burn just about anything liquid and combustible, but for the sake of your safety and sense of smell, avoid gasoline, creosote or other unrefined fuels. The best fuels are alcohol and kerosene. The latter is cheapest but it smells worse than alcohol and makes more soot. Both are less likely to explode than gasoline.

LIQUID·FUEL·STOVE

Warning: This stove works quite nicely when handled with care and caution, but it is basically hazardous. Never use it inside a tent, house, vehicle or boat. If possible, keep a fire extinguisher handy, even if it is just a pail of dirt or sand. Because the fuel is liquid, water will not snuff it out.

Now that you've mulled over these warnings, here's how to build and use the stove:

Punch several holes around the upper half of the can. Fill the can halfway with sand, dirt, sod, paper or pine needles. This stuff will act as a wick for the fuel. Add half a cup of your favorite fuel and carefully drop in a lighted match.

Don't peer into the can; you might lose an eyebrow. Pass your hand carefully over the can, well above the top, to test for heat. Alcohol burns almost invisibly and even a kerosene fire can be difficult to see on a bright sunny day.

This fire is not for barbecuing; one taste of a kerosene-sooty hamburger will demonstrate why.

If the fuel burns up before the food is cooked, *allow the stove to cool* before adding more. Hot kerosene and alcohol give off fumes that are very explosive.

Large Tin Can Stove: This might be called the restaurant version of the common hobo stove. It is used extensively in Mexico and Central America for roadside taco stands and is as close as many poorer people get to a kitchen range.

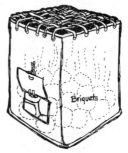

LARGE TIN·CAN·STOVE

Use a clean five gallon metal can, round or rectangular. If the can has had the top cut out punch a row of holes around the top edge and run heavy baling wire across from side to side, forming a crude grate. Now cut a rectangular hole in the side of the can where it meets the bottom of the can, a sort of doorway for the fuel. File or round the sharp edges. Make the hole about the size of a paperback novel. The door will be your lower draft, too, so you might want to get fancy and cut a piece of tin or foil to close it up so you can regulate the flame.

If your can has not been opened before, punch holes in the top—the very top—and use it as a stove top. If the fire doesn't get hot enough, enlarge your holes to allow more air to be drawn through.

Tin Can Oven: Here's a homemade version of the Coleman oven that won't win any beauty contests but nonetheless bakes food. It is lightweight

TIN·CAN·OVEN

but bulky, and completes the full line of Hobo Appliances. Here's how it's made: Cut the top of a rectangular five gallon can (a shiny clean or new can) on three sides and carefully fold the flap back. This is the oven door. Sharp edges should immediately be filed down or bent over with pliers.

Now punch a row of small holes (use a nail, icepick or punch) down the middle of the two opposite sides. Look at the drawing.

Run strong wire between these opposite rows of holes to form a crude grill or rack. This will support those mouth-watering apple pies and baked casseroles. Making the oven grate is even easier if you can find a ready-made grill that fits into place and can be secured with wire.

Place the oven on top of your camp stove (larger camp stoves work best) or support it over a fire with metal tent pegs, rocks or bricks. Insulate the bottom of the oven with sand, gravel, rocks, bricks or heavy tiles. This layer will act as a heat sink and give a more even, constant temperature. Pizza anyone?

Tin Can Lantern

I call this ingenious device a *campesino* flashlight. It is used by country people (*campesinos*) throughout Mexico and Guatemala. For night-time hiking, an activity I definitely don't recommend but sometimes find myself doing for one reason or another, this type of light is very useful. It may not be as intense as a battery light, but it can be made anywhere and its softer, more diffused beam reduces night blindness. Several lanterns will illuminate an entire campsite. Their rich warm glow is the perfect background to a relaxed evening of fireside stories or mindless wave listening.

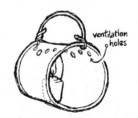

TIN·CAN·LANTERN

The most practical lantern size is a one-gallon tin can, though both smaller and larger cans also work.

Here's how: remove one end of the can and lay the can on its side. Punch a small hole near each end with a nail or awl. Rig a simple wire handle between the two holes. String won't do; the lantern gets hot and the string will burn through.

Now punch several holes around the area of the handle (which is now the top of the lantern when in use). Don't put too many holes directly under the handle or it may get too hot to hold. These holes provide an air draft for the candle.

Next put a candle inside the can below the handle and toward the back. It should be about one-third of the length of the can away from the closed end. A short nail punched through the underside of the can makes a good securing point for the candle or just drip some wax and stick the candle butt in that.

Light the candle and see how it burns. If it's too tall the lantern will soot up or the candle may melt itself. Both problems can be cured by using a shorter candle. Enlarging the draft holes may also help, but too much air flow will burn up the candle quickly. Short stubby votive candles (without a glass holder) are excellent, especially in a smaller can.

If your candle must be pared down, save the extra bits of wax. Melt and pour the wax into improvised molds with a wick of string, cotton threads or strips of your most ragged pair of undershorts (if cotton). Molds can be made from foil, paper, cardboard toilet paper rolls, clam shells, the covers of this book, etc.

Warning: Don't leave a lantern unattended; it is a fire hazard of the first order! Never use a tin can lantern inside a tent!

Stoves: Care and Feeding

Camp stoves need clean fuel for reliable operation. I once set off on a long hike without bothering to check the condition of the kerosene I'd bought at a local service station. It turned out to be both dirty and contaminated with water. My stove gasped, belched and erupted dirty flame, but refused to burn properly.

To avoid this problem, religiously use a good filter such as a chamois, both when filling the fuel bottle and later, when refilling the stove itself. To be even safer, pour your fresh fuel into a clean, dry glass jug and let it sit for half an hour. Can you see dirt or greasy blobs of water at the bottom? If so, decant the fuel off carefully, passing it through at least one filter. Discard the last inch or two in the glass container. Repeat this process before every trip.

A few minutes spent fussing with the fuel will save untold hours of teeth-gnashing, not to mention cold meals. A rule of stove use says: the stove will conk out only in the middle of a meal or just before the coffee perks. Plan ahead.

Spare parts are a simple and inexpensive precaution: carry O rings, gaskets, wire orifice cleaners, generators or whatever else it takes to keep your stove cooking. If you don't need it yourself some other camper will — and will bless you heartily for being prepared.

Even the cleanest burning stoves and lanterns have a tendency to smell after hard use. Pack the stove in a sturdy closed container or sack. A wooden box, large coffee can with plastic lid or a bucket makes a good organizer/container. Clean your stove regularly and wash it with warm soapy water, taking care to dry and clean small orifices or jets. A stove is a working tool that needs attention and servicing. A bit of extra effort will be well rewarded with dependability.

When not in use, especially for a month or more, dump the fuel from your stove. Stale kerosene and gasoline can cause serious clogging and erratic burning. The Northwest is so chilly and damp that I 'winterize' my kerosene stove by filling the tank to the brim with cheap rubbing alcohol. An empty fuel tank invites condensation and corrosion.

Wipe the stove down thoroughly with a light machine oil and wrap it in clean rags. Fuel bottles deserve similar treatment.

Caution: Over the years I have observed and participated in a number of stove and lantern-related accidents that all have one thing in common: a few critical moments of impatience and carelessness. The classic stove disaster goes like this (for all types of fuels and stoves): at the moment of lighting the stove, the camper is distracted and/or the match goes out and/or the stove fails to catch properly.

Here comes the disaster: rather than turn off the fuel quickly, the impatient camper strikes another match. In that seemingly brief time between turning on the fuel and lighting the second match, enough fuel or fuel vapor accumulates to create a Towering Inferno in a tent, van or lean-to, followed by the usual screams, curses and smouldering aftermath. If the fuel is kerosene the results will be a big sooty flame; with gasoline, white gas or propane, the flame will come after the explosion.

A friend learned this one the hard way, on a long solo canoe trip. Such carelessness caused his gasoline stove to explode in his face. He survived, after paddling almost fifty miles with severe burns that scarred him badly for life.

It may sound dramatic but the best approach to handling a stove is to think of it, *treat it,* as a potential bomb. Give the stove your full undivided attention and if it acts up, don't resort to kicks and threats. When normal operating procedures don't get normal results, it's time for common sense alternatives: clean the stove, check all parts and gaskets, replace the fuel or start gathering buffalo chips.

My brother and I were very nearly blown to Kingdom Come by careless handling of a propane bottle. We had made a quick run to town from our campsite to refill the stove bottle. The tank was quite heavy when fully charged and I assumed, from past experience, that it would ride safely on the floor behind the front seat of our van. I hadn't anticipated a deer in the road, however. As I swerved to avoid the startled animal we heard a metallic *Clang!* from the rear of the van.

Before I could slam on the brakes the air was dense with escaping propane. Rob instinctively tossed his cigarette out the passenger window or we'd have gone off like a Fourth of July fireworks display. As I brought the van to a screeching halt he dove over the back seat and twisted the valve closed.

By chance (*"Freak Accident Claims..."*) the tank valve had struck the handle of my tire pump and opened almost half a turn (in spite of a standard type safety shield around the valve knob). So it goes...secure your fuel bottles well!

Coleman Stoves: Care and Cleaning

Coleman gasoline stoves can be used with both white gas (naptha) and unleaded automobile gasoline.

"What? Use car gas in my stove? It says on the Coleman can that..."

Forget it; the main difference between Coleman fuel (white gas) and unleaded gasoline is additives that clog up the stove's generator. (Coleman lanterns don't work as well as stoves on unleaded gas but they will give light.) If you use unleaded gasoline you'll have to clean the generator *regularly* to remove these deposits before they plug things up beyond the point of no return (which takes about two to four weeks, using the stove every day). We clean our generator every week or two... or three or four if it seems to be burning well. Just don't let it get too dirty or you will have to replace the generator.

Unleaded automobile gasoline burns with a stronger odor than white gas and the flame is often yellowish. Keep the stove's tank well pumped up with air and try to avoid long periods of simmering. If you do use the stove for simmering foods, turn the flame up very high for a few moments before shutting the stove off. This helps clean out accumulated carbon inside the generator. The more you simmer, the more frequently you'll have to clean the generator. Here's how to do it:

Step 1: Loosen (counterclockwise, to the left) and remove the packing nut located just behind the control knob. Your control knob probably isn't as large as the one shown in the illustration; we broke ours and carved a replacement out of driftwood.

Step 2: Remove the long skinny 'needle' from inside the generator tube. Be careful: there's a very delicate tip section that is easily damaged. If your generator is hopelessly choked with carbon, removing the needle will be difficult or impossible. If it just won't come out you'll have to replace the entire generator assembly. Soaking the generator in solvent might eventually dissolve or loosen the deposits, but don't count on it.

Step 3: Loosen the generator tube by turning it to the left, counterclockwise. Use a wrench; pliers tend to chew up the soft metal.

Step 4: Remove the tube and shake out the long coiled spring that sits inside. If it won't budge drag it out with a hooked wire, needle-nosed pliers or some other improvised tool. Once again, if it refuses to cooperate, the generator tube may be beyond cleaning. This is why it is important to do this cleaning procedure frequently.

Step 5: The object of this crucial step is to clean up the needle, the spring and the inside of the generator tube without bending any of the parts (though the spring is relatively tough and flexible) or altering them so that they won't work properly.

I prefer to use a stiff wire brush or very fine sandpaper. Big chunks of carbon can be carefully scraped away with a sharp knife but don't cut the

CLEANING

THE GENERATOR OF YOUR··· **COLEMAN**

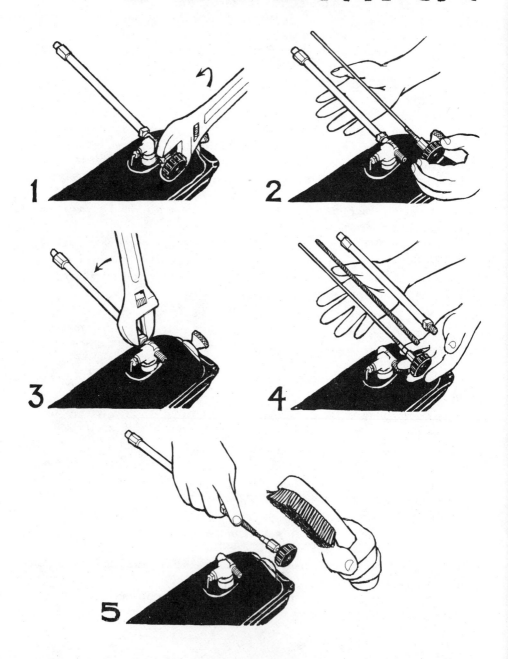

metal, especially on the delicate needle. Try laying the needle on a piece of flat smooth wood. This prevents bending. The method shown in the last step of the illustration is also good.

After you've removed the generator tube and spring, slip the needle back inside the spring and slip both of these back inside the tube. Let a couple of inches of the spring and needle extend out beyond the end of the tube and brush them lightly with the wire brush. Don't bend them! This method works best if the parts aren't heavily encrusted and can be cleaned with *light* strokes.

Be patient: if you screw something up here you'll have to dig out your firewood saw.

Step 6: This step isn't illustrated; it's just the other steps in reverse. To reassemble the generator, first slide the spring inside the tube. Screw the tube (spring inside) back onto the tank assembly. Get it tight but not ridiculously tight. The tube should screw in most of the way with finger pressure. If it won't go you've probably got the threads crossed. Take it off and try again. Cross threading will really foul things up and may ruin the tank assembly too.

OK, now slide the needle and control knob *very carefully* back inside the tank and on into the generator tube. The delicate tip of the needle must go inside the spring. Do this gently. If the tip section bends or catches on something, stop — pull the needle out — straighten the tip and try again. These reassembly procedures should go quite smoothly, but if you do it too fast you'll probably regret it.

Tighten the packing nut behind the control knob and you're done.

WARNING: Test your stove after this procedure and if it doesn't work properly, I strongly advise you to replace the generator with a brand-new one. Cleaning the generator can extend its life but when in doubt, don't risk using one that is faulty. These stoves use gasoline and gasoline is just plain dangerous. Faulty generators may gush fuel into the burner or give a very uneven flow of fuel, with dangerous spurts at unexpected settings of the control knob. If your generator acts like this, get rid of it.

Staying Healthy Outdoors

A rather dismaying proportion of the normal injuries and ailments we associate with life in the great outdoors can be traced directly to the camp kitchen. The list of hazards reads like the story-line for an episode of M.A.S.H.: cuts, puncture wounds, burns, scalding, smoke inhalation, indigestion and diarrhea...

Although I don't consider myself to be accident prone or a hypochondriac, I do pay more attention to health and safety precautions while camping. After all, nothing takes the shine off a trip like stabbing

yourself with a filet knife (mine somehow hit just below my left eye) or doubling up with an attack of stomach cramps just as the trout start biting (I was three days from the nearest road).

Unfortunately, common-sense health precautions often come into direct conflict with the popular image of the independent, self-reliant, macho-survivalist camper/explorer who drinks from any stream without fear of microbe or mud, gobbles down any and all foods, and disdains city-bred notions of hygiene (especially dishwashing). This type of camper can usually be seen on the Evening News, waving a weak hand as the Action News Camera covers the dramatic airlift from some distant camp to the nearest aid station.

Most camping health problems fall into one of the following categories: burns; cuts, wounds and infections; and indigestion, diarrhea and intestinal disorders (including dysentery and food poisoning). For more spectacular injuries and ailments, consult a book on outdoor medicine.

Stomach troubles can be very aggravating while camping, especially if your friends aren't sympathetic or suffering along with you. Before we discuss cures, let's look at prevention.

Almost all intestinal problems can be avoided with a minimum of effort. To twist an old cliche: "An ounce of prevention is worth a pound of Tums and toilet paper."

Purifying Water

Purify all drinking and cooking water. Pure stream water is as rare as the California Condor. The safest approach is to purify everything, no matter how sparkling clean it may look. This includes high mountain streams, which have proven to be unsafe in most areas.

Here's how: boiling purifies water, but contrary to what most people believe, it takes time: *at least* thirty minutes of boiling at sea level and at least forty-five minutes at 7,000 feet. This is a lot of boiling and a lot of fuel. (A pressure cooker would probably reduce these times by half.)

Water purification tablets are very convenient but they taste awful. Let pill-treated water stand for at least thirty minutes before drinking.

Liquid bleach can be used instead of tablets: 8 to 10 drops per quart of water, then allow to stand for thirty minutes or more. If you purify a bucket of water at a time and leave it uncovered for several hours much of the bleach flavor will be dissipated.

Iodine can also be used, 5 to 7 drops per quart.

Small water purifying units for campers remove micro-organisms and also some noxious chemicals. They aren't cheap but considering the relatively high cost of purification tablets, their awful taste and inconvenience, a purifying unit looks much more attractive. Palco makes a plastic EPA approved unit that can purify 1,000 gallons of water.

A much more compact unit called the Pocket Purifier (also known as the Survival Straw) can be ordered at 1442 Camino del Mar, Suite N, Del Mar, California, 92014. This straw-type device will even purify urine (now that's thirst!). The fact that it actually fits into a pocket makes this purifier especially useful for people (like me) who can't resist 'just a sip' of creek water on a hot day.

Many people worry about the long-range side effects of water purification agents such as bleach, tablets and even portable purifying units, which often give the water a distinct chemical flavor. Because we spend so much time camping (including several years in the back country of Mexico and Guatemala), Lorena and I have become very interested in alternatives to chemical purifiers. Like many natural alternatives, however, it is difficult to back up our home and folk methods with hard scientific evidence and laboratory reports. We do know, however, that the following precautions have worked for us and many of our friends.

Lime juice has anti-bacterial qualities and we often add it to our drinking water, preferably in liberal amounts. Allow it time to work, an hour or more.

Garlic is a powerful natural cure and preventative for many intestinal problems, from parasites to infections. When travelling in areas where the water is suspect we take several small cloves a day, raw, washed down like 'horse pills' with water or food. Garlic is also an important ingredient in our menu and we frequently add much more than is called for in a recipe. (Garlic also soothes insect bites.)

Lorena scoffs at this next measure but I've used it in a pinch. Stare intently at the water to be used, focusing your mind into a cleansing beam as you chant, "Pure! Pure! Pure!" Repeat three times if the water is especially dirty.

Diarrhea, Dysentery and Food Poisoning

Diarrhea is quite common while camping, often as a result of a sudden change in environment and normal eating habits. (Which is why doctors call it 'traveller's diarrhea'.)

If you can't always avoid diarrhea, you can certainly take a few steps to ease the discomfort and hasten recovery.

First, do not take anything that will stop bowel movement. The body needs to flush out, not plug up. This eliminates the use of Kaopectate and other classic diarrhea medicines. Using them will likely only prolong the problem and may even aggravate it, by forcing the body to delay healing.

A normal case of diarrhea is often more severe than a person expects: cramps, nausea, vomiting, chills and fever as high as 103° F. It lasts from one to three days and may end suddenly, leaving you weak but happy. Don't resort to antibiotics or 'liquid cork' until you've given yourself enough time for normal recovery.

Avoid coffee, black tea, alcohol, chiles, black pepper, raw fruit, anything greasy, spicy or extremely hot or cold. Rest and relax; it will probably go away.

For all internal ailments drink plenty of liquids. Beware of dehydration, especially in children. The following drink is recommended by the U.S. Center for Disease Control. It can be used for prevention of heat dehydration as well as relief from diarrhea.

Diarrhea Cocktail: Put eight ounces of fruit juice in a glass and add half a teaspoon of honey (or sugar) and a pinch of salt. In another glass mix eight ounces of water (mineral or carbonated is OK) and a quarter teaspoon of baking soda. Drink them down, alternating sips from one glass to the other. An adult should take several doses a day and a child at least four.

Many soothing herb teas are available at health food and whole foods shops. My favorites are camomile and other nerve tonics such as Sleepy Time. Rest is your best remedy and calming teas settle both your mind and your stomach.

Food Poisoning might be described as "diarrhea with a sense of impending doom." It isn't pleasant and though the symptoms for food poisoning are very similar to diarrhea, it tends to hit fast and hard. Fortunately it also ends quickly; a common variety of food poisoning lasts about 12 hours. Vomiting, uncontrollable diarrhea, gas and general despair can be expected. Remain calm, rest and follow the procedures given for diarrhea relief.

Dysentery is commonly and incorrectly used to describe diarrhea and even food poisoning. Having tried all three, I can testify that true dysentery is in a league of its own. If you suffer persistent intestinal problems (including constipation, depression and headache) by all means see a doctor. The treatment for dysentery requires more than over-the-counter medications.

Remember: simple diarrhea can hang on for days, especially if you don't take care of yourself and watch what you eat and drink.

Cramps: Stomach, Muscle and Menstrual

If this seems like an odd place for a discussion of cramps, I agree. However, our experience has shown that many people suffer from various cramps while camping, especially after exerting themselves, and don't know what to do about them. Take calcium: it helps the body tolerate pain and really seems to relieve the cramps themselves. I always suffered severe leg and foot cramps when hiking and kayaking. After I began taking hefty doses of calcium (1500 milligrams before bed) the cramps disappeared. Milk, cheese, greens, sprouts and sesame seeds are naturally high in calcium.

Calcium helps calm the nerves and I use it when I can't sleep.

Calcium also relieves the cramps and tension of the menstrual cycle.

Burns

Lorena keeps a vitamin E capsule handy and immediately squeezes a few drops of the oil on background burns from campfires, stoves, grates and hot pans. Some people prefer aloe vera gel for minor burns.

For more serious burns, clean gently with soap and warm water. Compresses of cool water or ice relieve pain, as does aloe vera gel or the juice of any succulent cactus, wet black tea bags and grated or mashed raw potatoes and onions. Vitamin E oil or cream can be used, but no salted grease, especially butter. Bandage with sterile, fine-meshed gauze. For serious burns drink lots of liquids; see *Diarrhea* for a special cocktail.

Infections and Wounds

Wash the wound with soap and water, or alcohol. If it is too painful to scrub, flush well with soapy water and hydrogen peroxide or soak the wound or infection in a bucket of warm soapy water. You have to clean out all those tiny particles of dirt and grime. Hot compresses used for 20 minutes, four times a day, will improve circulation around the wound. Lime juice is good on minor cuts or wounds, but stings like crazy.

Infections and wounds can be bandaged with crushed garlic compresses. Coat the surrounding skin with light oil (not industrial oil) before putting the garlic on. If the garlic burns, remove it, clean the skin and apply even more oil. The wound should be thoroughly cleaned three (or more) times a day and a fresh poultice applied. Goldenseal powder can be sprinkled on wounds and infections. Covering the wound with honey is said to prevent infection. Cover with gauze and/or cloth. We take extra Vitamin C tablets to prevent infection and even more if an infection gets started.

Puncture wounds should be cleaned as thoroughly as possible as they can infect rapidly if not properly cleaned. If infection sets in (pus and swelling) it may be necessary to enlarge the wound (time to bite the bullet) and clean it again.

Chapter 6
Cooking Tips & Techniques

Like many people I am fascinated by cooking tips, unusual recipes and novel ways to prepare familiar foods (or is it familiar ways to prepare novel foods?). Unfortunately, many cooking tips are like tidbits of gossip from the popular scandal sheets: they tend to strain common sense and credibility, if not good taste itself.

A friend who is as addicted to reading cookbooks, as others are fans of historical romances or crime thrillers, spends most of her time while camping trying out homemade and store-bought cooking gadgets, 'labor-saving' recipes and techniques, and ingenious methods for organizing the kitchen and camp.

She goes through cooking fads: once it was vacuum bottles and variations of slow cooking that required all dishes to be wrapped in sleeping bags and long underwear, thermal blankets and reflective foil. She was the only person I've met who could tell you the R-value of your sweater and suggest how it could be used to prepare a rice casserole overnight.

And then there was her Tin Can phase: tin can ovens, tin can stoves, tin can pots and pans, tin can bread baking, tin can soufflés . . . followed by Pre-Cut and Measured Meals sealed inside bags and plastic boxes, including garlic that was sliced and ready to sauté in oil (in a tiny plastic bottle next to the 1/64 oz. of oregano), a packet of tomato broth crystals and a 35mm film cannister of grated Parmesan. Her camping meals were sometimes compared to the conquests of major peaks: each hour spent actually cooking was backed up by at least eight hours of tedious preparation at home.

Our approach to camp cooking leans heavily toward simplicity, reliability and minimum work for maximum enjoyment. The purpose of these tips is to prevent cooking disasters, frazzled nerves and hot tempers. They'll also save you some money, time and even food.

Novices should pay special attention to the more basic tips, but even experienced camp cooks may find something to refresh their memories or spark a new idea.

Basic Camp Cooking

Before leaving home compare the capacities of your camping cups and spoons to a measuring cup and spoons. My favorite tin cup holds 12 ounces—a cup and a half. Knowing this in advance will keep you from having to guess about quantities.

• If camped on sand, insist (shout, swear, cuss, threaten) that others keep away from the kitchen area or walk with great caution when near the food to avoid kicking sand into the meal. 'Flip-Flop' sandals, for example, have a tendency to flip sand high into the air as a person walks by. Some of this sand will end up in your soup or salad.

"A little sand never hurt anybody" is a line you usually hear just before someone breaks a filling on a small rock hidden in the rice or noodles.

The kitchen area should be kept as neat and clean as a religious shrine and not allowed to become a hang-out for hungry camp followers.

• Store your provisions, and even cookware, as far away from stoves and fuel containers as you can. When backpacking, my stove and/or fuel bottles have a diabolical ability to spread noxious odors into the food. This is especially true of kerosene. The tiniest residue of fuel on your clothing or fingers is easily transferred to cook-pots, spoons and whatever else you touch while preparing a meal.

• The dishes and utensils should be clean and ready to use before the cooking starts. Arrange them and your ingredients close at hand. True 'one-pot' meals are the exception, and if you're like Lorena, you'll need at least two spoons to stir the soup. Nothing aggravates the cook more than having to interrupt the creative process with a frenzied session of dish scrubbing.

• When darkness approaches, have a flashlight in your pocket. Try to make yourself comfortable, close to the fire or stove. Send friends for firewood or forgotten utensils; just because you're cooking the meal doesn't mean you have to do *everything*.

• *True or False?* If one spud bakes in 40 minutes at 350° then two spuds will bake in 10 minutes at 1400°.

If you answered "True", I'm afraid you've won two hours of KP. When in doubt, use less heat and more time.

• Build your cookfires small or keep your stove flame low. This conserves fuel and reduces the chance of burning or overcooking your food. The nutritive value of many foods is also destroyed or decreased by very high temperatures.

• If your cookstove burns with a tight concentrated flame it may produce a 'hot spot' that scorches food and makes simmering difficult. You need a *heat sink* to distribute the heat: a round or square piece of thin tin or heavy gauge wire cloth (often called 'construction cloth') should do the trick. Aluminum foil works too, but not that well.

• The wind steals heat, not just from the fire or stove but from the cook pots themselves. If necessary, go to elaborate measures to protect your cookstove from the wind, but don't endanger yourself by cooking in unventilated spaces or very close to flammable materials, especially tents.

Cooking Methods

• When a recipe says 'simmer' or 'saute', the flame should be about as low as you can get it on a backpacking stove or cool enough that the food barely sizzles in the pan. 'Fry' or 'brown' means a hotter flame, though never so high that the oil or fat used will smoke.

• When frying and browning, heat the oil or fat before adding the food, especially if the food has been coated with flour or batter. This reduces the amount of oil absorbed during cooking and gives a crisper, more pleasing texture.

• To conserve cooking oil, soak a square piece of paper towel in oil and carry it in a tightly sealed plastic bag. Use this swab to wipe your skillet before frying. The less oil used while frying, the better—but at the same time you'll have to reduce the temperature for cooking or risk scorching both the food and the pan. Once you've tried cooking with very small amounts of oil, you'll be amazed at how well it works.

• If the food you're frying sucks up all of the oil in the pan but isn't quite tender, try this: pour or sprinkle a tablespoon of water into the pan and immediately cover it tightly with a lid. The lid will increase the temperature and the steam created will moisten both the food and the pan, and speed up cooking. This method works especially well for eggs and vegetables and when warming leftovers. Unfortunately, batter-fried foods may become rather soggy, especially if you add too much water for steam. Fried foods should be kept warm, but not tightly covered, and served up as soon as possible.

• Steaming and poaching are very useful cooking techniques for campers. Both methods are fuel efficient, use very little water and preserve nutritive value.

Note: Steaming and poaching *do not* mean boiling. Steamed foods are cooked in a small amount of water, just enough to produce hot steam. Ideally, the food will rest on a rack or small stones above the water level. A pot of potatoes, for example, can usually be steam cooked with a cup or less of water. The tighter your cook pot, the less water will be lost (and less heat energy required for cooking). (See *Cooking with Seawater* later in this chapter.)

In poaching, the food floats in water or broth that is kept at a simmer and is not allowed to boil. Poaching is a very good way to cook seafood.

• Herbs, spices and salt can be added to the water used for steaming and poaching. It takes just a pinch to give a distinct flavor. When the food is cooked, the water makes excellent stock or broth. In desert camping we always drink the water used in cooking (leave out the salt), or use it to mix with other foods (even bread dough).

• Cooking times for most foods can be reduced by reducing their size. A potato, for example, will steam much quicker if cut into small cubes. Some flavor and texture may be sacrificed but if fuel and water are scarce, cut your foods up.

• When cooking several foods together—such as fried or steamed vegetables—add the ingredients according to their texture, with the hardest first and softer thing later. Celery and carrots, for example, take much longer to cook than onions. Truly delicate foods such as mushrooms, sprouts and leafy greens require even less time. By adjusting cooking times to texture, the dish will be much more pleasing and tender ingredients won't turn into over-cooked blobs.

• When cooking with foil, place the shiny side of the foil inward, facing the food. This reflects the heat toward the food.

• When grilling, heat the grill very hot to prevent food from sticking. This will also sear grill marks into the food (especially fish and meat) and make it look like something off a *Gourmet* magazine cover.

For slower, lower temperature cooking, wipe the grill with cooking oil. (A grill can be oiled for fast searing and barbecuing, but if oil is scarce I prefer to let the food stick, then burn or scrape the grill clean afterward.)

• To prevent tender or small pieces of food from falling through the grill, spread out a piece of aluminum foil and punch it full of tiny slits or holes. Wipe the foil very lightly with oil, if you wish.

• Smoke itself can be added to a dish as a variation in flavor. If you don't have smoked meat or fish on hand, try smoking cheese for a few hours before using it to flavor a main dish. Cooked vegetables can also be lightly smoked or grilled over an open fire to add a seared flavor many people find enjoyable.

Food Storage

• Keep your fresh food in sight, not hidden away where it will be forgotten until something starts to reek. When travelling by vehicle we carry fresh foods in baskets with lids or cloth covers to keep flies off the bananas and tomatoes. A typical meal or snack begins with, "What's left in the baskets?"

• An important rule of good camp cooking is: *What you see is what you've got.* Don't fret over what you want or feel you need; use what's on hand and apply your talents to turning those ingredients into a good meal. Cookbook-trained cooks may find improvisation difficult at first, but hunger usually carries them through to success.

• Add salad dressings to individual portions if you think there might be leftovers. Undressed salads keep better. Most people use far more dressing than needed; add it a teaspoon at a time, dribbled over the salad as a second person tosses it with forks or spoons to evenly distribute the dressing. Stop before you think you've got enough or you'll probably use too much.

• When cutting a fresh onion, use the upper portion first. The lower root part will keep longer.

• Salt has an annoying tendency to get damp, harden and block the holes in the shaker. Cover with a plastic bag at night to keep the moisture out.

Preventing Spoilage

There's nothing quite like dipping into the food larder at the end of a long, hungry day to find that the tomatoes and bananas have gotten together with the peanuts and garlic to make a strange and disgusting sauce. Food spoilage is a constant problem while camping, especially if the weather is warm. Before you give up and buy a case of canned food, read over this section and plan your provisions and storage to take advantage of foods that resist spoilage or can be encouraged to last longer with simple precautions.

• When stocking up in advance, before heading into a remote area select fresh produce with special care. Buy some produce that is ripe and ready to eat, and some that is still green or hard.

• Cabbages and cucumbers are classic long-lasting foods. Buy the best you can and reject any that are very ripe or have started to spoil. Limes with thin hard skins and oranges with thin skins (very difficult to peel) last far longer than thick, easily peeled varieties. (Thin-skinned oranges are usually sold for juice.)

• To soften limes that have formed a very hard skin, drop them into boiling water for one minute. You can also roast them quickly right in the coals of a fire. You won't believe how juicy they'll be.

• Spoilage caused by natural bacteria on produce can be delayed for a considerable time by washing the food in a purifying bath. Use 5 to 7 drops of iodine or 8 to 10 drops (or more) of bleach. (This bath will also help kill parasites.) Soak the food for at least half an hour, then remove and drain until completely dry. Don't rinse it off; what little purification agent remains will also help retard spoilage and will have little, if any, effect on the flavor of the food.

Now wrap the individual pieces of produce in paper, taking care not to bruise or break their skins. Newspapers work fine but don't use plastic, aluminum foil or other impermeable wrappings. The food has to 'breathe'. Plastic bags are fine for food storage inside a refrigerator (dry air), but while camping they actually speed up spoilage by trapping moisture, heat and bacteria.

Arrange the wrapped food in baskets or boxes that have good air circulation, and store in a dark place or at least in the shade. In humid weather you may have to dry your food in the sun every morning to avoid rapid spoilage from condensation and dew.

If you are unable to purify the food first, try the wrapping method anyway.

• Check all the produce daily, using up any that is ripe or discarding any that shows signs of spoilage. Under ideal conditions a green tomato will keep for weeks. Cucumbers, onions (don't soak), limes, cabbage and other fairly durable fruits and vegetables will also last a surprisingly long time.

Emily Post and The Great Outdoors

• The American Way of Eating is a democratic scramble that can often lead to a camp free-for-all and hot tempers. If you've ever camped with someone who has a particularly greedy 'boarding-house reach', you'll understand why serving the food semi-formally can conserve peace and insure a fair distribution. Some people fill their bowls as if facing imminent starvation, others absentmindedly take more than they should and then go through painful apologies, self-recrimination and embarrassed attempts to shove half their food onto another's plate.

The solution is simple: the cook or an assigned helper serves the meal. This can become a very pleasant ceremony since it insures that everyone will gather at one time and will have the opportunity to admire and compliment the food. And special flourishes — a sprig of fresh mint on the rice — won't be gobbled up before all can give appropriate oohs-and-aahhs of delight.

Lorena and I learned this custom in Mexico, and a friend there pointed out an interesting side benefit: a wise cook will arrange the food on the plates as attractively as possible, spreading the food out so that it appears to be much more generous than it would normally appear.

Lorena once laid out a beach-side banquet by serving everything but the main course in oyster and scallop shells. The portions were doll-sized but they seemed to surround us.

• Meals can also be served in courses, with enough interval to allow the appetite to be dulled before the next dish is offered. Since most of us over-eat or eat much too quickly, you're doing people a favor rather than depriving anyone. This also helps stretch food when supplies are low.

Small Touches

Little touches usually don't take much time but they can have a surprising impact.

One of the greatest arguments against a super-simple or scornful approach to camp cooking is that food can be a very valuable weapon against depression, crankiness and Blue Mondays.

I've yet to make a long camping trip that went perfectly, and even short outings may include off-days or afternoons. Food can provide a valuable lift, a time to sit back and reflect on what's happening — or to forget the rain, the blisters and the slow leak in your air mattress.

• The cook should be prepared to put out a special effort when others begin to show signs of foul humor. "I've got something kind of special in mind for dinner tonight" can perk up a gloomy morning or give that extra burst of energy needed to reach the next campsite. And even if the "something special" turns out to be a measly quarter ounce of chocolate bar or a spoonful of dried mushroom in the gravy, make a big noise about it.

• Plain, ordinary cooked rice or potatoes become rather special when garnished with a dash of paprika, dried parsley flakes or sesame salt. One thin slice of salami, chopped quite small, will give the illusion of extravagance when carefully arranged over a mound of spaghetti. A few bean sprouts sprinkled over a salad, taco, main dish or even a bowl of stew gives the food a 'fresh' look. Mushrooms (fresh or dried and reconstituted), sliced olives, bits of salted anchovies, minced fresh vegetables or paper-thin slices of onion, purple cabbage and lettuce are also quite tasty and colorful.

• Lorena likes to arrange our bowls and utensils on a clean, bright Mexican bandanna, with a wildflower as an improvised centerpiece or a handful of wild berries to be savored one at a time throughout the meal. These flourishes aren't gimmicks but simple ways to enhance your enjoyment of camping.

• A friend uses a change of names to perk up his companions' interest and appetites. "I learned this from reading the menu at the high school cafeteria," he told us. "Chicken a la King meant chicken in gravy. Tuna a la King was...you guessed it, tuna in gravy. I name my dishes and then try to turn the name around. Like my Creole Cabbage. If I need something fancier I call it 'Cabbage Creole' or even 'Cabbage Louisiane'."

What makes the cabbage taste Creole?

"What's that got to do with it?" he answered. "If I'm scrambling eggs in Oregon I call them 'Eggs Montana'. If I'm in Texas the exact same eggs are 'Eggs Oregon' or if you want to get fancy, really gourmet, 'Eggs Pacifica'. The ingredients don't count; it's all in the name and how you serve them."

Name changes are useful but once your companions catch on, try minor variations in flavor to extend your menu and increase eating pleasure. When provisions are very limited, small changes are especially useful.

Variety

• Good camp cooks are often like magicians; they amaze and entertain by creating illusions and stretching reality. Let's imagine that you're on a long hike and are down to a final, treasured fresh orange. Will you eat it in one juicy spree or slice some paper thin to garnish a cooked dish and serve chunks of orange for dessert? Don't forget the peel: it can be shaved, grated or dried, and used to flavor other foods or beverages.

• We often cook one food two ways to give the illusion of greater variety. On the beach we'll eat fresh fish sliced thin and raw (the Japanese *sashimi*

appetizer) and portions of the same fish batter-fried, grilled or in soup. This stretches meager supplies and seems more satisfying than one larger portion of a single dish.

Rice is another good example: take the portion allotted for the meal and set aside one third for a rice dessert with milk, honey and cinnamon. In many cases you'll find that you still have leftovers from the main rice dish, even though you'd expected it to be eaten up.

• Variations in flavor and appearance literally make the meal more interesting to those eating it and hopefully more satisfying. A friend described a memorable meal of limpets foraged by a large group of campers on an Alaskan beach. These tough little shellfish are flavorful but could they satisfy a dozen starving people? The solution was to create an impromptu Limpet Cook-Off, with a minimum of time and ingredients.

They ate limpets steamed, raw, boiled, on the half shell, with lime juice and finally, lightly poached and dunked in melted butter. Several hundred limpets were eaten in a meal that none of the participants will soon forget.

• We made a long boat trip on the spur of the moment, with almost no time at all to shop or gather food carefully. I grabbed whatever looked good and not too perishable: onions, garlic, potatoes, limes, cabbage, cooking oil, salt, bananas and honey. A typical meal (breakfast, lunch or dinner) would be fresh fish cooked on a stick (see *Recipes*), chopped cabbage with lime juice dressing and a potato or onion baked in the fire. By the end of the trip our taste buds were as sensitive as a cat's whiskers. A simple variation such as a tablespoon of minced onion in the cabbage salad was noticed and really appreciated. One meal was just broiled fish followed by roast bananas and melted honey. Ambrosia!

• On an extended backpacking trip we learned another simple fact of camp cooking: Strong flavors are sometimes more satisfying than subtle flavors. We found ourselves munching raw onions and even whole cloves of garlic. I remember eating a cucumber, skin and all, and wondering why I'd always peeled them.

• Simplicity is the next lesson: *When in doubt, leave it out.* Too many cooks add a pinch of this and a piece of that, just because it's on hand, not because the dish really needs another flavor or ingredient. Such simple dishes as baked potatoes garnished with minced green onions are often more memorable than multi-flavored stews or giant fried concoctions that taste okay, but all taste the same.

• Which brings me to 'glop', a four-letter word that has no place in a good camp cook's vocabulary. Campers who equate eating with the grosser body functions substitute these 'dishes' for the most elementary yet genuinely tasty meals. Open a package of dried beef: dump it into boiling water. Open some dehydrated vegetable mix: dump it in, too. Here's some instant rice: dump it in. How about this stuff: Yeah, dump it in. Wait a minute, that was instant tea. Ah well, what's the difference? Stir it a few times; I think it's burning. How does it taste? Like sh...*glop!*

In more civilized cultures a cook would be consigned to the rack for even considering such a gastronomic atrocity. If you must eat glop please do so late at night in the privacy of your own tent.

Spices

• Some cooks add herbs and spices shortly before serving a dish, others prefer to add flavorings earlier. I like the 'early' method for two reasons: it allows you to control the flavor of the dish as it cooks and makes it easier to use miserly quantities. In frying or sauteing, for example, a few pinches of herbs look like quite a bit when there's nothing but oil in the pan. If you add the herbs later, when the pan is stuffed with rice and noodles, a few pinches will seem insignificant and you'll be tempted to add much more. In most dishes, adding more of anything at the last minute is usually a waste.

• Use spices one at a time until you're able to predict what the resulting dish will taste like. Use them sparingly, especially if the dish will also be intended for leftovers. As the hours go by spices tend to taste stronger. This can be used to advantage: I like to add just a 'touch' of finely grated Parmesan cheese to plain leftover rice, let it age overnight and then reheat and serve in the morning. A miserly amount of cheese imparts a rich flavor by the next day. (I consider strong cheese in small quantities to be a spice.)

• Be very careful with 'hot' spices such as chili, black pepper and curry. I once made a short desert hike with a guy who demanded a 'man-sized' portion of chili powder in our evening taco sauce. I am not impressed by people who make a great show of eating hot chiles, so I obliged him with a sauce that would have stunned a mule. Unfortunately, my practical joke backfired. In the following twenty-four hours he drank enough water to sustain half a dozen camels for a week, forcing us to detour from our intended route to the nearest water hole.

• To impress friends who don't believe that you can cook, use what I call the 'NATO Cooking School Method' for an instant reputation as an international chef. Simple fried spuds, for example, become '*Papas Romana*' by sauteing cooked sliced potatoes (I use leftovers) and sprinkling them with a pinch of oregano and a tablespoon of Parmesan cheese.

The key is to associate a spice with a national cuisine and improvise from there. Here are a few of the more obvious combinations: cumin and chile give a Mexican flavor; curry or cumin and *too much* chile is East Indian; ginger root for Chinese; soy sauce for anything vaguely Oriental (sprinkle a few sprouts on top and call it Oriental Delight); oregano, olive oil and Parmesan for Italian; any pastel-colored sauce for French; paprika (in quantity) for Hungarian or East Bloc; white sauce and black pepper for Scandinavian.

With regional dishes, 'steamed' translates to 'New England style' or even 'Bavarian' (well outside of Bavaria, anyway), mild red chile is Southwestern, too much chile is 'Texas-style' and anything very bland or overcooked is best called 'English'.

• Spices are also associated with various moods and states-of-mind. Want to bring a homey holiday atmosphere into a camp scene that is dull and depressed? Mix up bite-sized pieces of dry bread, biscuit or tortilla with onion, garlic and sage; saute in butter or margarine, add a shot of water for steam and cover tightly. The very aroma of a Christmas dinner! Serve with rich brown gravy and Christmas carols.

It works at breakfast too: an uninspiring puddle of oatmeal suddenly smells very rich and comforting when sprinkled with cinnamon and a pinch of nutmeg.

• Don't limit spices to cooked dishes, sauces and salad dressings. Oregano, for example, can be sprinkled on sandwiches and tacos. Mexicans sprinkle mild and hot chile powder on fresh slices of fruit, cucumber and even sweet corn. Once you try it you'll understand why; as with most new and apparently unusual combinations, it's best to trust your taste buds rather than your intellect.

Honey and Sweeteners

• Honey has many uses other than as a sweetener for beverages, breakfast cereals and munchies. Read the fine print on processed food labels and you'll see that sugar is a major ingredient in everything from salad dressing to canned string beans. Sweetening tends to enhance flavor (especially for those who've eaten sweetened foods all of their lives — the case with most of us), and gives vague satisfaction to our unconscious 'sweet-tooth'.

• Try this: Prepare a simple tomato spaghetti sauce. Now add a quarter cup of honey (in a quart of sauce) and simmer for fifteen minutes. Taste the difference?

I use honey in sauces and beans (most people won't believe that there's honey in my gringo-style chili) and salad dressings. Honey is excellent in sweet-and-sour sauces, marinades (especially for teriyaki style foods), as a baste for barbecued meat and fish and for smoking many seafoods.

Cooking with Seawater

Fresh water for drinking and cooking is often scarce while camping near the sea. On our ocean kayaking cruises, fresh water is a major concern. In Baja, even the most unappetizing brackish wells were used to fill our water jugs. We soon learned that drinking water could be stretched by mixing it with seawater for cooking. If only a few cups of water are saved daily, this will add up to a significant quantity, even on a week-long outing.

First of all, forget those lurid survival-at-sea stories you might have read about poor, sun-parched wretches going mad from drinking seawater. Seawater is extremely salty, but in reasonable amounts it will do you no harm and may even be good for you. (If you're troubled by constipation a 'dose of salts' will do the trick.) After all, salt and minerals found in seawater are also important to your body's metabolism.

• In very warm weather, fluid loss through sweating helps to lower and regulate your body temperature. Without adequate salt the system would go haywire. For this reason we sometimes take salt tablets while exerting ourselves heavily in warm weather. Headache, cramps and fatigue are symptoms Lorena and I have come to recognize as the signal for an overdue dose of salt.

To save on fresh water, however, we often take regular sips of seawater. (Try a sip or two every hour, then adjust this to your body's own requirements.) Salt tablets are supposed to be taken with a large measure of drinking water — but by sipping seawater regularly instead of using tablets, you shouldn't jolt your system with too much salt at one blow. At the same time you'll take in fluid that would otherwise have to come from your canteens.

• Using seawater for cooking eliminates the use of salt, of course, in the recipe. Depending on your own taste and the salinity of the seawater (seawater near river mouths, for example, is much less salty than seawater taken from shallow bays) the following mixtures can be adjusted to use more or less saltwater.

• Noodles can be cooked in a mixture of half seawater and half fresh water, but no salt should be used at all in the sauce or garnishings. The 50-50

mixture, however, is too salty for boiling vegetables, especially potatoes, which seem to absorb a great deal of salt as they cook. Rice is also 'salt sensitive' and a mixture of at least three parts fresh water to one part seawater is best.

• Seawater can be used in soups, stews, mush and beverages. Use a conservative amount and don't get carried away in your enthusiasm to save fresh water or you'll overdose on seawater.

• If more water is needed while cooking, *taste* the food and broth carefully before adding more of the freshwater-salt mixture. As water evaporates off, salt is left behind in the food. This can add up to quite a strong dose of salt. Lorena's tolerance for salt is much higher than mine so I always taste the food and say "Enough!"

• Salt should never be used in cooking beans (they won't soften properly), though seawater can be added once they've become tender.

Simmer the beans slowly, with a tight lid, using only enough fresh water to keep them covered. Once the beans are tender or almost-tender, you can begin adding saltwater. Remember: any water that is added to beans as they cook should be very hot or boiling.

• We use 100% seawater when making tortillas and find it also works (undiluted) in other breads.

• Undiluted seawater can be used for steaming—but not for boiling, unless the food to be cooked is shellfish, whole eggs, or is sealed within a pouch. For steaming, keep the food above the level of the seawater in the pot: small stones, seashells, very clean and dry sticks (not green or with bark), a wad of aluminum foil; any of these can make an improvised steaming rack. The broth, unless diluted with fresh water, will not be usable except in medicinal doses.

• Seawater isn't just salty, it also has a distinct flavor. We've sometimes noted a slight bitterness in rice and noodle dishes prepared with seawater,

but it wasn't strong enough to be objectionable — especially when drinking water was just too precious to waste at all.

High Altitude Cooking

• Cooking at high altitude requires adjustments in cooking time, liquid, sweeteners and leavening (baking powder, yeast, etc.). As a general rule, use more time and liquid and less of everything else. However, unless you do a lot of cooking above 10,000 feet (especially baking), don't worry too much about the effect of altitude on your recipes.

• Above 5,000 feet increase cooking times by about 10% per 1,000 feet gained. Since we don't use a timer, we cook food until it's obviously done; it's that simple. Just be patient and don't crank up the stove so high that it wastes fuel and scorches the food.

• Liquids boil away at lower temperatures as the altitude increases, so be prepared to add more. Keep a tight lid on pots to avoid losing too much steam. Above 5,000 feet add 10% more liquid (one slosh per cup).

• Pre-soak dried foods and cut fresh foods into thinner or smaller pieces to speed up cooking. Use more pre-cooked and instant foods.

• Above 5,000 feet decrease sweeteners by 10%, and baking powder by 10% for each 1,000 additional feet gained — until at 10,000 feet, for example, you've reduced baking powder in half (50%). Again, our experience is that camp cooking is too inexact to be much affected by 10% this-way-or-that.

Substitutions

Flour

• Use ⅛ cup less of whole wheat flour per cup of white flour recommended.

• Add ¼ cup wheat germ to ¾ cup white flour to equal 1 cup whole wheat.

• 1 Tbsp of flour (for thickening) = ½ Tbsp cornstarch or 2 tsp quick-cooking tapioca.

Sweeteners:

- 1 cup of honey = 1¼ cup sugar + ¼ cup liquid.
- 1 cup sugar = ¾ cup honey less ¼ cup liquid or 1 1/3 cup maple sugar or 1 cup corn syrup less 1/3 cup liquid.
- 1 cup syrup = 1 cup sugar + ¼ cup liquid.
- 1 cup molasses = ¾ cup sugar + ¼ cup liquid.

Fat and Oil:

- 1 cup butter = 1 cup oil or shortening + 1 tsp salt.

Cream:

- 1 cup heavy cream = ¾ cup milk + 1/3 cup butter or margarine (melt if used in liquid form).

Sour or Buttermilk:

- 1 cup milk or ½ cup evaporated milk + 1-2 Tbsp lemon juice or vinegar.

Yeast and Baking Powder:

- Yeast and baking powder are interchangeable. We prefer the flavor of yeast although it needs at least 15 minutes to rise. Baking powder is quicker but it destroys some B vitamins. A rule of thumb is to use ½ to 1 tsp of either per cup of flour.
- 1 tsp baking powder = ¼ tsp baking soda + ½ tsp cream of tartar.

Final Thoughts

- Don't trust your memory or taste buds when some variation or new idea you've tried in camp creates a successful dish. Write it down, preferably in the margins of the recipe section in this book. By keeping close track of the amounts of ingredients and staple foods you actually use while camping, as well as specific recipe variations, you'll simplify both meal planning and cooking for the next trip.
- If this book is too bulky or heavy to carry while camping, cut out the recipe section with a razor blade and hold the pages neatly together with a simple plastic manuscript binder. These binders are semi-rigid lengths of narrow plastic sold in stationery stores. They are very cheap and can be cut to length with a knife or scissors. Make an improvised cover of stiff paper or plastic and you've got your own personalized Field Edition.

Chapter 7
Recipes

All of our advice about recipes can be summed up in one simple statement: *Don't take recipes too seriously.*

We use recipes in much the same way we use maps and compasses: to guide ourselves in a general direction toward an uncertain goal, usually along the path of least resistance. If a recipe calls for half an onion and we've only a tablespoonful on hand and — well, why not? Or we'll substitute something, usually garlic.

Cooking can be a mechanical by-the-numbers process or it can be highly creative, entertaining and even suspenseful. Will this variation on corn bread amaze and astound our friends or will they smile weakly and crumble it into the weeds at their feet?

The recipes included here have evolved over countless camping trips by van, backpack, mule, kayak and sailboat. They are constantly changing as we learn more about food. Use them as a starting point or as a backup for your own recipes and variations.

Here's what's ahead:

Soups & Stews 192
Quick 1-Vegetable Soup
Very Quick Tomato Soup
Thick Stew with Gravy
Onion or Garlic Soup
Teresa's Lima Bean Soup
Simple Chowders
Bob's Fish Head Soup
Beans 196
Beans in Broth
Refritos: Refried Beans
Bean Chili
Beans & Cheese Melt
Miracle Bean Ball
Bean Supreme
Split Pea or Lentil Soup
Sandwiches & Tacos 200
Egg
Melted Cheese & Seafood
Grilled Cheese
Cheese Rabbit (Rarebit)
Salad
Suggestions
Tacos & Tortillas
Fried Tacos, Quesadillas
Tortilla Pizza
Simple Enchiladas
Burritos
Gorditas
Eggs 206
Hardboiled
Scrambled
Omelettes
Poached
Eggs with Beans
Eggs with Rice
Eggs with Sausage/Salami
Creamed Eggs
Rabbits in Their Holes
Stove Top Casserole
Fish & Seafood 210
Stone-Age Baked Fish
Fish Roasted On-A-Stick
Foil Baked Fish
Simple Fried Fish
Seafood Tempura
**Smoked Fish & Meat,
Jerky** 212

Smoked Fish
Quick Smoked Fish
Smoking and Drying Meat
Noodles & Pasta 215
Boiled Noodles
Very Quick Spaghetti
Instant White Spaghetti
Fast Macaroni & Cheese
Golden Noodles
Cheesy Noodles
Instant Seafood Linguini
Cashew Noodles with
Cauliflower
Rice & Bulgur 220
Rice Suggestions
Fluffy Steamed White
Rice
Steamed Brown Rice
Brown Rice in a Pressure
Cooker
Quick Mexican Rice
Oriental Fried Rice
Rice & Cheese Casserole
Rice & Smoked Fish
Casserole
Mushroom Rice with Nuts
Rice Casserole—or Cake
Bulgur Wheat
Potatoes 226
Potatoes without an Oven
Fast Baked Spuds
Mashed Potatoes
Instant Potatoes
French Fried Potato Slices
Mexican Potato Cakes
Yukon Spuds
Potato and Fish Hash
**Breads, Biscuits &
Tortillas** 230
Thick Flour Tortillas
Sweet Fried Tortillas
Leftover Tortillas
Pancakes & Pan Bread
Fried Biscuits
Breadsticks
Dumplings from Scratch
Quick Dumplings
Quick Biscuit Mix,
Crackers & Tarts

Fried Bread & Biscuits
Very Simple Fried Bread
Basic Bannock Bread
Corn Meal Cakes
Cooked Cereals 237
Table of Measures
Hot or Cold Bulgur
Cereal
**Sauces, Gravies,
Marinades & Dips** 239
Vegetables 244
**Drying Fruits &
Vegetables** 245
Salads 248
One Vegetable Salad
Cabbage Salad
Fresh Sprouts
World's Most Compact
Salad
Very Quick Carrot Salad
Fast Macaroni Salad
Fast Potato Salad
One Bean Salad
Cold Fish Salad
Simple Fruit Salad
**Dressings &
Croutons** 252
Oil & Vinegar
Homemade Mayonnaise
French Dressing
Nancy's Dressing
Crumb Topping &
Croutons
Snacks & Desserts 254
Popcorn
Toasted Nuts and Seeds
Simple Rice Pudding
Key Lime Pie & Pudding
Fruit Gobbler
Beverages 257
Cowboy Coffee
Y & B Energy Drink
Hibiscus Punch
Dried Fruit Punch
Quick Fruit Punch
Energy Drinks
Corn Energy Drink
Rice Energy Drink
Oatmeal Energy Drink

Soups & Stews

Soups and stews are especially prone to that familiar cooking malady called mono-flavoritis, when the cook reaches automatically for a pinch-of-this and a dash-of-that. A single-flavored soup can be much more interesting and economical and takes just a few minutes to prepare. (Also see *Beans: Split Pea or Lentil Soup*.)

Quick One-Vegetable Soup

½-1 cup	sliced or minced vegetable, from carrots to cauliflower	***Additions***	
		leftover cooked rice, noodles	
2 Tbsp	butter *or* 1 Tbsp oil (or less)	2 Tbsp	minced green onion tops
1 qt	water, mild stock or bouillon	1	raw beaten egg, add slowly
	salt and pepper	dash	soy or Worcheshire sauce
½ tsp	oregano, basil or mild chile		

The smaller you cut your vegetable, the faster the soup will cook. Sauté the vegetable(s) in the butter or oil until they're tender. Add the water or broth, salt and herbs to taste. Cook for a few more minutes and serve.

Variations: The variations on this recipe are obviously considerable, but among my favorites: add a handful of unpeeled raw shrimp five minutes before serving, while the soup is scalding hot. Slurp the soup and dip the shrimp out with your fingers. The shrimp won't be mushy and overcooked and you might want to dip one or two in hot mustard.

Add milk to your soup but don't let it boil or the milk will separate.

Very Quick Tomato Soup

Mix equal parts of tomato juice or reconstituted tomato crystals with your favorite bouillon or vegetable broth. Heat and serve. Garnish with celery salt.

Thick Stew with Gravy

This is a richly flavored, one-dish meal that will fill three pots and a washtub if allowed to get out of hand. Here's a simple trick that will help you chop the vegetables for the stew: heap them in the pot you intend to cook them in. Before the pot is full or overflowing, stop chopping; you've got enough stew-makings.

We also use the one-vegetable method: one potato, one carrot, one onion, etc., or the one-cup method: a cup of carrot, a cup of onion...

On short trips we will prepare the ingredients at home, packing them in plastic bags. This reduces weight and waste. For two people with leftovers:

4-6 Tbsp	butter, margarine or oil		*Additions*
2	small-medium spuds	1	average zucchini or summer squash
1	large carrot	several	green beans
1	medium onion	1 cup	small mushrooms
2	stalks of celery with tops		meat
	garlic — lots		

For the Gravy

¼-½ cup	flour (half white, half brown)	2	small bay leaves
	salt and pepper	pinches	rosemary, thyme or marjoram
1 tsp	oregano		water or stock

Cut the vegetables into bite-sized pieces, but leave the mushrooms whole or just slice them in half. The gravy is what makes this stew outstanding so now mix the flour and spices in a strong bag or large pot. Dump in the vegetables and give them a thorough shaking/mixing so they're well coated with the flour.

Heat the butter or oil in a large skillet and brown the floured vegetables over a fairly hot fire. If you goofed and used too many vegetables, cook them in turns, dividing the butter or oil in half or thirds. When nicely browned, cover the vegetables with water or stock, close the pan and simmer until tender. If your gravy is too thick, add more liquid. If your gravy is too thin, *don't add flour to the stew* or it'll turn lumpy. Use another pan to whip up a quick batch of gravy, then add it to the stew.

I often eat up most of the potatoes in my stew before the gravy and other vegetables are gone. To replenish the stew, just chop more ingredients and add them, unfloured, simmering until tender.

Meat eaters: Coat bite-sized pieces of lean raw meat with the flour mixture but don't combine the meat with the raw vegetables; handle it separately. The meat takes longer to cook (unless you mince it). Once it's floured and browned, add water and simmer until almost tender. Now combine with the browned vegetables and simmer until the vegetables are tender.

Navy (White) Bean Soup

1-1½ cups	Navy beans		*Additions*
¼ cup	minced onion, celery and green pepper garlic	2 Tbsp	butter or oil
			vegetable broth or bouillon
			several crisp bacon slices

Cook the beans as described in *Beans: Beans in Broth*, add the vegetables to the beans when they're almost tender and complete cooking.

If you wish, sauté the vegetables in the butter or oil (bacon fat is nice, too). Add this and garlic powder (if used) to the beans. Bouillon makes for tastier beans; reconstitute it with broth from the almost-cooked beans and stir it back in.

Onion or Garlic Soup

2 cups	sliced onion rings or 1 cup peeled garlic		grated cheese
2 Tbsp	butter or oil		*Additions*
2 cups	broth or bouillon		tomato sauce or crystals
	salt, cayenne to taste	1 tsp	soy sauce
	toast or croutons		

Sauté the onion rings or whole peeled garlic cloves until nicely browned, add the liquid and simmer for 30 minutes. Pour the soup on toast or toasted bread cubes, garnish with grated cheese.

Teresa's Lima Bean Soup

I'd always considered lima beans rather "blah" until I tried this traditional Mexican recipe served during Lent. If you've never tried Chinese parsley, *cilantro,* you're in for a new taste experience. Some people love Chinese parsley and others hate it. Either way, you can't ignore its distinctive flavor, but you may want to substitute regular parsley.

½-1 lb.	dry lima beans	1	small chile, canned or fresh, or chile powder to taste
	water or unsalted broth for cooking beans		
1	small onion chopped	1	sprig of cilantro
1	tomato, chopped or tomato crystals		salt
	garlic (don't hold back)		*Additions*
pinch	cumin		crumbled or grated white cheese

Cook the lima beans according to the basic procedures for regular beans (see *Beans in Broth*). Chicken flavored stock is very nice for this soup. Combine the vegetables, spices and cooked lima beans and simmer for at least 15 minutes. Add the Chinese parsley with the vegetables or sprinkle it into the soup as it is served. Crumble cheese into the soup and eat with hot bread or tortillas.

Simple Potato, Clam or Oyster Chowder

1 cup	minced onion		*Additions*
2 Tbsp	butter or oil	½ cup	minced celery
2 Tbsp	flour (white or brown)	½ cup	(or more) minced carrots
2 cups	raw diced potatoes		garlic
3 cups	hot water or broth		Worchestershire sauce
	milk, fresh or powdered		crisp bacon bits
		1-2 cups	raw clams or oysters boned seafood

Sauté the onion (and vegetables) until the onion is tender. Stir in the flour and spices and add the hot water. Add the potatoes and simmer until tender. Milk is added to taste after the spuds are cooked to avoid boiling and scorching the milk. Add the clams, oysters or boned seafood (such as cod) with the milk.

Bob's Fish Head Soup

1-2	onions, chopped	1	large fish head cut into pieces or 4-5 small split fish heads
5-6	cloves garlic		
1-2	tomatoes, chopped		
1-2	green chiles, chopped		water to cover fish
1 tsp	crushed oregano	4-8	pepper corns
	salt and pepper to taste	2	bay leaves
½ qt	water	3 Tbsp	Chinese parsley, (optional)

Sauté the onions and garlic until browned; then add the tomato, chiles, oregano, salt and pepper. Heat and simmer with ½ quart of water. Add the head or heads and enough water to cover. Add the pepper corns, bay leaves, more salt if needed and Chinese parsley.

Let the soup simmer (don't boil) until the fish is done.

Variation for the squeamish: Substitute ½-1½ pounds of fish filets for the head. Or: steam the head until tender, pick the meat off and add both meat and broth to the soup.

Beans

Beans have a way of getting out of hand. Like old coat hangers left in a dark closet, beans seem able to reproduce themselves in a closed pot. One cup of dry beans is enough for four generous servings. Two cups of dry beans is enough for two people for two meals plus a nice batch of refrieds. If you go beyond 2 cups of dry beans you're flirting with uncontrollable leftovers. (Also see *Soups and Stews: Navy [white] Bean Soup*.)

Beans in Broth

Inspect your beans for small rocks and debris, especially if you bought them in bulk. Give them a rinse or two in cold water.

1 cup	dry beans (pinto)	salt (after beans are soft)
2-4 qts	boiling unsalted water or broth	***Additions***
		fried or grilled sausage
1 Tbsp	oil or margarine	1 cup chopped onion
½ tsp	cumin	minced vegetables
½ tsp	chile powder	tomato flavoring of any
1 tsp	oregano	kind
	garlic to taste	

Bring a large pot of water to a boil. It is a hard and fast rule of bean cookery to never add salt until the beans are tender, or they'll never get as tender as they should. Add the beans to the boiling water and cook them vigorously, uncovered, until they begin to swell up. Reduce the flame to a simmer, cover the pot and cook until tender.

Keep plenty of water on the beans or the minute you turn your back they'll scorch. When they need water, add it *boiling hot,* not cool — or your beans will come out grainy and never soften properly. Beans are cranky.

When you reduce the flame, add the spices and chopped onion and whatever else strikes your fancy. The recipe given here produces Mexican style 'pot beans', traditionally served in their own broth, with fresh tortillas. They make excellent refrieds and put pressure-cooked beans to shame.

If you're using a campfire try this slow-cooked overnight method, what I'd call Graveyard Beans if Lorena would let me. Start your beans with plenty of water, preferably 3 or 4 quarts. The water doesn't have to be boiling. Add the spices right away.

Set the bean pot, tightly covered, close enough to the fire to bring the water to a light boil, but not so close that it blows off the lid. You might want to bank the cool side of the pot with sand, dirt or foil. Go to bed.

In the morning, your beans will be done or very close to it. If you didn't use plenty of water on the beans, however, or built an extremely hot fire, you'll have a burnt mess. Better luck next time...

Alternate method: Bring the beans to a boil 3-5 minutes, remove from the heat, wrap well in thick cloths and allow the beans to 'rest' overnight. Finish cooking the beans in the morning. Boiling for a few minutes and resting, even for just an hour, is the equivalent of cold-soaking beans overnight.

Store cooked beans in the shade, wrapped in a wet cloth. Bring them to a boil for five to ten minutes at least twice a day. This prevents spoilage.

Refritos: Refried Beans

This recipe is direct from a Mexican kitchen and makes outstanding refried beans. Two secrets that have frustrated gringo cooks seeking that authentic Mexican flavor: you've got to start with *frijoles de la olla* (see *Beans in Broth*), not canned beans or red kidney beans, and you must fry the beans in *manteca de cerdo*, pig fat, politely known as lard. In deference to Lorena's feelings about meat, however, we use oil and the refrieds still come out good.

3-4 cups   cooked beans
4 Tbsp   oil, margarine or lard

Drain the beans well and save the broth. Heat the oil and begin frying the beans, mashing and stirring constantly. If you don't have a bean or potato masher, a strong fork will do. After a few minutes add a shot of the bean broth. Don't stop mashing and stirring. Fry until the beans are almost dry again and then add more broth. Continue until you've used up all of the broth — one or two cups should do it — and the beans are the consistency of a thick paste. If you ran out of broth or spilled it, use a vegetable broth or mild bouillon.

Serve the refried beans with bread, tortillas or crackers, garnished with grated cheese, chopped lettuce and hot sauce. They also make excellent taco and sandwich filling, hot or cold.

Bean Chili

Chili is like stew, with more variations than you could sample in a lifetime. The ingredients listed are suggestions, not hard rules. Adjust the amounts to your own tastes and whims and your chili will taste just fine. For about 4 servings:

¼ cup	chopped onion		½ cup	ground cumin
¼ cup	chopped green pepper		2-3 cups	cooked beans
¼ cup	chopped celery			***Additions***
1 Tbsp	oil		¼ cup	honey, sugar or molasses
6 oz	can tomato paste or juice, or small can of V-8 juice, or tomato crystals and 1 Tbsp vegetable broth		½ lb	lean ground beef
			2	pork sausage links
			4	strips bacon
			1 cup	jerky, chopped
1 Tbsp	mild red chile powder			canned or fresh tomatoes
	Cayenne pepper to taste			

Sauté the vegetables (and/or meat) and spices until tender. Now combine juice or broth (and honey or sweetener) and the cooked beans and simmer for at least an hour. Add more liquid, water or juice as required.

Bean and Cheese Melt

2 cups	cooked beans		½ cup	diced onion or green pepper
½ cup	bean broth or bouillon			mild chile powder to taste (optional)
2 cups	grated or chopped cheese (cheddar or other, but not Parmesan)			

Heat the beans and broth and stir in the cheese. Keep the temperature low or you'll need a chisel to clean the pot. When the cheese is thoroughly melted, stir in the onion or green pepper and serve over toast, rice, noodles or what-have-you. Makes a good dip or taco filling, too.

Miracle Bean Ball

A friend introduced us to this amazing dish while climbing a volcano in Guatemala. It is perfect for backpackers, kayakers and those who enjoy camping with a minimum of cooking. The size of your Bean Ball depends, of course, on the size of your cook pots and your appetite. For starters, however, I suggest that you try this with about 4 cups of cooked beans, as described in *Beans in Broth*.

> 4 cups   cooked beans
> garlic powder to taste
> oil (not butter)

Read the recipe for *Refried Beans*. For this recipe, however, you'll want to use as little oil as possible, not butter or lard. Oil spoils slower than butter or lard and is milder in flavor. We add additional garlic powder (again, fresh garlic won't keep as long even when cooked into the beans), but you may not share our fondness for this flavor.

Refry the beans with broth and garlic powder, but no other ingredients. When they reach the consistency of proper *refritos*, keep frying and stirring, until they're very thick and beginning to dry out and crumble. Remove the beans from the pan and when they've cooled enough to handle, mold them into a cake, ball or cube. Allow this to cool thoroughly, then wrap it in a clean cloth or brown paper. Don't use plastic bags; they trap moisture and encourage spoilage.

A well-made Bean Ball will keep for an amazing (or is it 'dismaying'?) length of time, especially in cool weather. Our friend ate on his for four days and had enough leftover for several more meals. What his menu lacked in variety was made up for (he said) in convenience.

The Bean Ball is quite nutritious, especially when eaten with bread, tortillas and the occasional piece of raw vegetable or fruit. Eat it cold or slice and fry with onions. Mash with fresh tomatoes and herbs or fry it inside tortillas. Dissolved, it makes a good instant soup or beverage.

Bean Supreme

This dish makes a good snack, dip, taco and sandwich filling or even a main meal. If you count calories, prepare to ascend into a higher bracket.

2-3 cups	cooked beans, refried	2-3	eggs, gently beaten (optional)
1 cup	tomato sauce, paste or juice	dab	solid butter or margarine
¼-½ cup	melted butter or margarine	½-1 cup	Crumb Topping (See *Dressings & Croutons*)
1-2 cups	grated cheese		

Continue refrying the beans, diluting them with the tomato sauce or juice. While they're soft and mushy, stir in the melted butter, most of the cheese and the eggs. You want the beans to be the consistency of a very thick sauce, so simmer and stir slowly until it's ready.

Grease a baking dish or pan with butter and sprinkle with ½ of the Crumb Topping. Pour or spoon the beans into the dish, and cover with the remaining cheese and crumbs. Bake for 20 minutes or slow cook over a low flame until the cheese melts and eggs stiffen.

Serve with a Hot Sauce (See *Sauces, Gravys, Marinades & Dips.*)

Split Pea or Lentil Soup

This is a nourishing one-pot meal that can be a 'wet' soup or a thick hearty stew.

1 cup	split peas or lentils		carrots
8 cups	water or broth (unsalted)	2 Tbsp	butter or oil
	onions		garlic to taste
			salt and pepper

<table>
<tr><td>1 tsp</td><td>herbs: thyme for split
peas, oregano for
lentils</td><td>*Additions*
tomato sauce or
flavoring for lentils
crisp bacon bits</td></tr>
</table>

Rinse the peas or lentils and add them to the boiling water. Cover and simmer until tender (2-3 hours).

As the peas or lentils cook, heat the butter or oil in a skillet and saute the vegetable(s) until tender. You can just chuck all the ingredients (except salt) into the pot and stew it together, but sautéing enhances the flavor. The vegetables can be added at any time, but the longer they cook the softer they'll get. Add them 20 minutes before serving if you want a more distinct texture.

Serve with a pat of butter or margarine and whole wheat bread or crackers.

Leftovers: Lentils and pea soup, in particular, have a tendency to thicken dramatically as they cool. This can be used to your advantage. Deliberately cook off most of the liquid so that the soup or stew reaches the consistency of a thick pudding. When it cools it should be semi-solid, a heavy paste. This paste can be packed into bags or jars or left in the pot. At your next meal just add hot water, stir thoroughly and you've got soup again. The paste can also be warmed or sautéed in butter and served on crackers, bread or tortillas. We even eat pea soup paste cold, as a dip.

Sandwiches & Tacos

Whenever someone asks how we manage to live and travel on a budget that is less than many people pay in yearly taxes, I answer: "Egg sandwiches." We once met a fellow who travelled throughout Central and South America eating nothing but avocado sandwiches, splurging occasionally for an avocado salad.

A steady diet of one food, egg sandwiches or T-bone steaks, eventually becomes boring and unsatisfying. Learn to use fast sandwiches and tacos as a backup for those moments when you can't quite get up the energy to cook but need a nutritious meal. Sandwiches have fallen into disgrace in the U.S. because of their association with nutritionless white bread and fast food joints that crank out burgers and subs faster than Detroit can punch out hubcaps. Put imagination and good ingredients into your sandwiches and tacos and you'll be pleasantly surprised by these convenience meals.

Egg Sandwiches

In my opinion a well-crafted egg sandwich is better than an omelette, mainly because my egg sandwiches begin by making a mini-omelette, then dressing it up with bread, fresh bean sprouts, lettuce, mustard and other goodies. For one person:

		Additions
1	egg	mayonnaise
1 Tbsp	milk, broth or warm water	mustard, mild or very spicy
1 tsp (or Tbsp)	butter or margarine	lettuce
2	slices bread	bean sprouts
		Anything you'd put into an omelette or scrambled eggs.

There are so many egg sandwiches that I'll give you one of my favorites as an example: Sauté 1-2 Tbsps of finely minced mushroom and/or zucchini (fresh or reconstituted) with a clove of minced garlic. In a cup, bowl or bag, beat the egg gently with the milk or liquid. Pour this over the sautéed vegetable and cook slowly, folding in the edges of the egg to match the shape of your bread or tortilla (thick flour tortillas make especially good taco-sandwiches).

When cooked, remove from the fire and allow the egg to cool to eating temperature. Prepare the bread (toasting is nice) and lay the egg reverently between the slices. A searing hot egg will make your bread limp and wilt the lettuce and sprouts. Slice on a diagonal and serve with a flourish.

Melted Cheese and Seafood Sandwiches

2 slices	bread	2 Tbsp	grated or thinly sliced cheese
1-2 Tbsp	butter or margarine	1 tsp	water (optional)
small can	clams, crab, shrimp, etc.		tomato or chile sauce

A small can of clams, crab, shrimp, oysters or sardines will make several sandwiches when combined with cheese. Sauté a slice of bread in a Tbsp of butter or margarine and remove from the pan when browned. Lay a second slice of bread in the pan (you may need more butter) and cover it with about 2 Tbsps of finely minced seafood. Don't be afraid to be a miser; the flavor will come out as the sandwich heats.

Now sprinkle cheese over the sandwich, cover with the already browned slice of bread and cook slowly until the cheese melts. I like to cover the pan and if the sandwich seems to be going dry, add a tsp of water for steam. Serve with a tomato or chile sauce. This makes a great treat when prepared with smoked fish.

Grilled Cheese Sandwich

Just leave out the seafood from the sandwich described above and add a bit more cheese.

Fried Potato Burgers

leftover potatoes, mashed or hashbrowns	*Additions*
	minced onion
	lettuce
butter or oil	sprouts
bread	cheese

Flatten out a patty of leftover mashed or hashbrown potatoes and fry in butter or oil. Garnish with a bit of fresh minced onion, lettuce and sprouts. A slice of cheese is nice, too, either melted onto the potato or cold.

Cheese Rabbit (Rarebit)

1 cup	grated cheese	Worchestershire sauce (a dash)
½ cup	beer or broth	Dry mustard (a dash)

Melt the cheese into the beer or broth with the Worchestershire sauce and the dry mustard. Stir thoroughly and serve on toast, biscuits or tortillas. It's also quite good served with fresh sliced tomatos, sprouts, mushrooms, bacon and hashbrowns.

Salad Sandwich

Make a very small tossed salad from lettuce, cabbage or bean sprouts, add dressing and put it between two slices of bread or inside a tortilla.

For variety, make two sandwiches: one of salad and the other of cheese. Slice both in half and serve half of each to yourself and a companion. If there are half a dozen people in your group, make half a dozen different sandwiches, cut them into quarters and start trading back and forth. This is even more interesting if each person makes one sandwich, a true creative effort, and then shares it around.

Sandwich Suggestions

I can do severe damage to an eight ounce piece of salami at lunch or snack time. This same amount of salami, when sliced very thin, will make several satisfying sandwiches. The same goes for cheese, peanut butter, canned meat spreads, bean dips and whatever else will fit between two slices of bread or down the middle of a tortilla. Let the bread or tortilla provide the bulk and use other ingredients for flavor and variety. Good bread is very good food and if you slice it thick — and the salami and cheese thin — you'll eat well and save money at the same time.

Sandwiches are just the gringo version of the taco. For more ideas, read through *Tacos* and don't hesitate to try sandwich fillings that might seem off-the-wall, at least until you've eaten them.

Tacos and Tortillas

The true test of a tortilla is whether or not it can be eaten with pleasure when only slightly warm or even cold. Unfortunately, I've yet to find a brand of store-bought corn tortillas that can pass the test. Flour tortillas, however, can be eaten cold, especially if you've made them yourself. (See *Breads & Tortillas* for suggestions and instructions on making and storing tortillas.) Flour stays flexible and can be easily warmed on a hot rock, the hood of your truck or in a plastic bag left closed in the sun for ten or fifteen minutes. Corn tortillas, however, are made with lime and cold lime tastes too much like cement for most of us.

Unless you've been raised on tortillas you probably think of them as something quite different than bread. Don't: tortillas *are* bread, flattened and baked on a griddle rather than inside an oven. (Pocket breads are between tortillas and loaf breads.) Tortillas are wrapped around food rather than layered, as in a sandwich. The fillings and ingredients for a good taco are similar or identical to sandwiches: peanut butter, fresh avocado and tomato, tuna salad, refried beans or potatoes, strips of meat; you name it, it'll probably fit inside a tortilla.

For improved flexibility and enhanced flavor, tortillas are normally eaten warm or hot. When preparing tacos-as-sandwiches it's nice to prepare the fillings before warming the tortillas, arranging them so that everyone can dip in and create their own tacos. We usually sit around the stove or fire, heating the tortillas and passing them quickly to whoever is ready for another. Kids especially enjoy making up their own tacos.

Fried Tacos, Quesadillas

Quesadillas are basically cheese tacos, the Mexican equivalent of the grilled cheese sandwich. Vegetarians who travel in Mexico learn to love quesadillas, at least for the first month or two...

		Additions	
	corn tortillas	onion, minced	cabbage, shredded or
⅛-¼ cup	oil or butter	tomato, chopped	lettuce thinly sliced
	grated cheese	bean sprouts	chile sauce
			oregano

Some cooks fry tacos in a lot of oil; I prefer to use just enough to keep them sliding around in the pan. Mix the cheese, onion, tomato and oregano. Put two heaping spoonsful of this mixture into a tortilla and fold it gently in half. It may be too stiff to fold; if so, sprinkle warm water over the tortillas and wrap them in a jacket or hot towel for ten minutes.

Fry the taco until the tortilla is crisp and golden and the cheese is runny. Serve garnished with cabbage, lettuce and bean sprouts, with a hot sauce on the side. Cooked tacos tend to turn soggy so we eat them out of the pan, waiting impatiently by turns.

Variations: Fill with cooked beans, potatoes, rice or anything else close at hand.

Tortilla Pizza

We invented this one while camped on a remote Mexican beach. I have to admit that it looks more pizza-like the farther away you are from a pizza parlor. It works equally well with corn or flour tortillas. There are two methods for this pizza; here's the first:

		Additions
several	tortillas	mushrooms, onions,
1-2 cups	Rich Tomato Sauce (see *Sauces, Gravies, Marinades & Dips*)	peppers, anchovies, salami and other
1-2 cups	grated or sliced cheese	dream foods

Grease a skillet (or a large square of heavy foil) and lay down the first tortilla. Sprinkle the tortilla with cheese, whatever variations you're lucky enough to have, and a generous smear of tomato sauce. Cover this with a second tortilla, repeat the filling and so on and on until you've got a stack of tortillas about 1-2" thick. Cover the last tortilla with the remaining ingredients, close the pan or foil, and cook very slowly over the fire until the cheese is quite runny. A squirt of water, beer or wine will keep the pizza moist as it cooks. If it scorches a bit on the bottom, don't worry about it; the crisp cheese tastes great.

Second method: If you don't have a tomato sauce on hand, just saute onion, garlic and whatever else you've got in a few tablespoons of butter or oil and put this between the tortillas. Pour or dribble tomato sauce, paste, catsup or even V-8 juice between the layers.

Simple Enchiladas

What this recipe lacks in authenticity is made up for in convenience. As many cooks know, enchiladas are a simple looking dish that is time-consuming and messy to prepare. Burritos are a northern Mexican variation of the enchilada made with flour tortillas. For our purposes we'll use either corn or flour tortillas or even thin pocket bread.

	tortillas	¼ cup	finely minced onion
2 cups	Rich Tomato Sauce (see *Sauces, Gravies, Marinades & Dips*)		***Additions***
			chile powder to taste or canned jalapeño or serrano chiles, minced
2 cups	grated cheese		
1 cup	cooked rice or beans		yogurt or sour cream (highly desirable)
½ cup	finely chopped lettuce or cabbage		

Roll your tortillas tightly around a few tablespoons of grated cheese, beans and/or rice. If you like chiles, mince them and add to taste. Lay the rolled tortillas side by side in a skillet, baking dish or large piece of foil. Cover with the sauce and sprinkle a bit of cheese on top.

Seal tightly and simmer over a low fire. Add a squirt of water or tomato broth if the pan looks dry. Serve when the cheese is quite runny, garnished with onion, lettuce and sour cream or yogurt.

Burritos

'Little Burros' are a well-balanced dish that will carry you a long way, especially if eaten for breakfast. We prefer to make them in foil, wrapped individually for easy handling and cooking. Make some up at home, too, for the first day of the trip.

tortillas, preferably flour	cheese, grated or thinly sliced
beans, refried or cooked and drained	water or broth
green onions, one per burrito or 1 tsp chopped regular onion	***Additions***
	rice, cooked
	chile powder or chiles to taste

Wrap the tortillas around a generous portion of beans and/or rice garnished with as much cheese as you can afford. Lay a tender green onion or chopped onion on top of the cheese and add chile to taste. If your tortilla is very dry add a teaspoon of water or broth. This will steam soften the burrito. Seal up the foil packet tightly. Bake on the coals for 20-30 minutes and serve with chile sauce. (Burritos can be pan-cooked, too.)

Gorditas

Gorditas roughly translates to mean "Little Fat Ones" and if you eat enough of these you'll understand why. Gorditas are a variation on flour tortillas, but for our recipe we'll use a baked or fried biscuit type bread.

several biscuits (see *Breads & Tortillas*)	salt to taste
grated cheese	oil or butter

Additions	onion, minced
lettuce, cabbage or	chile sauce
sprouts, finely chopped	tomato, chopped

Heat a very small amount of oil or butter in a skillet and arrange the biscuits in the bottom. Sprinkle them with cheese, cover and cook until the cheese is soft or fully melted. Serve as is or garnish with other ingredients.

Gorditas can also be baked in foil. If they are dry or tough, add a Tbsp of water or broth to the pan or package.

Variations: Smear with refried beans, then add the cheese.

Eggs

Brown 'ranch' eggs cost more than white 'factory' eggs but they also have more flavor. When hiking or boating we carry some eggs hardboiled for immediate snacking and crack others into a wide mouthed plastic jar. Open the eggs one at a time into a cup, just in case one is rotten. Eggs will keep for weeks in their shells but boiled or broken open eggs should be eaten within a day or two. (See *Sandwiches & Tacos: Egg Sandwiches*)

Hardboiled Eggs

Most people overcook eggs. Seven to ten minutes in boiling hot water should hardboil them adequately; fry eggs gently, not hot enough to crisp or burn the thin edges.

Scrambled Eggs

Eggs have saved the day on more than one camping trip. The variations on the following recipes are beyond counting. Use the basic recipe and your imagination to keep eggs from becoming boring. For one person:

2	fresh eggs		*Additions*
1 Tbsp	butter, margarine or oil	¼ cup	or less thinly sliced,
2 Tbsp	minced onion		fresh zucchini
2 Tbsp	warm water or milk		garlic, fresh or pow-
	salt and pepper to		dered to taste
	taste		mushrooms

Additions		hot chile pepper, minced
¼ cup	garlic, fresh or pow-	cooked potatoes, diced
	dered to taste	cooked beans
	mushrooms	

Saute the onion and vegetables (zucchini and/or cooked potatoes are my favorite) until *just* tender. Beat the eggs gently with the water or milk and pour them over the vegetables. Cook slowly, stirring as little as possible.

Serve with bread, tortillas and hot sauce. This dish makes an excellent sandwich and taco filling, hot or cold.

Omelettes

This is a 'cheater's omelette' since it does not call for folding the egg mixture in half, a maneuver that I can seldom manage without turning the recipe into Scrambled Eggs.

2	eggs	*Additions*
1 Tbsp	butter, margarine or oil	fresh or dried parsley
¼ cup	sliced or chopped mush-	minced olives
	rooms, bean sprouts	fresh steamed greens
	or cheese (or all three	cooked meat, fish or
	if you're lucky).	seafood
2 Tbsp	warm water or milk	capers
	salt, pepper and garlic	fresh tomato
	to taste	

Sauté the mushrooms until barely tender (one or two minutes). Gently blend the eggs with water or milk (optional but gives a smoother, softer texture to the omelette). Pour the eggs over the mushrooms and cook over a medium heat. Add the bean sprouts and/or cheese after the eggs have solidified slightly.

Cheater's omelette: Cover the pan and cook slowly until the eggs are thoroughly congealed and the cheese melted. Watch the heat; a sealed pan cooks faster than you might expect.

Legal omelette: When the eggs are solid enough, slip a spatula under one half and double them over, somewhat like a folded taco. Cook slowly until the egg is fully congealed.

Poached Eggs

	water or milk
2	eggs per person
1 tsp	butter

Poached eggs do not require oil or butter for cooking and are easier to check than soft-boiled eggs. Heat 1-2 inches of lightly salted water or milk in a skillet or pot (or even a large metal cup) until scalding—but not boiling. Crack the eggs gently into the scalding water and cook for 3-5 minutes. Serve on toast, pancakes or tortillas with milk, gravy or sauce.

Eggs with Beans

2	eggs	*Additions*
½ cup	or more cooked, drained beans	minced onion
		garlic
1 tsp	butter, margarine or oil	dash of cayenne
		mild red chile powder

Heat the butter and add the beans, sauteeing until thoroughly warm. Crack the eggs directly into the pan, either over the beans or to one side. Stir slowly, mixing in the beans, or if you prefer, scramble and fry the eggs alongside the beans, mixing the two after the eggs have congealed. If you add minced onion it can be sauteed with the beans or served raw, as a garnish, after the eggs have cooked.

Eggs with Rice

I particularly enjoy this for breakfast. The texture of the rice is most pleasing if it has been cooked several hours earlier. Unless you're quite hungry, use just one egg per person.

1 or 2	eggs	*Additions*
½ cup	cooked rice	sesame seeds, raw or
1 Tbsp	butter, margarine or oil	toasted
	minced onion	any tender vegetable
	salt, pepper, garlic to	soy sauce or garnish
	taste	hot sauce or gravy

There are three ways to cook this dish:

• Sauté the onion and rice until the onion is tender, then stir in the egg and cook until well congealed or:

• Mix the rice, onion, egg and spices into a ball. Add more rice if it's very runny with egg. Form into a patty ½" thick and fry in hot butter or oil until browned. Flip and brown the other side. Serve as is, with gravy or hot sauce, or with another fried egg on top.

• Sauté the onion and rice until the onion is cooked, then set aside on a plate. Fry one or two eggs, sunnyside up, and serve them on top of the rice.

Variations: Substitute cooked noodles or cubed potatoes for the rice.

Eggs with Sausage or Salami

This is a variation of the Mexican truck driver's breakfast of eggs scrambled with spicy *chorizo* sausage.

2 Tbsp	or more finely minced sausage, pepperoni or salami		*Additions*
1 tsp	butter, margarine or oil		chorizo sausage
2	eggs		minced onion
			minced garlic
			hot peppers

Sauté the minced sausage or salami until it begins to get tough. This extracts the flavor, and if the meat is minced finely enough, won't detract much from the texture. Stir in the eggs and cook slowly until done. Serve with bread or tortillas.

Creamed Eggs

This is a very hearty meal that can be packed with more eggs or milk according to your needs and appetite.

1-2	hard boiled eggs per person, chopped	toast, tortillas or pancakes
½-1 cup	gravy per person	

Make a rich gravy (see *Sauces, Gravys, Marinades & Dips*) or cheese sauce. Add the chopped egg (you can use chopped fried egg), warm and serve over toast or what-have-you, including cooked rice, noodles or potatoes.

Rabbits In Their Holes

I know, the name is ridiculous but our friend Peter insists that is correct. In any case, the dish tastes good so feel free to rename it.

1 or 2	eggs	1	thick slice of bread or pancake or soft tortilla
1 Tbsp	butter or margarine		

Cut or chew out a hole about two inches in diameter in the center of the bread. Heat the butter and place the bread in the pan. Crack the egg and slip it into the hole, fry, flip and continue cooking until the egg is done. Because the fried bread has a French toast sort of flavor you might like to serve it with a dab of jam, honey or syrup.

Stove Top Casserole

2	eggs	¼ cup	(or more) cooked rice, beans or noodles
1 Tbsp	butter, margarine or oil	2 Tbsp	warm water or milk
¼ cup	sliced or chopped vegetable		salt, pepper and garlic to taste
¼ cup	grated or thinly sliced cheese		

Variations: Anything you'd enjoy in scrambled eggs or an omelette.

Heat the fat in a skillet or baking dish. Blend everything together except the cheese. You may want to crumble or separate the rice if it's cold and lumpy. Pour this mixture into the pan, sprinkle with the cheese, cover tightly and simmer over a very low flame until everything is congealed and cooked.

Fish & Seafood

Stone-Age Baked Fish

We learned this method camped on the Sea of Cortez. Take any tough skinned or heavily scaled fish and lay it very close to a hot fire or bed of coals. We do our fish on a rock, board or heavy beachcombed limb. Don't be impatient; this is a slow cooking method.

Turn the fish every 10 to 15 minutes, taking care to avoid tearing the skin. The skin and scales will toughen as they cook, forming a tight 'wrapper' that holds the fish's juices and flavor. The skin often scorches but it can be easily peeled away, revealing tender cooked flesh. Serve with appropriate grunts and groans of pleasure.

Fish Roasted On-A-Stick

This time-honored cooking method reduces the muss and fuss to an absolute minimum. Skewer a fresh fish from head to tail with a sharp peeled stick or heavy wire. Leave the guts, head and scales intact or, if you want, remove only the gills and scales. The guts and head add flavor. Removing them tends to dry out the fish.

Make shallow cuts on both sides of the fish. A light brushing of oil is nice. Rub the cuts with salt and herbs.

Prop the skewered fish over the coals of a fire or jam the end of the stick deep into the ground, angling the fish over the fire. (If you don't have any salt at all, dunk the fish in the sea several times as it cooks.)

Cook until tender and serve with tortillas, lime juice and hot sauce.

Foil Baked Fish

Remove the guts, gills and scales from small fish or fillet larger fish. Use a pan with a tight lid or a piece of foil. Rub the fish with butter or oil, sprinkle a few pinches of herbs (especially dill), salt, garlic, pepper, a slice or two of onion, a bay leaf, a sliced banana, pineapple...you name it, it'll probably taste good. Add a shot of beer, wine or water, seal tightly and place gently over the coals or on a grill. Bake gently, turning with care to avoid tearing the package. It shouldn't take more than 30 minutes.

Simple Fried Fish

flour (any kind)	*Additions*
spices	toasted sesame seeds
oil for frying	garlic powder
egg and/or milk	spices

Gut, gill and scale fish under a pound or fillet and skin larger fish, cutting the flesh into six inch long pieces. Roll the fish in flour (I add garlic powder, sesame seeds, spices), then dip the pieces into a beaten egg mixed with milk or beer. Roll them through the flour again and fry in hot oil until browned and just tender. This is a messy method but worth it. If you prefer an easier recipe, just roll the fish in flour and fry. (See *Soups & Stews: Bob's Fish Head Soup*.)

Seafood Tempura

Frankly, buying a box of pre-mixed tempura batter is easier than making your own, but when I'm full of energy it's worth the trouble to do tempura from scratch. This batter is quite good on all seafoods and slices of vegetables and fruit, especially bananas.

1 cup	white flour	water, beer, mineral
¼-½ cup	cornstarch (optional)	water or 7-Up
¼ tsp	salt	oil for frying
1½ Tbsp	baking powder	*Additions*
		1-2 egg yolks

Sift or stir the flour and cornstarch together, then mix in the other ingredients. Use enough liquid to make a thin batter. Stir it as little as you can and don't worry about lumps.

Dip bite-size chunks of seafood into the batter and fry in deep, hot oil. The batter should puff up and brown nicely around the seafood, forming a delicious light crust. Don't overlook the tempura. If your batter is too thin, add more flour and cornstarch. If it won't puff up, try more baking powder.

Serve with hot mustard, horseradish, soy sauce and toasted sesame seeds.

Variations: Any quick cooking fresh vegetable can be cooked in tempura.

Smoked Fish & Meat, Jerky

Smoked Fish

There are many ways to smoke a fish and after years of experimentation we've come to rely on what I call the Stone Age Method. Forget fancy smokehouses, portable smokers, hickory chips and other modern complications; the following technique produces the finest smoked fish I've ever had.

Preparing the Fish: The first 'secret' for high quality smoked fish is to clean the fresh fish as soon as possible, preferably right in the boat or on the shore. Cut out the gills and guts. Keep the fish damp and out of the sun. As soon as you get to camp remove the head (I often leave it on; heads are very tasty) and split the fish lengthwise, along the backbone, into two separate pieces or 'butterfly' it.

Don't fillet it; those bones add flavor and hold the fish together. Cut large fish into pieces that are easy to handle and not too heavy for the smoking grill.

Clean the split fish well, removing every bit of guts and blood, and rinse thoroughly in clean salt or fresh water. Lay the pieces out on a clean board, paper or cloth. Sprinkle a liberal amount of salt over both sides, taking care to hit all the nooks and crannies.

Don't smother the fish but use more salt than you'd want on a regular fried fish. Some of the salt will dissolve and run off into the fire later. The idea is to preserve the flesh with salt and smoke (both kill bacteria) without making it too salty to eat. You'll soon learn just how much to use. (You can actually smoke fish without any salt, but it won't keep as long and just doesn't have the flavor of salted fish.)

If the fish will be smoked within a few hours, place it in a cool shady place and allow the salt to soak in. Fish that will be smoked the next day should be salted very heavily or kept in brine (add enough salt to the water to float a raw potato or egg). The warmer the weather, the more salt you should use when storing raw fish.

The Smoker: After many elaborate construction projects, we've become firm believers in using a very simple smoker. It must be tended carefully to avoid burning up the fish, but when you taste the final product you won't begrudge the time. An open smoker actually works better in warm weather (especially humid beach conditions) than a smoker that is completely enclosed and traps moisture.

The basic idea is to suspend the pieces of fish about twelve to eighteen inches over the top of the coals. Support a metal grill with forked sticks, rocks or bricks or, if you don't have a grill, improvise one with green sticks. When the sticks begin to burn through, replace them and feed the burnt sticks into the smoke fire. Be careful; drops of fish fat can suddenly catch fire and send the whole works up in a mini-inferno.

To get fancier, build some sort of sides around the grill's supporting legs or framework. We use mats, fronds, cardboard, aluminum foil, pieces of tin and even newspaper. This traps the smoke and helps control the fire, especially on windy days. The fire should not be hot enough to scorch anything: the fish, the supporting sticks or the sides. This looks like a hobo set-up, but it's all the more satisfying because it will turn out really fine smoked fish and meat.

The Fire: Build your fire from dry wood but keep it small. When it starts to cool down later you can add more small bits of dry wood to rejuvenate it. Driftwood is fine, but don't use any that is painted or has tar stuck to it. (Tar is becoming a real problem on some beaches, the result of oil spills and passing ships pumping their bilges.) Pull out any wood that produces dark or obnoxious-smelling smoke.

Once the fire has burned down to a nice *small* bed of coals add several pieces of green wood. Give it ten minutes or more to heat up and produce smoke. As the wood dries it will begin to smolder and perhaps burst into flame. If this happens, beat out the flames with a stick and spread the coals around. Add more bits of green wood (if needed) and let it begin smoking again. This is where time and patience come in; nothing can substitute for a very careful watch over the fire to maintain constant smoke and the proper temperature. If you don't have green wood use dry stuff and watch the fire even more closely.

Place the fish on the grill with the skin side down. Test the fish by carefully touching the side facing the coals. If it's hot but not sizzling (fish that are fatty will gently ooze fat at the proper temperature), you've got it just right. The darkening of the flesh should be caused by smoke, not from cooking.

Leave the fish skin side down until the flesh has firmed up, then turn it gently. Very tender fish may fall apart at this point. The solution is to use a fine-meshed grill. Or place aluminum foil on the grill and punch *lots* of holes in it.

How long does it take to smoke a fish? It depends on several factors: the heat of the fire, the thickness of the fish, the degree of dryness and smokiness you prefer, and the length of time you'd like to keep the fish afterwards. Here a few examples: a thick slab of salmon or cod takes about six to twelve hours, start to finish. This is enough smoke to preserve the fish for at least several days, if not weeks. A 12" trout can be smoked in 2-3 hours.

Storage: Smoked fish should be kept in a shady, cool, well-ventilated place. We wrap ours in brown paper, newspaper or cloth (never use plastic) and keep it in a loosely woven Mexican shopping bag. The bag is easily suspended from the van, tent poles or a tree branch, out of reach of dogs and other pests. Check the fish every day or two; if mold appears on the surface don't toss it out. Put the fish back onto the smoke fire for an hour or dry it carefully in the sun. The mold won't hurt you and another round of smoking disguises its flavor.

Smoked fish does spoil, especially if you don't use enough salt or smoke (a hazard of thick fish). Give it a close whiff. Spoiled fish smells really awful.

Variations: Baste the fish as it smokes with a mixture of soy sauce, water, ginger powder and garlic. Don't use too much; as the fish dries out the flavors will be concentrated.

Uses: Smoked fish goes well in soups, casseroles, salads, tacos and other dishes that call for meat or fish. Tough smoked fish can be tenderized by soaking it in warm water.

Quick Smoked Fish

Prepare a smoke fire, exactly as for regular fish smoking, but build the grill higher and the fire hotter. This is a relatively quick process and you'd better plan on tending the fire closely or you'll end up with fish cinders.

Remove the gills (optional) and cut shallow slices in the sides of the whole fish, about an inch apart. Rub a generous amount of salt into the slices and place the fish on the rack. Don't gut the fish unless you're really squeamish; they give a special flavor. Turn the fish about every half hour or so. If the fire is the proper temperature, the fish will be thoroughly cooked and quite smoky within two or three hours. The more green wood you heap on, the more they'll have a rich smokey flavor. These fish are salty and go very well with chilled beer. Tear off chunks, wrap them in a fresh tortilla, garnish with lime juice and hot sauce...it's hard to beat!

Smoking and Drying Meat

Smoked and dried meat is an excellent camp and trail food. I usually try to prepare a supply before making a long back country trip.

Lean meat makes the best jerky. Fat eventually breaks down and gives a slightly rancid flavor. Fattier meats should not be passed over, however, especially if you don't intend to keep it around very long. Loin is excellent and more tender than most other cuts.

Boil a large kettle of water (seawater is okay) with enough salt to float a raw potato or egg (about 1-1¼ cups per gallon).

Cut the meat into long thin slices, thin enough to be translucent. Thick spots can be beaten out later. Don't try to make the slices as neat as commercial jerky or you'll just waste time and energy. Large strips are easier to handle, but small pieces can be used to.

Dump the thin slices of raw meat into the boiling brine, stirring constantly. You can add garlic and spices to the water or wait until later, and sprinkle them directly onto the meat strips. Don't turn your back; this is a fast operation. When the meat is gray on the outside (within a minute or so) remove and spread it out to dry. Discard the salt water.

An oven works great for the drying process, but I prefer an open fire (follow the instructions for *Smoked Fish*). If you use an oven put it on a very low heat. Spread the meat on the oven rack or in shallow pans. Don't use waxed paper; it melts. Prop the door open to increase air circulation.

The jerky will be done in four to eight hours, depending on the temperature and thickness of the meat. It's done when it bends but feels tough and is on the edge of brittleness. It will get more brittle as it cools, so don't overdo it.

• Try different flavors of jerky. I brush some lightly with soy sauce before drying. Garlic powder works great, but if you use garlic salt be careful or the jerky may be too salty. A mixture of oregano, garlic powder and dried mild red chile powder is good, though go very easy; the shrinking of the meat will concentrate the flavors.

• If the jerky is too salty, soak it in fresh water for a few minutes and redry it. Jerky that is too salty can also be added to soups and stews *before* other spices are added. Give it time to release the salt before adding more.

• When a fire isn't practical the meat can be sun dried. Put more salt on the meat to prevent spoiling since sun drying may take 2 or 3 days. Drape it over strings, wires or thorn bushes. The salt should keep flies away but if it doesn't, you'll have to cover the meat as best you can without blocking too much sun. When the sun goes down, take in the meat. Put it back out as soon as possible in the morning. Finish the drying off with a short session over a smokey fire to enhance the flavor.

Noodles & Pasta

There are two basic ways to cook noodles: boiled in lots of lightly salted water (the American method) or fried or sautéed, then slowly steamed. This second method is commonly used in Mexico. We've yet to find a better way to prepare pastas while camping, especially if you want to use a minimum amount of water, fuel, time and utensils. The Mexican method of cooking noodles creates innumerable possibilities for true one-pot meals, since all of the ingredients, from noodles to sauce and spices, are cooked together. (This also works for rice and other grains; see *Rice* recipes.)

Once you've learned the Mexican method you'll find it easy to convert regular noodle and rice recipes to one-pot meals. Whenever a recipe calls for

'cooked noodles' with other ingredients, just loosely calculate which can be added as the noodles steam in the pan. Harder vegetables go right in with the pasta as it's being sautéed while softer ingredients (cheese, mushrooms, tomatoes) can be added later, as the pasta steams. Practice with the recipes given here and you'll soon learn the technique.

Seawater can be used — with care — for cooking noodles. (See *Cooking Tips & Techniques: Cooking with Seawater.*)

Boiled Noodles

2 cups	noodles		1 Tbsp	oil
2 qts	water		1 cup	cold or ice water
1 tsp	salt			(optional)

For every cup of raw noodles or pasta you're going to want at least one quart of boiling lightly salted water. The more water the better; it keeps the noodles from sticking to each other and to the bottom of the pan. Water also dilutes away the starch from the pasta. Starch makes noodles gummy, a problem with cheaper pastas. The oil also prevents the noodles from sticking together.

Bring the water, salt and oil to a rolling boil and add the noodles slowly, not in one fell swoop. Keep the heat high and stir constantly to separate the individual noodles. Thick elbows take 12 to 29 minutes to cook, but thinner noodles may be done within 7 minutes. Give them a chew and when you suspect that they're done, remove the pot from the fire and set it aside for a few minutes. Now taste them again. Indecision often leads to overcooking.

Lorena pours a cup of cold water (ice water is best but ...) into the pot when the noodles are tender. Drain. The cold water helps separate the starch from the noodles and makes them less gummy. I prefer to just drain them, rinsing with water if there is enough.

Serve the noodles with a gravy, cheese sauce or a salad dressing (I especially like oil and vinegar).

If water is quite scarce, save the noodle water for soup stock or leave out the salt and drink it with a broth flavoring.

Very Quick Spaghetti

Elbow noodles are easier to sauté than long pastas but with practice you can do either. I often break spaghetti and fettucini noodles in half or quarters for easier stringing.

2 cups	uncooked noodles	¼ cup	celery, green pepper, zucchini minced
3 Tbsp	oil or margarine (with dash of olive oil)		tomato paste, juice or powder
3-4 cups	water, broth or bouillon	½ tsp	chile powder
½ cup	minced onion	1 Tbsp	honey or sugar
	garlic to taste		minced sausage or salami
½ tsp	oregano, thyme or basil	2 Tbsp	Worchestershire sauce

Additions

grated Parmesan or sharp cheddar cheese

Sauté the raw noodles in the hot oil until they begin to brown, then add the onion, garlic and any other vegetables you have, along with the spices. Sauté for a few more minutes but don't let the noodles scorch.

Now add the liquid, preferably pre-heated; don't worry about it, though, if it's cold. (The amount of liquid varies according to the type of pasta, temperature or the fire and the tightness of your pot lid. If the noodles need more liquid as they cook it can be added without problem. Too much liquid is easily remedied by removing the lid and slowly stirring and simmering until the desired consistency is reached.)

If this is to be a tomato sauce spaghetti, add the tomato paste or whatever you have with the liquid. Add the sweetener now, too, if you use it.

Cover the pan tightly and simmer for about 20 minutes. Test the pasta by chewing. If it's almost done but the liquid is gone add another ¼ cup of liquid and continue cooking.

A few minutes before serving, remove the lid, sprinkle on the cheese and re-cover.

As insurance again scorched spaghetti try this: when the noodles are still firm, with about 10 minutes cooking time to go, remove the pan from the heat and wrap it well in towels, clothing or what-have-you. Let it sit covered (don't open it) for at least 15 minutes and preferably 20 to 25. The noodles will continue slow-cooking without any danger of over-cooking.

Variations: If you are short on ingredients this spaghetti can be made with just the garlic, the onion or even a flavored broth by itself.

Instant White Spaghetti

2-3 cups	cooked noodles	5 Tbsp	butter, margarine or olive oil
2/3 cup	rich broth, hot	1 cup	grated cheese (or less)

Melt the butter in the hot broth and stir this into the cooked noodles. Serve with a generous topping of cheese.

With uncooked noodles: See *Very Fast Macaroni and Cheese.*

Very Fast Macaroni and Cheese

You can whip this up before your friends have the tent in place:

2-3 cups	cooked noodles (or rice)	garlic to taste
2/3 cup	milk	salt and pepper
¼ tsp	dry or ½ tsp prepared mustard	*Additions*
1-2 cups	grated or thinly shaved cheese	pinches of oregano, basil or chile powder

Mix everything over a low heat and, when the cheese is melted or your friends begin whining hungrily, serve.

With uncooked noodles: Sauté 1 cup of raw noodles in 3 Tbsp of oil or margarine until lightly browned. Add 2 cups of water or broth, cover and simmer until the noodles are almost tender (20 minutes). Lift the lid and stir in the milk, mustard, cheese and spices; re-cover, set aside from the heat for 10 minutes and serve.

Golden Noodles

This is another very fast dish that we often eat on gloomy days. If your friends are depressed call it Noodles El Dorado.

2 cups	cooked noodles (or rice or chopped spuds)		*Additions*
			chile powder (to taste)
2 Tbsp	butter or oil	1/3-½ cup	grated Parmesan cheese
⅛ tsp	paprika		
	salt and pepper		garlic

Sauté the noodles, rice or spuds over a fairly hot fire until nicely browned but not crisp. Noodles won't brown as much as potatoes so just use your judgement and get them good and hot without turning them into hard pellets. When they're close to being done add the spices and cheese and continue cooking for a few more minutes.

Cheesy Noodles

2-3 cups	cooked noodles, pasta	½ cup	milk with 2 beaten eggs, or —
¼ cup	minced onion		
2 Tbsp	butter or oil	1 cup	gravy or white sauce
	garlic and pepper	1-2 cups	grated cheese

	Additions	canned seafood (tuna)
¼ cup	minced green pepper and/or celery	or meat, jerky nuts and seeds, toasted
1-2 Tbsp	Worchestershire sauce	bread crumbs

If you've got an oven just mix everything up, pour into a lightly oiled pan and bake for 30-40 minutes in a moderately hot oven. On top of the stove or fire: sauté the vegetables until tender, then mix everything well, cover tightly and cook until the egg is congealed. Sprinkle extra cheese and a few sesame seeds or bread crumbs on top.

Instant Clam or Seafood Linguini

I've made this with many types of noodles and seafoods (fresh shrimp or lobster tails!), but my standard version is with elbow noodles and canned clams. This dish makes a great emergency meal, but once you've tried it you'll probably eat it regularly.

2 cups	dry noodles	1-2 cans	clams
	garlic: more than ever before	3 cups	water
4 Tbsp	butter or oil (with olive oil)		basil or parsley to taste

The more clams the better; the same with the garlic and butter. Real gluttons use one can of clams per person.

Sauté the pasta and garlic until lightly browned. If you're leery of garlic, fish it out now and discard. Drain the clams and save the liquid. Add the clam broth and water to the pasta, cover tightly and simmer for 15 minutes. Lift the lid and add the clams and basil or parsley. Simmer until the noodles are tender — another five or ten minutes should do it. Serve with garlic bread, biscuits or tortillas.

Variations: With raw seafoods such as shrimp, fish or oysters, add them 10 minute before serving and chop them up if they're very large.

If you don't have clams or seafood you can call this Garlic Delight.

Cashew Noodles with Cauliflower

2-3 cups	cooked noodles or pasta	4 Tbsp	butter or oil
½ cup	chopped onion		garlic to taste
½ cup	cashews		Parmesan cheese (or
1 cup	cauliflower (optional)		sharp cheddar)

Sauté the garlic in the butter or oil. When browned, remove and discard the garlic or, if you prefer, add it later, sprinkled in with the cheese. Now sauté the cashews, slowly and carefully or they'll scorch. Remove from the pan and set aside. Sauté the onion and cauliflower next. Now mix everything together with the noodles (reheat if necessary), smother in cheese and serve.

Rice & Bulgur

Rice Suggestions

Rice doesn't require much dressing-up to make a satisfying main dish. The trick is to cook your plain rice well so that it doesn't have to be disguised to be enjoyable.

Serve plain, steamed or fried rice with gravy, cheese sauce, vinegar and oil dressing (try heating it, too), chile sauces, a sprinkle of grated cheese, sesame seeds, peanuts, cashews and minced dried fruit. Cooked rice can be mixed with nuts, seeds and dried fruit, then wrapped in foil and baked in the coals. Add a few shots of water for steam.

Rice picks up flavors well and simple casseroles can be whipped up with a bare minimum of ingredients. Try Green Rice (lots of parsley, mushrooms and cheese), Curried Rice (curry and sautéed onions), Cheese Rice (onions again, with grated cheese) and so on.

One of our favorite breakfasts is just leftover rice fried with onions and garlic, then scrambled with one or two eggs. I'll add some chile if I have it and maybe a few nuts.

Leftover rice is very good in soups and stews and can even make a nice beverage and dessert. (See *Beverages* and *Desserts*.)

Bulgur, discussed at the end of this section can replace rice in any of these recipes.

Fluffy Steamed White Rice

Like most simple foods, rice is easy to prepare (once you know how) and just as easy to mess up. For four servings:

1 cup   raw white rice
         water or broth
1 Tbsp   oil or butter (optional)

Washing rice removes some nutrients, including the starch that can make the grains gummy. If I'm using my steamed rice for frying later with vegetables I'll wash it so that the grains separate easily. Otherwise, I forget the washing.

Put the rice in a pan with a tightly sealing lid and cover with cold water about ½" over the rice. Measure the water by placing your thumb with the tip just touching the rice. The water should cover your thumbnail. A Japanese friend taught us this method and it seems to work with any amount of rice, any reasonably shaped thumb and any pot. How? Don't ask me.

Add the oil or butter and cover the pan. Bring it to a boil, then reduce the heat to a simmer for 20-25 minutes. Don't peek, just keep the lid on and pray.

If you have a history of burning your rice, try this: remove the pot after 15 to 20 minutes (don't open the lid), wrap it in a thick towel or sweater and let it cook in its own heat for another 10 to 20 minutes.

Steamed Brown Rice

I use a simple and slightly inaccurate saying to remind myself how to cook brown rice: "Brown rice is twice as hard to cook as white rice." This means: use twice as much water as rice and cook it twice as long, 40 minutes versus 20 for white rice. Now that we're thoroughly confused here's the recipe:

1 cup	raw brown rice
2 cups	water or broth
1 Tbsp	oil or butter (optional)

Put water, rice and oil into a tightly sealing pot, bring to a boil, then reduce the heat to a simmer. Cook slowly for 40 to 50 minutes. For those who scorch rice, remove the pot, unopened, after 35 minutes and wrap well in towels or cloth. Set aside for another 15 to 20 minutes, then serve.

Brown Rice in a Pressure Cooker

Cook equal measures of brown rice and water (or broth) for 20 minutes.

If the rice looks old or especially hard, give it another 5 minutes. Every grade of rice cooks differently so be prepared to experiment. When in doubt, use less actual cooking time, wrap the pressure cooker in a towel and allow it to stand unopened for at least 15 minutes.

Quick Mexican Rice

This is an ideal one-pot camping dish with countless variations. Use this recipe when you just can't think of anything else. If you don't have vegetables, just add strong broth instead of water and the rice will be quite tasty. This dish is good for stuffing: baked fish, peppers, cabbage rolls, enchiladas, etc. For four generous servings:

1 cup	raw rice	1 cup	chopped onion
3-4 cups	water or broth		garlic, minced
2-4 Tbsp	margarine or oil		

Additions		most any cooked meat
¼-½ cup	carrot, thinly sliced	or seafood
1	tomato, chopped or	cheese
	equivalent paste,	canned chiles
	powder	mushrooms, other
1 tsp	oregano	vegetables
½ tsp	chile powder (to taste)	nuts and seeds

Sauté the rice, garlic and vegetables until the rice is browned. (If you use fresh tomato, hold it and add with the liquid.)

Add the liquid. We've found that enough water to cover the rice is usually sufficient, though brown rice may need more. Cover and simmer until the rice is tender: about 25 minutes for white rice, 40 minutes or longer for brown rice. If it looks too dry, add more liquid and if it's too wet, remove the lid and steam off some of the water. Five minutes before the rice is to be served I like to sprinkle it heavily with grated cheese.

Rice and Gravy: Serve plain cooked rice smothered in a thick gravy made with (all optional) mushrooms, cheese, chopped onion and canned meat or seafood (especially tuna) and hard boiled eggs. If the rice is added to gravy in the pan and stirred, it tends to form a 'glue stew'. Whenever possible pour the gravy over the heated rice.

Flavored Steamed Rice: Instead of water, add bouillon (one cube per cup of liquid) or broth to raw rice. An excellent smokey broth can be made by soaking half a cup of shredded smoked meat or fish in a cup of boiling water for at least 15 minutes. Add the jerky or smoked fish with the broth or sprinkle it on top of the cooked rice.

Fruit Rice: Substitute fruit juice for half of the liquid when cooking rice. Orange or apple juice is best; grape juice would probably be weird but who knows? Add chopped nuts and dried fruit, cook until tender and serve with a gravy-like sauce or with milk and honey as a dessert. Dried orange rind, finely grated, would also be nice.

Curried Rice: Curry is powerful stuff; add it to taste to already cooked rice, either plain or with the usual condiments. Curry goes well with nut and fruit rices.

Rice and Soup: Add cold cooked rice to stews and soups for 'body'. A cup of cooked rice soaked in a cup of very hot broth for five minutes will serve two people a fast nutritious meal.

Oriental Fried Rice

This dish takes a bit more planning and preparation than most of our one-pot rice recipes but it's worth it. On long expeditions we prepare this rice on Sundays ('Sunday' is any full day of rest).

Although freshly steamed rice can be used I hope you'll try to use leftover rice. The texture is much better for frying and traditional Oriental recipes demand day-old cooked rice. I steam my rice the night before and leave it open to the air to insure that it isn't soggy. Four generous servings:

4 cups	steamed rice	½ cup	sliced mushrooms
4-8 Tbsp	oil or margarine	1 cup	bean sprouts
	garlic to taste	¼-½ cup	sesame seeds
1 tsp	powdered ginger or		***Additions***
	several fresh slices		soy sauce to taste
1 cup	chopped onion		tofu
¼-½ cup	sliced celery		nuts and seeds,
½ cup	sliced carrot		especially sunflower
¼-½ cup	chopped green pepper		eggs
½-1 cup	chopped Chinese cab-		cooked meat or seafood
	bage or any leafy green		

A well-prepared Oriental rice won't be soggy and the vegetables will be cooked but firm, even crunchy. To maintain control you'll want to cut up your vegetables and arrange them by texture. Slice them Oriental style: on an angle, in thin bite-sized pieces. Put the harder things: celery, carrot and onion in a bag or bowl; the green pepper in another; the mushrooms, greens or cabbage and sprouts in another. Make sure that your companions observe this procedure. A lot of cursing and arm waving is good, too, to enhance your image as a selfless chef.

If your sesame seeds aren't toasted do it now, before you add oil to the pan. Sesame oil is common in Oriental dishes and the toasted seeds will give a wonderful flavor to the rice.

I enjoy egg in my fried rice and to keep this operation to one skillet, scramble the egg(s) now, in just a bit of oil or butter, and set aside.

Sauté the sliced garlic and ginger in the oil until both are well browned. Remove and discard the ginger (Lorena eats it like chips) but save the garlic, if you wish. (Add powdered ginger and the crisp garlic later, with the vegetables.)

Now for the fun and drama: we'll be doing some fairly wild frying here so the bigger the pan, the better. Our 10" skillet will be well-filled by this recipe.

Heat several tablespoons of oil or margarine until quite hot but not smoking hot. Add the harder vegetables. Fry, stirring constantly. When they begin to look very shiny and just slightly tender, add the green pepper, stir some more, then the greens, the mushrooms, the sprouts... As soon as the sprouts are stirred in add the rice and the sesame seeds. When the rice is thoroughly heated, gently mix in the scrambled eggs, heat for a few moments and serve. If your friends aren't impressed, you're camping with the wrong crowd.

Rice and Cheese Casserole

This is the 'Old Reliable' recipe that just never seems to lose its appeal. The variations are countless, everything from fresh lobster or mushrooms to toasted sesame seeds.

1 cup	raw rice, white or brown	2 cups	broth or water (3 for brown rice)
2-4 Tbsp	oil, butter		
1 cup	chopped onion (or less)	2 cups	grated cheese (or more; use some Parmesan too)
¼ cup	chopped celery and/or green pepper		
	garlic to taste		***Additions***
		½ cup	milk beaten with 2 eggs

Sauté the raw rice for 5 minutes, then add the onion and vegetables and continue cooking until the onions are tender. Add the broth or water, cover tightly and steam about 10 minutes. Add the cheese and cook another 10-15 minutes, until the rice is done.

Variation: For already cooked rice sauté the vegetables until tender, then stir them into the rice. Add ½ cup of milk beaten with one or two fresh eggs and the cheese, mix well, then cook over very low heat in a tightly sealed pan or bake until the egg is thoroughly congealed and the cheese well melted. (About 30 minutes in a moderate 300°-350° oven.) If you don't have eggs, add powdered milk until the milk is fairly rich and creamy and continue as described. The more cheese, the better.

Rice and Smoked Fish Casserole

Like many casseroles, this dish gets better and better as a leftover. Because the smoked fish is already preserved, the casserole can be kept without refrigeration for at least a full day or two. If you substitute fresh seafood or meat, eat it up sooner.

3-4 cups	cooked rice, preferably brown	½-1 cup	smoked fish, deboned, flaked
1-2 cups	chopped onion	½-1 cup	cheese, including some Parmesan
	garlic to taste		
2-4 Tbsp	oil or butter		***Additions***
1 tsp	thyme (very desirable) pepper (optional)	¼ cup	toasted sunflower or sesame seeds

Sauté the onion and garlic until the onion is tender. Add the spices and smoked fish and simmer until hot, then stir in the rice and cheese. Cook slowly until hot (or bake at 350° for 30 minutes) then remove the pan from the fire, wrap in a heavy towel and allow it to sit at least 15-30 minutes before serving. Don't add the salt until you've tasted the finished casserole; the smoked fish may be salty enough as it is.

Mushroom Rice with Nuts

1 cup	raw rice, white or brown	4 Tbsp	oil or butter
1 cup	chopped onion	2 cups	broth or water (3 cups with brown rice)

½ cup	sliced almonds or other nuts or seeds	*Additions*	
1 cup	sliced or whole mushrooms	½ cup	grated cheese, or more

Sauté the raw rice until very lightly browned (about 5 minutes) then add the onion, mushroom and nuts and sauté until the onions are tender or the rice is browned, whichever comes first (and hopefully together). Add the broth and cover tightly, steam until tender and fluffy. If you add cheese, just sprinkle it over the rice ten or fifteen minutes before it is done.

With already cooked rice: Sauté the onions, nuts and mushrooms until the onions are tender. Now add the rice, stirring frequently, and the cheese. The broth won't be used since you've already cooked the rice.

Rice Casserole . . . or Cake

This is a main dish or a dessert; you've got until we get to the nutmeg to make up your mind.

2 cups	cooked rice	2 Tbsp	butter, margarine or oil
1	beaten egg	½ tsp	each nutmeg, cinnamon and vanilla and —
1 cup	sour milk		
½ cup	flour	¼ cup	honey or sugar
1 tsp	baking soda		*or*
½ tsp	salt		oregano, garlic and pepper

Mash the cooked rice lightly with a fork, mixing in the eggs, flour and milk. If your milk isn't sour, don't worry about it. Add the baking soda and salt, the melted fat or oil and . . . time to decide: for a rice dessert add nutmeg, cinnamon and vanilla (½ teaspoon of each) and the sweetener. Blend everything well, form it into patties and fry in hot oil or butter until browned and thoroughly warmed. Serve with jam or syrup, yogurt, cream, etc.

As a main dish: Instead of nutmeg and sweetener, mix in the spices (some sweetener can be used if you wish) and form into patties, fry and serve as is or with a gravy. The mixture can also be baked or cooked in an oiled pan over a low heat. Grated cheese on top is nice.

Bulgur Wheat

Bulgur is wheat that has been parboiled, dried and cracked. It makes an excellent substitute for rice. In fact, bulgur is one of the most versatile grains we have, though most cooks are unfamiliar with it. Bulgur can be used cold, as a salad, dropped raw or cooked into soups, prepared as a hot cereal or in a variety of main dishes, especially one-pot casseroles. Campers will find this highly compact multi-use food very useful.

Because bulgur is harder than white rice and noodles it takes more water and more time to cook. However, bulgur also expands more than you'd probably expect and half a cup of raw bulgur will make 2 to 3 very generous servings.

In general, cook one part of bulgur with 3 to 4 parts of water or broth and use half as much bulgur as the amount of rice or noodles called for in a recipe. For example, a one-pot rice dish that uses 1 cup of rice can be made with ½ cup bulgur (and 1½-2 cups water).

Bulgur is easily prepared by soaking. Measure out a portion of bulgur, add boiling water, wrap well (or use a wide-mouthed vacuum bottle) and set aside overnight or for a few hours. This bulgur can be used in any recipe calling for cooked rice or noodles. This is also an excellent method for preparing bulgur as a breakfast cereal. (See *Cooked Cereal.*)

Experiment with bulgur recipes — the texture, for example, can be adjusted considerably by adding more or less liquid when cooking. I'm sure you'll find, as we have, that bulgur is much more than just a novelty food. (Also see *Salads: Bulgur.*)

Potatoes

Potatoes Baked Without an Oven

Scrub the potatoes, dry them and wipe lightly with cooking oil. To get fancy give the spuds a sprinkle of garlic powder, herbs and minced onion. Wrap tightly in aluminum foil (shiny side facing inward) and place the potatoes directly on top of the coals. On a stove, put the wrapped spuds in a heavy closed skillet. Turn every ten to fifteen minutes. The potatoes will be cooked within 30-40 minutes. Test with a fork or sharp twig; when done, a potato can be pierced easily to the center.

This cooking method works for other vegetables as well, especially onions, carrots, squash or anything tough.

Leftovers: Slice or chop and sauté with onions (raw or cooked) in butter or oil. Serve with fried eggs.

Chop and mix into a salad. See *Fast Potato Salad.*

Mash and mix with other ingredients. See *Mashed Potatoes.*

Fast Baked Spuds

Slice unpeeled spuds lengthwise into halves or quarters. Wipe lightly with oil or margarine (butter tends to scorch) and sprinkle with paprika, garlic powder, salt and pepper. Wrap in foil (a flat packet with spud slices side by side or individually) and bake on top of the coals until tender, usually within 30 minutes.

Variations: About 10 minutes before the potatoes are tender, open the packet and sprinkle grated or sliced cheese (Parmesan or cheddar) over the spuds.

Serve with a hot sauce, vinegar and oil salad dressing or mayonnaise.

Mashed Potatoes

Mashed spuds can be as simple or as complex as you wish. If you use all of the Additions, you'll have a one-dish meal. The amounts given here are for modest individual servings. I'd easily double or even triple the amount of potato used, especially if it was to be a main course or if you want leftovers.

1 cup, handful or average	*Additions*
spud per person	butter, oil or salad
milk, cream or broth	dressing
egg	minced onion
salt, pepper, spices	parsley

Cut potatoes into egg-sized pieces. We leave the skins on; they are flavorful and nutritious. Steam in a small amount of lightly salted water until just tender, not mushy. Don't boil and drown the potatoes; it isn't necessary and dilutes their flavor.

When cooked, drain off the water and save it for soup stock, making breads or for mixing with dried milk or bouillon.

Mash the potatoes (a fork will do) and add milk (enriched with powdered milk or a very rich powdered milk) or eggs. It is easy to overdo the liquid, so go slow and add a few squirts at a time. Broth or bouillon can be used with or instead of milk. Butter, cooking oil or salad dressing will also give a creamier texture and add flavor.

Mexicans use mashed potato as a taco and sandwich filling, served hot or cold.

Leftovers: Form into patties and fry in butter or oil until nicely browned. Serve with grated cheese, hot sauce or gravy.

Dissolve into soups, hot broth or gravy as a thickener.

Form leftover patties into flat cakes, balls or biscuits and roll them in sesame seeds. Fry in hot oil or butter until browned or bake in foil for 20 minutes.

Shape the leftover spuds into a flattened donut about the size of a pancake. Heat a tablespoon of oil or fat in a skillet, add the potato donut and crack an egg or two into the hole. Fry and flip, serve as is or with gravy or sauce.

Form leftover spuds into egg-sized balls and place them gently on top of thick stews or beans; heat for at least 15 minutes and serve. Your potato dumplings can also be browned in hot oil or butter first.

Instant Potatoes

I always transfer dried potatoes to a suitable container, burn the factory packages and promptly forget the mixing instructions. The following should be typical for off-the-shelf dried potatoes; 3 servings (stingy ones):

¾ cup	water	½ cup	milk
1 Tbsp	margarine or butter	¾ cup	potato flakes
1/3 tsp	salt		

Bring the water to a boil, add the salt and butter, remove from the heat and add the milk and potatoes. Stir gently and serve.

For 2 servings of Potato Buds (Betty Crocker):

2/3 cup	water	¼ tsp	salt
2 Tbsp	milk	2/3 cup	Potato Buds
1 Tbsp	butter or margarine		

Heat everything but the Buds to a boil, then remove from the heat, add the Potato Buds, stir and allow to stand for 30 seconds, then whip the potatoes with a fork and serve.

Variations: As you reconstitute dried potatoes add one or even all of the following: dill, paprika, bacon bits, garlic, minced raw or dried onion, a fresh egg (decrease liquid added), grated cheese, fresh or dried parsley, mushrooms.

French Fried Potato Slices

If this doesn't satisfy your greasy junk-food cravings, nothing will. I love french fries with fish or beans, but they also make a good filling snack.

1 potato per person	grated Parmesan cheese
oil	minced green chile
salt to taste	hot sauce
Additions	vinegar or lime juice
garlic and chile powder	

Cut well-scrubbed but unpeeled potatoes into ¼" thick rounds (slices). As they dry off on a cloth or piece of paper, heat ¼-½" of oil in a skillet. Get it hot but not smoking hot. Fry a big handful of potato slices until lightly browned but not fully cooked. Remove and drain for at least five minutes.

When all of the slices have been fried once and drained, refry them a second time until fully browned and crisp on the outside. The thinnest slices will become potato chips.

Serve garnished with salt, pepper, garlic salt, mild chile, lime juice, vinegar or hot sauce. *Or:* sprinkle lightly with Parmesan or heavily with cheddar cheese and chopped green chiles, wrap in foil or warm in a closed pan until the cheese melts. (Use leftover oil for frying or bread-making.)

Mexican Potato Cakes

These fried cakes keep well and we usually make enough at dinner to have leftovers for breakfast, served with eggs. In Mexico, potato cakes (called *tortas de papa*) are served as a taco filling or floating in a rich tomato sauce. We are impatient and usually nab them right out of the pan, sizzling hot.

2/3 cup	mashed potatoes	1-2	eggs, separated
½ cup	grated cheese or more		*Additions*
	oil or butter for frying		sesame seeds

Separate the yolk from the egg white. Beat the white with a fork or whisk until it's stiff and fluffy, then beat the yolk (just mildly; it won't fluff up at all). Stir the beaten yolk into the beaten white. Got that?

Mix the cheese and the mashed potatoes (if you use herbs, add them now) and form the mixture into round patties. Dip the patties in the egg and fry in ¼" of hot butter or oil until browned.

If you like sesame seeds, roll the patties in toasted seeds before the egg mixture.

Yukon Spuds

John Kibbons is a wilderness guide in Alaska. Some of his tall tales may be hard to swallow but his recipes go down very easy. Like many of his outdoor lies, this dish has a surprise ending.

1	large spud per person, sliced in ¼" thick rounds	1-2	green peppers, chopped
		1 cup	grated or thinly sliced cheese per person
1	small onion per person, chopped or sliced		butter (a lot)
several	crisp bacon strips (optional but desirable)		salt and pepper

Grease or butter a skillet, preferably a deep one, or better yet, a Dutch oven. Cover the bottom of the pan with potato slices and sprinkle with cheese, onion, green pepper, bacon and dabs of butter. Salt and pepper to taste as you add another layer of spud slices, more cheese, onion, bacon, etc. Do at least three layers, topped with whatever cheese and stuff that's left over. Cover tightly and slow cook over the coals or in a 350° oven for about an hour, or until the spuds are easily pierced with a fork.

Here's the twist: remove the lid, cover the pan with a large plate and turn everything upside down. If the potatoes are stuck to the pan with crisp cheese, scrape it clean and serve it all; the overcooked cheese will be salty and rich with butter.

Potato and Fish Hash

Norwegian fishermen call this *plugfisk*. With a cup of strong coffee and a brilliant sunrise, it's a great way to start the day.

2-4	steamed spuds		garlic
2-4 Tbsp	butter or oil	1 cup	cooked fish, deboned
1	medium onion, chopped		and flaked
			salt and pepper

Cut the steamed potatoes into bite-sized pieces. I cook them the night before so they'll be firm and fairly dry. Heat the butter or oil and sauté the onions and potatoes (we add garlic). Just before they're done, add the fish and continue frying until the potatoes are browned and the fish is thoroughly warmed. Serve with fried eggs and liberal amounts of catsup.

Variations: Smoked fish or meat, canned meat. Sauté the onion separately, mix with the cubed potatoes, smother in cheese and bake or heat over a low flame until hot.

Breads, Biscuits & Tortillas

If seawater is available it can be used instead of fresh water in bread and tortilla recipes. Be sure, however, that you eliminate all other salt from the recipe. Salt-water can be used to activate dry yeast but fresh water works better.

Leavening: Yeast and baking powder are interchangeable. Use equivalent amounts of either but allow yeast doughs to rest in a warm place for at least 15 minutes. The leavening can be eliminated entirely from most bread recipes but your bread will be flatter and much more dense.

Tortillas and fried breads are often made without leavening, though it is nice to let the dough rest for 2 to 3 hours. This improves the flexibility and texture of the dough. At the least, allow the dough to rest for 15 minutes.

Baking powder bread mixtures should be stirred just enough to blend the ingredients. Yeast mixes, however, need more stirring.

Salt is important in any bread but sweeteners are not. We sometimes use sugar to help activate dry yeast, especially in cool weather; a teaspoonful should do it.

Flavored breads and tortillas are very simple to prepare and the variations are endless. I like to mix toasted sesame seeds into tortilla dough or roll out the tortillas over a sprinkle of seeds. Carraway seeds, poppy seeds, dill seeds, mild chile powder, garlic powder, pinches of cumin and even grated cheese can be mixed into all types of bread doughs.

A basic bread can be baked, fried, griddle-cooked or roasted (as bannock). Each cooking method will give a distinct flavor and texture to identical batches of dough. Don't get in a rut: experiment with bread and create your own recipes and cooking techniques.

To rejuvenate stiff or stale bread and tortillas, warm them in a hot pan or directly over the coals of a fire, then wrap in a thick cloth. Moistening the cloth will also help soften the bread.

Dried milk is often added to camping breads to increase their nutritive value. Unfortunately, cooking reduces the food value of milk. Drink your milk to get the most benefits from it.

Thick Flour Tortillas

This bread is our all-time favorite and on long camping trips we'll try to make tortillas about every other day. Don't be discouraged if your first batches of tortillas aren't perfect. Like all basic foods, it takes practice to get them just right.

4 cups	flour (half white and half brown is best)	1 Tbsp	dry yeast *or* no leavening
2-4 Tbsp	oil, shortening or lard	1-1¼ cups	warm water
½-1½ tsp	salt		***Additions***
1 Tbsp	baking powder *or*	½ tsp	sugar

In a large bowl or bag, mix the flour, salt and oil and the baking powder (if you use it instead of yeast). Yeast gives bread a much nicer flavor than baking powder and it's probably better for you. The few minutes it takes to mix up the yeast is well worth it. If you don't use any leavening, it's nice to let the dough rest 15 minutes or more.

Mix the yeast with the sugar and ¼ cup of warm water. Allow to stand until foamy, usually 15 to 30 minutes. The sugar is optional but speeds up the yeast's development.

Mix the flour with the yeast, working it with your hands and adding more water as needed. Every flour is different but we usually add about a cup of water while kneading. You want a dough that won't quite stick to your bowl or fingers.

Form the dough into a ball, cover with a cloth and set aside. With the yeast, let the dough double. If you have the time, punch it down and let it rise again. For baking powder, let it set for 15 minutes to an hour (more resting won't hurt but the dough may begin to stiffen).

Cooking the tortillas is the critical part of the operation. We use a tin griddle placed over a very hot fire, but you can use an ungreased griddle or frying pan on a stove. The tortillas will be cooked fast and hot to keep them from drying out too much. Very dry tortillas become crackers.

Squeeze off a lump of dough the size of a small egg. Flour your hands liberally, as well as a rolling pin or bottle and whatever surface you'll flatten the tortillas on. We've used driftwood boards, the blades of paddles, a car hood...

Flatten the dough ball with the palms of your hands and then iron it out with the rolling pin until it's uniformly ⅛" to ¼" thick. If it's not round, don't worry, it'll taste as good as the others. Pick the tortillas up and slap it vigorously three or four times from the palm of one hand to the other to shake off excess flour. Tortilla dough is tough and flexible so don't be leery of throwing them around.

Lay the tortilla on the hot dry griddle. If the temperature is just right, bubbles will pop up in about 30 seconds. When the tortilla begins to smoke, flip it over. A well-made tortilla will inflate after being flipped. Don't pop it; the steam inside is cooking the dough.

When it stops steaming or begins to sag (or starts scorching), remove and wrap in a thick cloth. Constant flipping will make your tortillas tough and stiff, so try to get them cooked with just one flip. Practice and pay close attention or your tortillas will overcook.

These tortillas will keep for days and should soften nicely when reheated. Flour tortillas can be kept in a plastic bag (corn tortillas go sour quickly in plastic), but watch them closely after two days for mold or transfer them to a cloth or paper wrapper.

Sweet Fried Tortillas

This is the Mexican equivalent of the donut.

tortilla dough (see previous recipe)	oil for frying
3 eggs, beaten	sugar

Mix the eggs into the tortilla dough and fry the raw tortillas in lots of hot oil until brown and crisp. Sprinkle liberally with sugar or smear with honey and serve while still hot.

Leftover Tortillas

Leftover tortillas can be puzzling. What can be done with half a dozen rock-hard corn or flour discs? Here are a few ideas:

• Keep corn tortillas wrapped in paper or cloth, not plastic. If the tortillas can't breathe they'll quickly go sour. Flour tortillas, however, can be kept for up to three days in plastic. After that, transfer them to paper or cloth or they'll mold. (The lime used for processing corn can become quite bitter in a plastic bag or container.)

• Sun dried corn tortillas can be used for snacks. When brittle-dry garnish with refried beans, hot sauce, grated cheese, vegetables or even peanut butter.

• Bake tortillas in a warm (not hot) oven until crisp to make chips.

• Tortilla chips: this is the Mexican version of Doritos. Sprinkle corn tortillas with heavily salted water and allow to dry. Chop or break the tortillas into pieces (cut into small triangles if you start with fresh tortillas) and fry in hot oil until golden and crisp. Fried chips absorb a great deal of oil; eat them within two days or they'll turn slightly rancid.

• Sauté hard flour tortillas in butter. When soft, sprinkle grated cheese on top, roll tightly, and eat like a breadstick.

• Cover chips with grated cheese, minced onion and tomato, canned or fresh slices of chile pepper, layer in a pan or foil packet and bake until the cheese melts. Douse with hot sauce or catsup.

• To soften a really stiff tortilla, heat a skillet until it's quite warm but not searing hot, drop in a tortilla and a teaspoon of water, cover tightly for 15 seconds and serve. Too damp? Use less water and/or less time in the pan.

Pancakes and Pan Bread

I was never much of a pancake fan until Lorena used this recipe. It takes a bit more preparation than some pancakes but the difference, especially if you use the fluffy egg whites, is dramatic.

2 cups	flour (we use 2/3 cup each white, brown, corn)	1 Tbsp	sugar or honey
		2 cups	milk, sweet or sour, or water
1 tsp	salt	3	eggs
2-3 tsp	baking powder	½ cup	oil, melted butter or margarine
1 tsp	cinnamon		

Mix the flour, salt, baking powder, cinnamon and sugar. If you use honey, dissolve it in the milk or water. Mix the milk or water (and honey) in a second bowl or bag, with the egg and oil or melted butter. Combine this with the flour mixture and rest for 15 minutes in a warm place (you and the batter). Fry the pancakes on a hot, lightly greased griddle or skillet. Avoid flipping them more than once or they'll go flat and heavy.

For extra fluffy pancakes: Separate the egg whites from the yolks and add the yolks to the milk mixture. When the batter has rested for 15 minutes, beat the egg whites stiff and fluffy with a fork or whisk. Gently stir them into the batter and fry.

Sweet Pan Bread: Make up the pancake batter, fill a lightly greased skillet or pot an inch or so deep with batter. Cook slowly in the coals or bake.

Fried Biscuits

As you may have noticed by now, the recipes for simple baked and fried breads are all quite similar. Small changes in ingredients, however, can have surprising results in terms of texture and flavor. This is a favorite recipe we use when craving oil.

2 cups	flour (we mix white, brown and corn)	3-6 Tbsp	shortening or oil
2-3 tsp	baking powder	1 cup	boiling water
1 tsp	salt		oil for frying

Mix half of the flour with the dry yeast. Combine the warm water with the shortening, sugar and salt and mix it in with the flour and yeast. Beat for the dough into inch thick balls, then flatten them out. (Flour the back of this book and use it as a press.) You want patties about ¼" thick. Fry in oil or butter until browned and thoroughly cooked. If you wish, cook the biscuits on a dry griddle, like tortillas. Serve with honey, jam or gravy.

Breadsticks

Make these at home and stuff them in your shirt pocket to munch as you travel.

3 cups	flour (white, brown or mix)	2 Tbsp	shortening, oil or margarine
1 cup	rolled oats, instant or regular	1 tsp	salt
1 Tbsp	or packet of dry yeast		*Additions*
1¼ cups	warm water (approx.)		sesame or poppy seeds
		1 Tbsp	sugar

Mix half of the flour with the dry yeast. Combine the warm water witht the shortening, sugar and salt and mix it in with the flour and yeast. Beat for 3 to 5 minutes, then stir in the second half of the flour and the oats. Cover and let the dough rise to double its size in a warm place. Punch the dough down, wait 10 minutes, then begin shaping the breadsticks.

Cut the dough into equal sized pieces (12 to 24) or tear off lumps and roll them between your floured hands until they're the size you like. We make ours ½" to ¾" thick. Lay the sticks on a greased baking sheet and let them rise until they've doubled in size. Bake for 20 to 25 minutes in a 375° oven.

Variation: Mix sesame seeds into the raw dough.

Dumplings from Scratch

Dumplings are basically balls of bread. They can make a full meal out of a simple pot of soup, stew or even broth.

1 cup	flour (½ white, ½ whole wheat)
¼ tsp	salt
⅛-¼ cup	oil or melted butter
½ cup	water or milk
1-2 tsp	baking powder *or*
1 Tbsp	yeast (both optional)

Additions

¼ tsp	herb(s)
	garlic to taste
¼ cup	minced onion
½ cup	grated cheese
¼ cup	toasted sesame seeds
1	egg

Mix the dry ingredients, butter or oil, and any additions. Add the water, but if you use an egg reduce the water to just 2-3 Tbsp. You want a dough that is wetter than bread dough but not runny. If you use yeast, allow the dough to rest in a warm place for 15-60 minutes.

Spoon the dough into a scalding hot or boiling pot of soup, stew or broth. Cover the pot tightly and don't peek! Small dumplings will be cooked in 5 minutes, larger ones take 10 to 15 minutes.

When the dumplings are cooked remove them and drop in another batch. Over-crowding leads to gummy messes.

Quick Dumplings

Store-bought biscuit mixes can make short work out of fixing dumplings. Add any or all of the Additions suggestions above and follow the same cooking directions.

1 cup	biscuit or corn bread mix
¼-1/3 cup	water or milk

Quick Biscuit Mix, Crackers and Tarts

Prepared biscuit mixes can simplify your bread making. We use Krusteaz's whole wheat type.

2 cups	biscuit mix
2/3 cup	milk or water

Additions

grated cheese
minced canned green chiles
dried onion
garlic
sesame seeds
honey
cinnamon

Mix the milk and biscuit flour with a fork and add any of the variations you care for. Flatten the dough out on a floured surface to the thickness of a pie crust. Cut into whatever shape you want and to make it look like crackers, poke the dough with a fork. Bake at 400° for 8 minutes or fry in butter or hot oil.

Variations: Brush with melted butter, egg white or milk, sprinkle with cinnamon and sugar and bake.

Fold raw dough squares or triangles over fillings: cooked meat, fish, cheese, jam, what-have-you. Press edges of the 'tart' with a fork to seal and fry.

Fried Bread & Biscuits

5 cups	flour	2 tsp	oil or melted fat
1 tsp	salt	2 cups	warm water
5 tsp	baking powder		

Mix everything well and form it into cakes or patties about ¼" thick. Fry until well browned in hot oil or cook as a tortilla on a hot dry griddle or pan.

Very Simple Fried Bread

3 cups	flour	water
½ tsp	salt	oil
2 tsp	baking powder	

Mix flour, baking powder and water to form a thick batter. Heat oil in a skillet and spoon or pour in enough batter to cover the bottom of the pan. Fry slowly. This recipe may not win awards from Betty Crocker but it'll keep you in bread.

Basic Bannock Bread

Bannock is a frontier style bread that is simple, nourishing and entertaining to cook. Give everyone, restless children and yawning adults, their own stick and wad of dough.

1 cup	flour		warm water
pinch	salt		*Additions*
1 tsp	baking powder	1	handful of raisins
1 Tbsp	butter, margarine or oil		

Mix all of the ingredients until you've got a pliable dough that is neither too sticky to get off your fingers or so dry it won't stretch and bend. Work it around for a while, then form it into long sausage-like rolls. Wrap these in a loose coil or spiral around green sticks that have been peeled and warmed in the fire. Toast the bannock slowly over the coals until browned and fully cooked. Serve plain or with jam, syrup or honey.

Cornmeal Cakes

1 cup	corn meal	1	egg, beaten
½ tsp	salt		oil or butter
½ tsp	baking soda		*Additions*
1 cup	sour milk or water		raisins

Combine everything but the oil or butter into a thick batter. Heat the oil and fry the dough as patties or cakes until well browned.

Cooked Cereals

Mush is an elemental food, a sort of manna in liquid form. Although processed 'instant cooking' cereals are the most popular, less refined cereals are more nutritious, much less expensive and surprisingly simple to cook. With the addition of a few ingredients such as cinnamon, honey, dried fruit and milk, unprocessed grain cereals can be tasty wholesome meals, useful for snacks and dinner as well as breakfast.

The difference between a good bowl of mush and a serving of unappetizing paste is often a matter of the cook's attitude. Mush seems to invite ridicule and disrespect as well as a macho-disdain for simple cooking procedures and directions. Mush disasters make good camp stories but lousy meals for those who have to choke them down.

Very few breakfast cereals require much actual stove time and even the least processed types — rolled rye and oats, bulgur, seven grain, etc. — need only a few minutes of actual boiling. The secret, in fact, is to avoid cooking the cereal longer than needed to start it softening, then remove from the flame and set aside. Wrap the pot well and allow it to sit for 15 to 30 minutes. The cereal will be tender, with a firm texture rather than gummy, and will have a full rich flavor.

My procedure for cooking cereal is automatic, regardless of the type of cereal I'm using:

Measure and heat the water, adding a dash of salt, cinnamon, honey to taste, raisins, banana chips, nuts or minced dried fruit. Cover and bring slowly to a boil.

Stir in a measured amount of cereal — 'eyeballing it' is only for experienced cooks — boil for a few minutes (see cooking times below), simmer for a few more, then wrap and set aside. This is an almost infallible method that can be adapted to any cereal. The general rule-of-thumb: cook processed cereals for no more than 2-3 minutes before wrapping and setting them aside, and hard, unrefined cereals no more than 5-7 minutes.

Leftover mush is widely touted as an excellent ingredient for breads and pastries. I find it about as convenient as leftover egg whites and twice as sticky. Lorena insists on packing leftover mush into plastic bags for later use; I face the problem head-on and bury it.

The finer the texture of your mush, the more difficult it will be to get the pot clean when the meal is over. I have literally had to sandpaper mush off an aluminum kettle. To avoid this, serve the mush and then immediately fill the pot back to the brim with water. In the desert, such extravagant water use is impossible and I merely wipe out the pot and forget about it. The hardened mush cooks away into other foods and won't be noticed.

No matter how often I cook mush I can't seem to accurately recall the proper proportion of water and cereal. Here then are some typical cooking instructions:

Cups Required for 2 Servings

Cereal	Measure	Water + ¼ tsp salt	Cooking Time (minutes at sea level)
Quaker Minute Oats	2/3	1 2/3	1
Old Fashioned Oats	2/3	1½	5
oat flakes, unrefined	2/3	1½	5 (chewy) 20 (creamy)
oats, rolled, quick	¾	1½	8
oat groats	½	2	soak, simmer 45
Scotch oats	½	1½	25 plus 2 resting
hot granola	1	2	1 (chewy) 7-8 (creamy)
7 grain	½	2	7-10
Wheat Hearts	½	2	2-3
Malt-O-Meal	1/3	1 2/3	1
Cream of Wheat, regular	1/3	2-2¼	10
quick	1/3	1¾-2	2½
instant	1/3	1 1/3-1½	30 seconds plus 1 minute resting
wheat flakes	2/3	1½	5 (chewy) 15 (creamy)
quick	2/3	1½	1 6-7 (creamy)
wholewheat farina	¾	2	10 plus 5 resting
cracked wheat	½	1½	7-10 uncovered
Quick Grits	1/3	1¼	4-5
corn grits	½	1½	45

Note: measures, cooking times and servings were taken from the instructions on the cereal packages and may vary slightly from one brand of cereal to another.

Hot or Cold Bulgur Cereal

This is an excellent time-saving method for preparing the next day's breakfast as you lazily sip your evening tea. For two servings:

½ cup	raw bulgur	2 Tbsp	honey
1½ cups	boiling water	handful	raisins
¼ tsp	salt	dash	cinnamon

Pour boiling water over the bulgur and stir in the other ingredients. Cover tightly and insulate the pot well. In the morning, add milk to the cereal and reheat or just eat it cold. (This method works with any long cooking cereal.)

Sauces, Gravies, Marinades & Dips

A clever cook uses sauces the way a bricklayer uses plaster — to conceal mistakes and irregularities. Sauces convert leftovers into 'new' dishes, disguise plain rice or noodles, give fresh interest to old vegetables and otherwise make camp cooking a lot easier. Most sauces will keep for at least a couple of days without refrigeration, even in warm weather. Your best bet, however, especially if it's a hot day, is to cook them every morning and evening. A spoiled sauce won't kill you but it might taste rather odd.

Rich Tomato Sauce

This is an excellent spaghetti sauce but we also use it liberally on rice, potatoes, fried tacos, fish, melted cheese sandwiches, eggs... you name it, most any dish can stand a few spoonfuls of a good sauce. The quantities of ingredients are very loose.

When hiking, Lorena likes to prepare a tomato sauce at home a day in advance. Cook off most of the liquid so that the sauce is a rich paste. In camp, thin out the sauce with water and/or a shot of red or white wine.

¼ cup	minced onion	4 Tbsp	oil or olive oil and butter
¼ cup	minced garlic (or less, to taste)		tomato sauce, puree or crystals

pinches oregano, basil, thyme, rosemary, pepper

Additions

¼ cup green pepper
¼ cup minced celery
¼ cup minced carrot
¼ cup minced zucchini

1 cup chopped tomatoes
fresh or dried chile peppers
fresh or dried pine-apple bits
¼ cup honey and two Tbsp vinegar
bouillon or broth

Sauté everything but the tomatoes and tomato sauce until the hardest vegetables are tender. Add the chopped tomatoes (optional) and the spices; simmer for half an hour or a day, the longer the better. Keep the sauce liquid with bouillon, broth, water, tomato juice and small shots of red or white wine.

Red Chile Sauce

We use chile sauces on just about everything, including salads. Don't overdo the chile or the sauce will be too hot to enjoy. Macho chile eaters rarely appreciate the fine flavor of a properly balanced chile sauce, which never assaults the senses or the stomach.

If you don't like chile at all, leave it out; the sauce will still taste quite good.

2 ripe red tomatoes, chopped small
1 medium onion, minced
garlic, as much as you can handle, minced
salt to taste

1-2 Tbsp lemon/lime juice or vinegar
chiles, fresh or canned, minced, to taste
½ tsp oregano
¼ tsp cumin

Lime juice tends to neutralize the hotness of the chile but you can also cool them down by removing the seeds and inner white veins. Wash your hands after handling chiles; a burn in the eyes or nose is nothing to laugh about. Serve this sauce as is or cook it for awhile.

Green Chile Sauce

With a little practice you'll be able to whip up a chile sauce that is tastier, far cheaper and more appealing than anything that comes from a bottle.

6-10 small green tomatoes (the type covered with a leafy membrane)
or
3 regular green tomatoes

1 medium onion, minced
2-3 garlic cloves, minced
1 green chile (or less)
salt to taste

Chop up the tomatoes (use pulp and juice, too) and mash all the ingredients together with a strong fork until the sauce is spooning consistency. Simmer until fully cooked (15-30 minutes) and serve hot or cold. This is a rather tart sauce that can liven up a dull portion of beans or a serving of plain steamed rice.

Golden Sauce

4 Tbsp	melted butter or margarine	2 Tbsp	lemon juice or vinegar
1 Tbsp	prepared mustard		

Blend the ingredients well with a fork or shake them in a bag or jar. Serve over cooked or raw vegetables.

Homestyle Gravy

2-3 Tbsp	flour (white, brown, corn or mixture)		*Additions*
			bits of crisp fried bacon
3-4 Tbsp	oil, butter or bacon fat		shredded smoked meat
2-3 cups	milk, water, bouillon or stock		mild red chile (with the flour)
	garlic and herbs to taste	1-2	eggs (raw, after the liquid has been added)
	salt and pepper		a dollop of red wine...

Brown the flour well in the oil or fat, stirring constantly to avoid scorching. Add the liquid a quarter cup or less at a time, not all at once. Dilute it slowly, stirring out the lumps and allowing the gravy to reheat before adding more liquid. The first half cup will probably combine with the flour to form a thick paste.

If your gravy is too thin, just keep stirring patiently and it'll soon thicken. Gravy also thickens considerably as it cools, so if it looks a little too stiff in the pan, it'll probably turn to pudding by the time you serve it.

It takes ten or fifteen minutes to make a good gravy, but it's time well spent. Add the herbs whenever you want to.

Variation: Sesame or Nut Gravy: toast ¼ to ½ cup of seeds or nuts in an unoiled skillet until nicely browned. Remove from the pan and cool. Add the toasted seeds or nuts as you brown the flour for the gravy. Serve over plain rice or noodles.

White Sauce

White sauce is just another name for white milk gravy. Follow the instructions for Homestyle Gravy but use white flour and don't let it get very brown. Butter or margarine is preferable to oil or lard. Thin the gravy with milk and add paprika or one herb.

Variations: Add ½ teaspoon of curry powder to make a curry sauce. Sauté 1 teaspoon of minced onion with up to one cup of mushrooms when browning the flour for the sauce.

Cheese Sauce

This sauce is really gravy with melted cheese. I much prefer cheese sauce made from a brown flour and milk gravy rather than a white gravy. The brown gravy has more flavor and looks healthier than a pale sauce. In any case, just mix:

1 cup finely grated, shaved or chopped cheese into a bubbling gravy (2 cups) that is a bit more 'watery' than normal. The cheese will thicken the gravy.

Mock Hollandaise Sauce

Mix equal parts of melted butter or margarine with fresh lemon juice or vinegar. Serve over fish or vegetables or as a dip.

Sashimi or Seafood Dips

Thinly sliced raw fish is a delicacy we often enjoy while boating and beach camping. Tasty dips are an important part of the sashimi arrangement and while kayaking in Baja we carried a small set of matched scallop shells to serve our dips.

Note: If sashimi makes you squeamish, try the dips on cooked seafoods, especially fried oysters, steamed clams, whole steamed shrimp and battered fish filets.

The following are our personal favorites; many other dips and dip combinations can be improvised from commonly available ingredients. Use individually or blend some together.

soy sauce
Chinese or dry mustard
  (prepared with vinegar
  or water)
canned chile pepper
  juice (mix with soy
  sauce and dried
  mustard)

mustard and catsup
  mixed with horse-
  radish
tofu sauce (by Westbrae)
toasted sesame seeds
sesame salt
horseradish, dry or
  prepared

Make up small servings of a few tablespoons. As they're tasted and eaten up, replenish them or create new combinations.

Sesame Salt

Sesame salt is a traditional Japanese garnish and salt substitute. We use it on salads, popcorn, seafood, casseroles and just about anything else that needs salt.

5-8 Tbsp   sesame seeds
  1 Tbsp   salt

pinch   garlic powder (optional)

I like my seeds well toasted. Grind the seeds coarsely with a mortar and pestle or electric blender. Not too fine, or the sesame salt will compact and tend to harden. Mix in the salt with a fork or add it as you grind the seeds. Use in place of regular salt.

Universal Sauce and Marinade

We use this on everything from shishkabob to salads. It keeps well and can be freshened up from time to time with new and different ingredients.

2/3 cup	salad oil (mix in some olive oil, too)	1 tsp	garlic powder
			Additions
2 Tbsp	powdered butter (Butter Buds)	¼ cup	vinegar or lemon juice
		½ tsp	of other spices
½ tsp	thyme	1 tsp	dried vegetable broth
½ tsp	salt		or a bouillon cube

Try basting grilled fish and meats with this sauce or sprinkle it over fried or baked potatoes, tacos, cold beans...

Teriyaki Sauce and Marinade

You haven't lived until you've tried this on fresh venison tenderloin or mahi-mahi.

¼ cup	soy sauce		*Additions*
¼ cup	sugar or honey	1 tsp	worchestershire sauce
1-3 Tbsp	powdered ginger	1 tsp	dry or prepared mustard
1-3 Tbsp	garlic, fresh or powdered	2 Tbsp	lime juice
			chile powder to taste
			herbs

We personally prefer more garlic and ginger; 3 Tbsp each gives the sauce real zing. Mix the ingredients and marinate the raw foods for at least half an hour. Cook over open coals if you can, basting constantly with leftover sauce.

This sauce makes an interesting glaze for smoked foods; just baste it on from time to time.

Yogurt

Yogurt can be cultured while camping from a vehicle or boat and, if you're dedicated, even while hiking. It is an excellent way to use dried milk. Yogurt makes a very nice dressing for vegetables, tacos, salads and casseroles. With fruit or honey it is both a dessert and a breakfast.

Many people go through elaborate yogurt rituals, claiming that its preparation is somewhere between Art and Science. Our method is simple and reliable.

1 cup	boiling water	1 cup	yogurt culture *or*
1 cup	cold water		¼-½ cup unpasteurized
1 cup	dry powdered milk		yogurt
		1	clean plastic or glass jar

Mix the cold and boiling water together (this combination gives the proper temperature) with the milk and yogurt culture or fresh yogurt. Pour the mixture into a jar, cover and set it in the sun or other warm place. We put ours into a spare ice chest or wrap it in a sleeping bag or jacket and set it in the sun.

Avoid handling the yogurt until it is firm, usually about 6 to 10 hours. Make fresh batches frequently or your yogurt culture will go sour.

Vegetables

Unless we're camping from our van and have access to an assortment of pots and pans, we prefer to eat our vegetables mixed with staples such as beans, rice or noodles, usually in a one-pot dish. This can get boring, however, and even hikers can afford to occasionally serve a vegetable as a side dish. Whatever your circumstances, here are some simple vegetable suggestions:

Steamed: Cut the vegetable into bite-sized pieces and steam it slowly in a tightly covered pot or skillet. Use half a cup of lightly salted water. A few small rocks in the bottom of the pot will keep the vegetables above the water.

When tender enough to be pierced with a fork, serve the vegetables with margarine or butter, a salad dressing or a gravy. I enjoy vinegar or lime juice, varied with a pinch of some favorite herb and a sprinkling of grated Parmesan cheese.

Baked in Foil: Lay the vegetables (whole or in pieces) on a piece of foil and dribble oil over them. Sprinkle with salt and herbs. A shot of water, broth or wine will give extra moisture and steam. Cheese may be sprinkled over the vegetables but it tends to scorch, so use it sparingly.

Close the foil tightly and bake on top of the coals, according to the recipe for *Baked Potatoes Without An Oven.*

Shishkabobs: Cut the vegetables into chunks according to their texture: harder ones such as celery should be cut smaller than quick cooking mushrooms or green pepper. Use fruit too, especially pineapple. Skewer on heavy wire, brush lightly with oil and cook slowly over the coals, basting if you wish with a sauce or marinade.

Shishkabobs are fun but they often become maddening when the best morsels fall from the skewers into the coals as they become tender. To prevent this while preserving the shishkabob mood and flavor, plunge your skewered vegetables into the flames for a few moments or hold them quite close to the coals. The idea is to lightly sear the vegetables without cremating them. Pull them out and wrap the entire shishkabob, skewer and all, in foil. Lay these packets on the coals, turning frequently until they're done, usually about 15-20 minutes.

See *Soups & Stews* and *Salads* for more vegetable ideas.

Drying Fruits & Vegetables

There are as many techniques for drying food as there are ways to skin a cat — and some are just about as messy. One simple fact tends to be obscured by expert advice on the subject: before food became a science and technology, 'primitive' people routinely dried many types of fresh foods. They did this without blanching, ascorbic acid, forced air dehydrators, freeze-drying and other recent innovations. The techniques used today do enhance the flavor, appearance and shelf life of the dried foods, but for those who wish to save time and money and  won't be hoarding their food to use after Armageddon, the age-old methods should do quite well.

Start by selecting ripe foods of high quality. We keep an eye open at the local supermarket for foods that are reduced for quick sale, *i.e.* still good to eat but too ripe to keep in the store any longer. Ironically, Americans often think a fully ripened fruit or vegetable is too ripe or even rotten. Bananas, for example, reach the peak of flavor and sweetness when the skin is dark yellow and spotted with brown. This coloring marks a banana that is ideal for drying, though you'll want to take it home and dry it immediately, not tomorrow or the next day.

Mushrooms are another bargain; those too tough to be eaten raw in salad are often sold very cheap or even thrown away. Ask the produce manager about the store's policy on over-ripe foods. You might well make an agreement to buy such foods on a regular basis at big discounts.

Preparation and Processing: Wash the food well and cut out or pare off obvious bad spots. Don't go crazy, however, or you'll soon find yourself throwing away useful food. Save celery tops and don't skin anything unless you really must. Even then, you might find a use for the peel in stock for soups and stews.

The simplest guideline is to slice hard foods thin and very tender foods thick. The thinner a food is cut, the quicker it will dry. If you're using drying racks, however, a lot of thin slices will occupy a much greater area than a few thick ones.

One of the simplest compromises is to grate or shred the food, either with a fancy food processor or a flat grater. Spread the shredded food out on a flat tray, plastic screen or clean board. Place in the sun, an oven or a dehydrator.

Soaking in ascorbic acid (vitamin C) prevents browning in apples, apricots, pears and peaches and increases the vitamin C content in other fruits. Add 1 teaspoon to half a gallon of water and leave the fruit in this bath as you go through the slicing and other procedures.

Blanching stops enzyme action in food (primarily used in drying vegetables) which leads eventually to spoilage. Unless you intend to dry large stocks of food or hold it in storage for long periods of time, don't bother with blanching.

However, slow-cooking vegetables, such as beets, are often blanched until tender, then cut and dried. This greatly reduces cooking times in camp. Cooking times are also reduced by slicing the vegetable very thin or shredding it. You'll lose some texture, of course, but not all.

If you blanch your foods do it by steaming, not boiling. This preserves food value and gives a firmer texture.

A compromise between blanching and not blanching is to buy frozen vegetables. They're already blanched, as well as washed, peeled, sliced and otherwise made ready for drying.

Food Dehydrators and Alternatives: There are enough reasons not to buy or build a food dehydrator that we gave ours away after a few months of sporadic use. First of all, a food dehydrator will be relatively expensive and bulky. Next, how much dried food do you and your family actually use in a year's time? Unless you're seriously interested in drying food, you should be able to supply your camping needs quite easily by sun or oven drying. Our food dryer was supposed to process the excess from a large garden, but we soon found that it was much less work to freeze the foods — and they looked and tasted better frozen rather than dried.

The most obvious alternative to a food dehydrator is an ordinary electric, gas or wood range oven or, if you live in a sunny area such as the southwest, open-air drying. To turn your oven into a food dehydrator simply prop the door open a few inches and adjust the heat to its lowest level. The broiler can also be used for very fast drying, but you'll want to keep a close eye on the food to avoid disasters. Extra racks can be installed by propping them up with bricks, tin cans or oven-proof cookware. This will give enough surface area to dry quite a lot of food within one day's time.

Oven racks themselves don't make good drying racks, however, because the metal rods are too widely spaced. Use them to support homemade wooden frames covered with plastic screening (don't use the broiler on these!) or dry your food on cookie sheets, aluminum foil, boards or even cardboard (a fire hazard for sure; we cover ours with foil). Some food will stick, but by turning it every 15 or 20 minutes until it firms up you shouldn't have too many problems.

Note: Don't use galvanized screening for drying food; chemicals in the metal can be drawn out by acidic foods.

If you have a wood range try suspending racks or baskets over the stove top, plenty high enough to eliminate any chance of scorching or burning. We often dry small quantities of food on the upper warming shelf.

Food can also be dried over furnace registers, but if your house is dusty this can turn into a mess.

Sun Drying: We learned basic sun-drying for fruits and vegetables while travelling in Mexico. In rural areas, refrigeration is just a dream and the people can seldom afford to preserve food by canning. Their solution is simple: slice the fruit or vegetable or just mash it flat, then drape it over a line, thorn bush, clean board or rock or what-have-you. (We used the roof of our van.) Place in the direct sunlight and turn frequently. Take the food in at sundown and put it out again bright and early the next morning. Some will fall in the dirt (rinse and start over), some will be stolen by crows and children will nab a bite here and there. Within 1 to 3 days, however, the majority of the food will be dry and can be packed away in bags or jars.

Outside sun drying can be speeded up by improvising a solar dryer. Our version, which won't win any Golden Hammer awards, is just a large wood framed window propped up against an outside wall at the sunniest spot on the porch. Staple black plastic sheeting to the wall and floor; this will absorb the heat of the sun and speed up drying. Prop up racks of food behind the window and close off the two ends with more plastic, cardboard or pieces of wood. Don't seal it too tight or moisture won't be able to escape.

Glass, plexiglass or clear plastic sheeting can also be laid over the top of an open cardboard box lined with black plastic. Punch holes in the sides of the box to allow moisture to escape and place the food inside. Prop the box toward the sun: instant solar food processor!

Drying Times: Fruits and vegetables will usually dry well in an oven within 4 to 8 hours, depending of course on temperature, thickness and air circulation. Sun dried foods take 1 to 3 days. Well-dried foods should be flexible, not brittle, when fully cooled. To test it for moisture, place the food in a tightly sealed jar. If moisture forms on the glass within a week, you've got too much moisture. (This method also distributes the moisture evenly among the pieces of food.) Remove the food and dry it for another hour or so.

Quick dried foods that haven't been processed or blanched should keep quite well for several weeks to months. If you have doubts, freeze the dried food and dry it again for an hour or two just before you go camping.

Zucchini is especially good dried. It can be eaten raw like potato chips.

Salads

One Vegetable Salad

One vegetable salads are popular in Mexico, where they often brighten up a simple plate of beans and rice. Put a bit of care into the preparation and arrangement of the salad: slice tomatoes into even wedges, for example, or cut carrots and cucumbers on an angle, Oriental style. Portions are up to your appetite and larder, but any or all of the following make nice salads.

tomato (I like uncut
  cherry tomatoes)
zucchini, sliced thin
  with the skin
onions, sliced (marinate
  one hour in dressing)
cauliflower or broccoli
  (the tender flowerlets)

cucumber
Napa cabbage (Chinese)
beets (grated)
sprouts, bean or seed
carrots

Simple salads call for simple dressings: lime or lemon juice; mild red chile powder; salt, pepper and a single herb such as oregano or basil; mayonnaise, etc.

Cabbage Salad

Cabbage isn't easily damaged so you might like to make up a salad at home and pack it into plastic jars or bags. Leave out the tomatoes, however, or you'll have a mess.

2 cups	grated or finely sliced cabbage (mix red and white)	½ cup	finely chopped celery, green pepper or grated carrot
	dressing		tomato chunks
	Additions		dried minced pineapple or fresh chunks
½ cup	raisins		
¼ cup	nuts and seeds	1 Tbsp	finely grated orange rind or fresh sliced orange pieces

The basic salad is just the cabbage with a dressing of oil, vinegar and herbs (see *Dressings & Croutons*), everything else is optional. Cabbage goes well with sweets so I often make a simple dressing of honey and lime juice or vinegar. Dress the salad on your plate so that leftovers can be cooked as a quick cabbage soup.

Fresh Sprouts

Fresh sprouts are a nice addition to almost any casserole, salad, sandwich or taco. On long trips sprouts may be your only green vegetable and though they might seem rather insignificant at home, you'll really appreciate sprouts after a few days in camp.

Mung bean sprouts are common in restaurants and stores, but for camping we prefer alfalfa seed sprouts. A teaspoon of these tiny seeds will grow into a couple of cups of sprouts. Alfalfa sprouts are very tender and can be eaten as soon as they begin growing, usually within two to three days of starting.

The technique for making sprouts is quite simple and can be used by backpackers as well as other campers. Place 1 teaspoon to 1 tablespoon of alfalfa seeds (or ¼ cup mung beans or lentils) in a wide-mouth plastic jar. Cover the seeds with an inch of fresh water and soak overnight. Cover the jar mouth with a clean cloth, bandanna or fine-meshed screen. Secure the cloth or screen with a strong rubber band or string. The seeds must never be sealed completely or they'll suffocate and die.

Many people advise that sprouts be kept in complete darkness but we just keep them out of the direct sunlight.

Drain the sprouts (use the water for cooking and drinking) and give them a fresh rinse at least once a day, more often if the weather is dry or hot. In three to five days you'll have a fine mess of sprouts. To insure a steady crop, start a new batch every day or two.

Many people advise that sprouts be kept in complete darkness but we just keep them out of the direct sunlight.

1 tsp	alfalfa seeds, sprouted	1-2 Tbsp	salad dressing
¼ cup	raw bulgur	1 Tbsp	minced onion
½ cup	cold water	½ tsp	herbs (optional)

salt to taste
Additions
lettuce or cabbage
tomato

cucumber
green pepper
any salad vegetable

Soak the bulgur in the cold water for 3-4 hours and drain if necessary. Toss the bulgur, sprouts, dressing and other ingredients together and serve. Makes two generous servings.

Very Quick Carrot Salad

2 cups	grated raw carrot	¼ cup	chopped nuts and seeds
2 Tbsp	lemon juice or vinegar	¼ cup	raisins
	Additions		bean sprouts
1 cup	chopped celery		salad dressing to taste or 2 Tbsp honey or sugar

Mix everything well and serve. This salad can also be made with raw cucumber, cabbage or beets. If you're not sure about adding a sweetener, just set aside a few bites of salad and add a dab of honey or sugar. This salad is easily prepared in a plastic sack.

Fast Macaroni Salad

I use elbow noodles for this salad, but any small pasta will do. In a pinch I've prepared it from broken spaghetti noodles.

2-3 cups	of cooked noodles (cold is best but hot okay, see *Noodles*)	¼ cup	minced celery or green pepper
½ cup	minced onion		garlic and chile powder to taste
	dressing (mayonnaise *or* oil and vinegar)	½ tsp	celery, dill or caraway seeds
	Additions		boned smoked fish
¼ cup	minced raw or cooked carrots	whole	peeled shrimp leftover beans, well drained

Gently mix the ingredients and serve.

Fast Potato Salad

Served hot or cold, this salad is one of my favorite camp dishes. It can be jazzed up to make a complete meal or kept simple for a side dish or snack.

1	steamed potato per person (baked works too)		***Additions***
	minced onion (about ¼ cup per person)	1	hard cooked egg per person, chopped
	salt, pepper, garlic to taste		minced celery
			olives
	dressing (mayonnaise, oil and vinegar, mustard and mayonnaise)		fresh mushrooms
			parsley
			bean sprouts
			minced green pepper
			pinch of chile powder

Cut the spuds into bite-sized pieces, add the onion, spices and dressing and mix gently. Allow to rest for fifteen minutes or eat immediately.

One Bean Salad

2-3 cups	cooked beans, well drained (See *Beans in Broth*)	¼-½ cup	dressing (oil and vinegar is best)
½ cup	minced onion		***Additions***
	garlic to taste		tomato chunks or a squirt of tomato juice or broth

Mix and allow to marinate for a few hours — or eat at once. This salad makes a tasty taco filling. It can be also be eaten hot.

Cold Fish Salad

Use any smoked, canned or cooked fish or sea food. Tuna is the standard but we've used shark, lobster, crab and trout. Served with a bread, this salad can easily make a full meal. For two servings:

1 cup	deboned, flaked fish		***Additions***
¼-½ cup	minced onion	½ cup	chopped lettuce
	salt, pepper, garlic to taste	¼ cup	minced celery
			bean sprouts
	mayonnaise: enough to moisten the mixture		olives

Mix gently and serve with toast, tortillas, crackers or crisp fried potatoes.

Simple Fruit Salad

One fruit salads allow you to savor and appreciate the flavor of the fruit. Bananas can overwhelm the flavor of grapes in a mixed salad and quickly become mushy. Cut your fruit attractively and experiment with dressings.

1 cup	fresh fruit, sliced or chunks (preserves juiciness)	dressing to taste	
¼ cup	seeds and nuts	***Additions***	
		pinch of salt	
		grated coconut	

The dressing is the trick; equal parts of sweetened condensed milk and mayonnaise or just plain sweetened milk mixed with orange or pineapple juice, a dash of nutmeg and cinnamon.

My favorite fruit salad is Mexican style: slices of fruit garnished with fresh lime or lemon juice and sprinkled with chile powder and salt. Try this on an orange, pineapple or an apple and you'll see what I mean.

Dressings & Croutons

The term 'salad dressing' is misleading since most dressings go very well on fried potatoes, rice, noodles, fish, tacos and even sandwiches.

Oil and Vinegar Dressing

I like to make up a full cup of dressing so that it has a chance to age before it's used up.

¾ cup	salad oil (including olive oil if possible)	¼ tsp	salt
¼ cup	vinegar, lime or lemon juice	¼ tsp	pepper
		1 tsp	oregano, basil, marjoram, thyme, parsley or?
1 Tbsp	garlic, powdered or fresh crushed	1	chicken bouillon cube, mashed (optional)

I use one herb in addition to the garlic (Lorena hates pepper so I add it to my salad later). When the level drops in the jar, I'll top it off with more oil, vinegar and herbs. The flavor changes constantly and never gets boring.

Individual servings of dressing can be as simple as dribbling 1 Tbsp of oil over the salad, followed by a generous squirt of lime juice or vinegar and a pinch of herbs.

Flavored vinegars make good simple dressings. Just add a tablespoon or two of your favorite herb(s) to a cup of vinegar.

Handmade Mayonnaise

Lorena likes this dressing so much I sometimes call her Madame Mayonnaise. Whipping up a batch of mayonnaise never fails to impress fellow campers, though many groan when called upon to help beat the mixture.

1	egg yolk	1 cup	(or less) salad and/or olive oil
pinch	salt		
1-2 Tbsp	lemon/lime juice or vinegar		***Additions***
		1 tsp	garlic powder, herbs, dry mustard

Combine in a large bowl the egg yolk, salt, lemon/lime or vinegar (2 Tbsp makes a more tart dressing) and herbs (thyme or dill and caraway seeds are Lorena's favorites). Beat *vigorously* with a fork or wire whisk. Add cooking oil, drop by drop or ½ teaspoon at at time, beating constantly. Be patient; it takes a while. The amount of oil needed varies, but once the mayonnaise forms and solidifies, you're done. Fresh egg mayonnaise should be used up within 12 hours or less if the weather is warm.

Did your mixture curdle rather than turning to mayonnaise? If so, you probably added too much oil, too fast. Save the curdled mixture. Put another egg yolk into a clean bowl and begin whipping, adding the curdled mixture, drop by drop. This should make mayonnaise.

If you have a blender, use both the yolk and white of the egg, blending slowly as you add the oil.

French Dressing

½ cup	mayonnaise		salt to taste
½ tsp	vinegar or lemon juice		tomato paste, catsup or tomato crystals
1 tsp	honey		
½ tsp	paprika		

Whip the ingredients with a fork, adding just enough tomato flavoring to turn the dressing a rich orange color.

Nancy's Dressing

This is an excellent example of how two common ingredients can make a surprising and tasty combination. I hope it inspires you to experiment for yourself.

applesauce	mayonnaise or prepared salad dressing

Mix equal parts of applesauce and mayonnaise, blend gently with a fork and serve on salads.

Crumb Topping and Crouton Sprinkle

Sauté bread, cracker or tortilla crumbs in lots of butter. I am a sesame fiend so I also add sesame seeds, already toasted, for more flavor. When the crumbs have browned nicely, sprinkle them on noodles, rice, potatoes or fresh salads. They're also quite good in soups.

Snacks & Desserts

Frankly, we prefer to use prepared foods for desserts: dried fruit, candy, snack type high energy bars, or very easy to prepare desserts such as popcorn, rice pudding or tortillas with jam, honey or peanut butter. Elaborate desserts take very careful preparation and by the time we've fixed a main meal we're usually too tired to continue cooking. For those who wish to indulge I highly recommend the book, *Natural Snacks 'n' Sweets* (see *Recommended Reading*).

Popcorn

Get the best (usually most expensive) popcorn; it will give a much higher yield and be tastier and more tender than cheap stuff. Most people use too much oil (butter will scorch): add enough to coat the bottom of your pan well, plus a tablespoonful or so.

Heat the oil until it's almost smoking, then add enough popcorn to almost cover the bottom of the pan. Lorena puts four kernels in first. When they pop she adds the rest. If your pan is shallow, use less popcorn. Our 10" frying pan takes ½ cup of kernels.

I begin shaking right away, though gently. This coats the popcorn evenly with hot oil and gives a better rate of popping, with fewer 'old maids'. Others shake infrequently — it's up to you. I continue shaking until the main volley subsides, then remove from the fire and uncover. Covered popcorn will toughen quickly.

Dust liberally with garlic powder, parmesan cheese, mild chile powder, herb salts, dried vegetable broth, well toasted sesame seeds, Butter Buds or real melted butter, melted honey or granulated white or brown sugar.

Lorena's favorite is butter (or Butter Buds), garlic and dry vegetable broth. In camp tests on friends, garlic powder and parmesan cheese also rated high.

Toasted Nuts and Seeds

I prefer to toast my own nuts and seeds for two reasons: it saves money and home-toasted nuts and seeds have a fresher, more interesting flavor than store-bought. The following method is widely used in Mexico and works on just about any nut or seed. It is excellent for squash seeds, a treat that most gringos toss into the garbage.

A large iron skillet works best for this operation but most anything will do, even an aluminum pot, though you'll have to watch it carefully to avoid scorching.

1 cup	raw nuts or seeds or mixture	*Additions*
½ cup	water	chile powder to taste
	salt to taste or soy sauce	garlic powder to taste

Heat your pan but don't get it searing hot. Mix the water with the salt and spices and the nuts or seeds. Dump this into the pan and begin stirring slowly. Use a spatula or wooden paddle if you have one. The water will soon begin to cook off, leaving the nuts or seeds coated with the spices and damp enough to resist scorching. Continue stirring. Sesame and squash seeds will begin to pop when well toasted, but peanuts, sunflower seeds and other nuts won't. You'll have to judge by eye and odor when they're done. It's best to remove them from the heat—and the pan—before they're obviously brown.

Many people, myself included, prefer slightly scorched nuts and seeds, but it's easy to overdo it. Allow the nuts to cool and give them a taste. Too raw? Back into the pan...

For entertainment value we often do the toasting in camp, varying the flavors of small batches and eating them hot from the pan.

Simple Rice Pudding

Cooked rice, white or brown	*Additions*
milk	nutmeg
honey	vanilla
cinnamon	raisins
	dried fruit

Mix whatever you have of the above ingredients, to taste, and serve warmed or cold. Makes a good hot evening dessert or a nice breakfast. Leftover rice pudding tends to be thick stuff, but try serving it drenched in a melted honey and butter mixture.

Variations: Use oatmeal, bulgur or any grain instead of the rice.

Key Lime Pie & Pudding

The beauty of this dessert is that it doesn't require cooking, yet makes a dramatic presentation, especially when you're camped in places where pies are seldom seen.

1 stick	(4 ounces) butter or margarine	6-8 oz.	sweetened condensed milk
1-2 cups	graham cracker or cookie crumbs		juice of 2 limes

Mash the crackers or cookies into crumbs and mix with the butter (a fork works nicely). Pat this mixture into a pie pan or bowl (plastic is okay since it won't be cooked) so that it forms a pie-like crust. Now mix the milk and lime juice. This will jell into a thick pudding. If it doesn't, add more lime juice. Pour the pudding into the crust and serve.

Variations: Add raisins, nuts, fruits and dribble more condensed milk on top. Without the crackers this makes a good pudding.

Fruit Gobbler

I love the name; it makes me want to plunge my nose into a steaming bowl of the stuff. For 2 to 3 people or one glutton:

3-5	apples, peaches, pears or equivalent berries	dash	salt
½ cup	sugar or 1/3 cup of honey	1 cup	pancake mix or biscuit mix
½ tsp	cinnamon	¼-1/3 cup	milk

Slice the fruit (reconstitute and chop dried fruit) and place it in a small skillet, baking pan or pie dish. Cover with honey or sugar, the cinnamon and a dash of salt. Mix the pancake or biscuit mix with milk until it's the consistency of pancake batter — kind of runny. Pour this over the fruit.

Bake for 45 minutes at 350-375° or slow cook over the fire until the fruit is tender and the batter firm. Serve with milk, cream or yogurt. At home I gobble with ice cream.

Variation: Jam Gobbler: Spread a thick layer of jam or jelly in the bottom of your pan, add the batter and cook.

Beverages

Cowboy Coffee

Some people abandon all pretense of civilized behavior while camping and drink nothing but instant coffee. I refuse, though I will concede that my glass coffee pot, brass grinder for whole beans and filtering systems are best left behind on backpacking and kayaking trips. When conditions are rough, Cowbow Coffee will keep you from stooping to instant imitations of the real thing.

The grind of coffee needed for Cowboy style is not normally sold to the public so skip the prepared and canned coffees and buy whole beans. Have them ground *fine*. By 'fine' I mean dusty fine. Some coffee sellers balk at grinding coffee this much. Be firm.

Bring your water to a rollicking boil, preferably in a blue or black chipped enamelled Cowboy Coffee Pot. As you remove the pot from the fire swiftly dump in the ground coffee, stirring it well to avoid lumping. I use about a generous teaspoon of coffee per large cup, plus one for the pot.

Wrap the coffee pot in a shirt, towel or jacket and allow it to age and mellow for ten minutes, seven if you just can't wait. Never, ever let the coffee boil once the grounds have been added. If you do, you'll create a pot of Fishermen's Coffee, a brackish bitter fluid unfit for human consumption.

When the coffee is 'rested', pour it gently into cups (heavy china mugs with cracked handles are best). The extra-fine grounds should have settled to the bottom by now, but if they haven't, strain the brew through a clean bandanna, the tail of your flannel shirt or a fine-meshed copper wire sieve. My sieve is the size of a large thimble. It is worth a trip to Mexico to buy one if you're serious about Cowboy Coffee.

Y and B Energy Drink

This tasty soup-like drink is loaded with protein (about 8 grams from the yeast) and B vitamins. It also tastes good, especially if you use flaked brewer's yeast rather than the finer, more concentrated torula type yeast. Novice yeast eaters might like to start with one tablespoon of yeast in their drink until they've acquired a taste for the stuff. (It can be done, as I will personally testify, and you'll soon come to enjoy the rich flavor of the yeast.)

2 Tbsp	flaked brewer's yeast	**Additions**
1 Tbsp	dried vegetable broth *or* bouillon cube	add cold rice or noodles for body
1-1½ cups	hot water	shredded smoked meat or fish
dash	soy sauce (optional)	crackers, bread or shredded tortillas

Leave a spoon in the drink and stir frequently to keep the yeast in suspension. B vitamins may cause a 'rush': a flushed and tingling sensation on your face and arms, like a sudden heat rash. This goes away quickly; once your body is used to the vitamins you won't notice any flushing.

Hibiscus Punch

Hibiscus flowers are used to give herbal tea mixtures a rosy tint and tartness. Buy the flowers at food co-ops, health food shops or specialty food stores. This punch is quite refreshing and can be combined with other fruit drinks or booze (gin, vodka, grain spirits).

1 cup	or small handful dried hibiscus flowers	*Additions*
		orange juice
1 qt	boiling water	lemon juice
	honey to taste	grape juice
		cranberry juice

Steep the flowers in boiling water until it cools to drinking temperature. Remove the flowers and reuse them again or leave them in the punch until it's polished off. Add the sweetener and if you have it, a few ounces of any fruit juice.

A few hibiscus flowers can also be added to drinking water and canteens to offset the flavor of purifying agents.

Dried Fruit Punch

¼-½ cup	dried fruit			*Additions*
2 cups	boiling water	¼ tsp	allspice
1 tsp	(or Tbsp) honey	1 tsp	butter
pinch	cinnamon		milk
		drop	vanilla
		1 Tbsp	(heaping) dark rum

Steep the dried fruit and spices for 15 minutes or more in the hot water. If you intend to use the fruit for cooking — in the next morning's mush, for example — fish it out and set aside. Stir in the honey and butter and serve hot, or hold the butter and serve the punch cold. If you have orange peel, it can be used instead of fruit. This punch mixes well with rum or brandy.

Quick Fruit Punch

One of the side benefits of camping, especially on long outings, is that we re-discover so many things we can get by *without*, from television shows to over-rich foods. The following drink might be your first step toward a simpler lifestyle. If nothing else, it tastes good and is amazingly inexpensive.

2-3 qts	cool water	honey to taste
1 lb	fresh fruit	

My favorite fruit for this drink is cantaloupe, followed closely by strawberries, pineapple, limes and watermelon. Combinations are also good but beware of blending too many flavors into blandness.

Blend, mash or furiously chop the fruit, taking care not to lose too much of the juice. Add the fruit to the water and just enough sweetener to be noticeable. Go easy; this is supposed to be a refreshing drink, not a syrup. Allow the punch to rest for 15-30 minutes and serve.

If you serve it with ice, start out with less water or it'll be too diluted. This drink is an excellent weaning beverage for children and adults who are addicted to soda pop.

Energy Drinks

Aside from the obvious psychological benefits of a good hot beverage, many of the drinks described here are low-cost sources of food and energy. They are based on *atole*, a kind of watery gruel that has been used for thousands of years in Latin America. The word 'gruel', however, sounds like something you'd spill on your shoes so I'll call them Energy Drinks. These drinks can be used as snacks, nutritional complements or even quick meals. I'll give basic recipes but don't stop there; you can add everything from raw eggs to brewer's yeast to these beverages.

Just about any cereal that requires cooking can be made into an Energy Drink. Cream of Wheat is especially good and cooks very quickly. I've used 7 grain cereal mixes too, but they tend to be scratchy when chug-a-lugged.

Corn Energy Drink

There's nothing quite like a tall glass of hot cornstarch to start the day! Talk about carbohydrate loading: cornstarch is almost 90% carbohydrate by weight. Take my word for it, this stuff tastes better than it sounds. For two large servings:

1 qt	milk or water	***Additions***
1	cinnamon stick *or*	raisins
	1 tsp ground cinnamon	dried fruit, minced
½ tsp	vanilla (optional)	carob or chocolate
5 Tbsp	cornstarch	powder
	honey or sugar to taste	instant coffee or similar
		soluble beverage

Heat the milk or water to the boiling point. Water-based *atole* isn't nearly as good as milk, but it's fine in a pinch. Add the cinnamon stick now and the raisins or dried fruit (fresh fruit can be used, of course, especially bananas, well mashed).

Dip out half a cup of the hot milk and blend in the cornstarch. When the cornstarch is completely dissolved, stir it into the remainder of the milk and sweeten to taste. In general, the sweeter the better.

Cook over a low heat for 15 minutes, stirring constantly. Try to avoid boiling the milk; it could scorch. If the drink gets very thick, dilute it with more milk or water.

To enhance flavor and nutritional value, add powdered milk, brewer's yeast, a well beaten raw egg, protein powders...

Serve garnished with a dash of cinnamon. Cheers!

Rice Energy Drink

If this looks suspiciously like heavily diluted rice pudding you're right. As a matter of fact, most puddings and creamy dessert fillings make good drinks when diluted with milk.

1-1½ qts	water	small can sweetened
½ cup	rice, white or brown	condensed milk *or*
1 tsp	cinnamon	dried milk
pinch	salt	*Additions*
	honey to taste	raisins, dried fruit
		fresh banana, mashed

Salt the water and bring it to a boil. Add the rice and cook until it is quite tender and fluffed open. Brown rice may require more water to keep it thin and drinkable. When the rice is cooked, remove from the fire and add the canned milk or enough powdered milk to make a rich drink. Add the cinnamon and sweetener. If you use dried fruit, add it with the rice or at least 10 minutes before the rice is cooked. This is a good way to prepare cheap starchy rice since the starch acts to thicken the drink and provides carbohydrates.

Oatmeal Energy Drink

This is our favorite of the Energy Drinks and about the easiest to prepare.

½-1½ cup	oatmeal	honey to taste
1 qt	milk	*Additions*
1 tsp	cinnamon	dried or fresh fruit

The more oatmeal you use, the thicker and heartier the drink. We prefer regular rather than instant oatmeal. Instant oatmeal tends to dissolve but some people prefer a beverage that doesn't require occasional chewing.

Heat the milk to the boiling point and add the oatmeal, sweetener, the cinnamon and whatever fruit or flavorings you like (see *Corn Energy Drink* for suggestions). Cook stirring constantly, for 15 minutes, diluting as necessary. A blob of butter looks and tastes good on top of a mug of Energy Drink.

Appendices

Recommended Reading

Natural Snacks 'n' Sweets by Stan and Floss Dworkin, Rodale Press. Wholesome snacks and sweets with simple and easy to prepare recipes.

Laurel's Kitchen: A Handbook For Vegetarian Cookery And Nutrition by Laurel Robertson, Carol Flinders and Bronwen Godfrey, Bantam. A cross between *Joy of Cooking* (vegetarian style) and Adelle Davis, loaded with good recipes that can be adapted (often simplified) for camping. Highly recommended.

Joy of Cooking by Irma S. Rombauer and Marion Rombauer Becker, Signet. Invaluable aids to all cooks; filled with useful tips, suggestions and recipes.

Diet For A Small Planet by Frances Moore Lappe, Ballantine Books. "This book is about protein..." how much you need, where to get it, meatless meals, saving money, etc. An invaluable aid to meal planning.

James Beard: The author of many cookbooks on outdoor cooking, seafood, breads, pastas and so on. His recipes range from the simple to the staggering and his approach and style are always entertaining and informative. His seafood recipes have sent us directly to the beach several times.

Let's Eat Right To Keep Fit by Adelle Davis, New American Library. Tells you how to eat but doesn't offer recipes. It is a classic but you may prefer something lighter like *Laurel's Kitchen*.

Handbook Of The Nutritional Contents Of Foods (also known as **Composition of Foods**) prepared for the U.S. Department of Agriculture, Dover Publications; 190 pages, $5.00. Almost 200 pages of detailed and often boggling tables, listing everything from calories to trace mineral contents of common and uncommon foods. A sort of food almanac and trivia trove.

Euell Gibbons: Foraging for food isn't complete without one of Mr. Gibbons' wonderful books in your knapsack or clam bucket. His books remain classics on the subject and are very comprehensive. (*Stalking the Wild Asparagus* and others.)

Gorp, Glop & Glue Stew: Favorite Foods From 165 Outdoor Experts by Yvonne Prater and Ruth Dyar Mendenhall. The Mountaineers, 715 Pike St., Seattle, WA, 98101. Recipes, anecdotes and mini-biographies that are like my favorite fish head stew: it reads much better than it sounds. Entertaining, humorous, informative and even outrageous. The real-life experiences of a diverse group of campers and outdoor enthusiasts. We recommend it highly.

The New Healthy Trail Food Book by Dorcas S. Miller, East Woods Press, 820 East Blvd, Charlotte, N.C. 28203. A concise look at nutrition, trail foods, food values and complements. Pamphlet-length, but sold as a book. ($3.95 for 79 pages).

Foraging Along The California Coast by Peter Howorth, Capra Press, 631 State St., Santa Barbara, CA 93101. How to find and collect everything from clams to striped bass, with good clear tips on equipment, cleaning and preparation, and recipes. Applies to most any North American coast. We recommend it highly.

Roughing It Easy by Dian Thomas, Brigham Young University Press and Warner Books. An 'idea book', with suggestions on everything from selecting a campsite to baking pineapple upsidedown cake on an open fire. Appeals to many people who like to improvise gear; many of the cooking hints involve homemade utensils from tin cans. Volume Two has more ideas but repeats much of Volume One.

Packrat Papers edited by Betty Mueller, Signpost Books, 8912 192nd SW, Edmonds, WA 98020. Subtitled *Tips on food (and other stuff) for campers, backpackers, and those who travel lightly.* There are two volumes, each about 90 pages, absolutely loaded with interesting tips and information gleaned from Signpost Magazine, one of the oldest and best camping publications.

Make It and Take It: Homemade Gear For Camp and Trail by Russ Mohney, Pacific Search Press, 715 Harrison St., Seattle, WA 98109. Money-saving do-it-yourself cookware, fishing gear, seafood traps, packs, self-inflating mattresses, tents, camera hitches, utility bags and more. Very clearly written and illustrated. The publisher also does nice cookbooks; ask for a catalog.

Equipment and Food Sources

Trial and error are effective teachers, but when it comes to buying mail order food and equipment, the errors can be both costly and frustrating.

• Quality, prices and service can vary dramatically from one company to another; your only assurance of getting what you want, when you want it — and at a good price — is to request catalogs months in advance. Look them over carefully, comparing prices, shipping charges, guarantees and special deals. REI Co-op, for example, gives a yearly rebate to members and has a toll free ordering number; use it for inquiries and technical questions, too.

• Don't order anything until you've got all the catalogs you need to make a detailed cost comparison. List everything you need on a sheet of paper, then write down the prices from each company. A quick look will tell you which company gives the best bargains.

• If you don't want substitutions, say so; do you really care if your bowls are red or yellow? Mark "no substitutions" only on those items you really care about.

• When time is limited don't accept back orders. They'll hold your money (if you send a check) until the item is back in stock. This can take time.

• Before spending large amounts of money, make an initial small order to test quality and service. This is time consuming but it can save headaches in the long run. A good mail order supplier will fill your order fast. Any order that is delayed more than three weeks is too slow, no matter what excuse you may be given.

Recreational Equipment, Inc. (REI Co-op), P.O. Box C-88125, Seattle, WA 98188. REI is big and handles everything from ski equipment to camping foods and backpacking gear. Prices and service are good; they have a toll free ordering number. In 1981, Co-op members received a 14% rebate on their purchases. REI now owns Mountain Safety Research.

Indiana Camp Supply Inc., P.O. Box 344, Pittsboro, IN 46167. Indiana's catalog is done on cheap newsprint, looks funky and costs $1. On the other hand, they have good prices and gave us the best service of any large mail-order house. Their selection of first-aid items and books is outstanding.

Eastern Mountain Sports, Inc., Vose Farm Road, Peterborough, NH 03458. A big company, with a catalog similar to REI's.

The Ski Hut, P.O. Box 309 Berkeley, CA 94701. Disregard their name; this company has a wide assortment of outdoor gear.

Early Winters, 110 Prefontaine Place South, Seattle, WA 98104. Unusual and interesting (and often rather expensive) outdoor equipment, though not as broad a selection as the companies listed above.

The North Face, 4560 University Way NE, Seattle, WA 98105. Tents, bags, clothing and some general camping gear.

Campmor, 205 West Shore Ave., Bogota, NJ 07603. General camping gear and food.

Northwest River Supplies, 214 N. Main, P.O. Box 9186, Moscow, ID 83843. We have found their quality, prices, service and good humor to be far better than most other mail order houses. Highly recommended, they carry everything from rafts and wet suits to whitewater hardware, books and miscellaneous camping gear.

Camping Foods

Trail Foods Co., P.O. Box 9309-B, North Hollywood, CA. 91609. Freeze-dried foods.

Richmoor, P.O. Box 2728, Van Nuys, CA 91404. Freeze-dried.

Stow-A-Way Industries, 166 Cushing Highway (Rt. 3-A), Cohasset, MA 02025. Freeze-dried, dried and 'survival pack' whole foods; equipment and books. Toll free number.

Index

- A -

A, Vitamin, 38-39
ABC's of Camp Cooking, 149-50
Additives, food, 57
Alcoholic beverages, 65
Alfalfa sprouts, 249
Aloe vera, 173
Aluminum box, 111-12
Aluminum clipboard, 128
Aluminum foil, 109; 104; 177; 179
Apron, 109-10; 107
Atole, 259-60
Awnings, 136-37

- B -

B, Vitamin, 39
Backpacker's Kitchen, 103-4
Backpacking Stoves, 127-28
Bagels, 66
Baja, kayak trip planning, 13-16
Baking pans, 107; 102
Baking powder and yeast, 189; 230-31; high altitude, 188
Bandannas, 117; 104
Bannock bread, 236
Barbecuing, 161; 162
Bare Bones Kitchen, 107-8
Basic Camp Cooking, 176-89
Baskets, 133; 107
Beans, 62-63; recipes, 196-200; with eggs, 208; soup, 194-95; salad, 251; cooking with seawater, 187; storing, 63; sprouts, 249-50
Bean masher, 107
Bell peppers, 82; 83
Berry picking, 86
Beverages, 63-65; recipes, 257-60
Beverage bag, 64; (see also *Spice Rack*, 81)
Biscuits, 234-36; 230-31
Blender, 118; 107
Bob's Fish Head Soup, 195
Booze, 65
Bottles, plastic, 104; fuel, 128; see *Containers*
Bottle opener, 104

Bouillon cubes, 64
Bowls, 110; 104; salad, 107; in dime stores, 102
Boxes, storage containers, 133
Brass Stove, 99-100
Breads, Biscuits & Tortillas, 230-36; 65-66
Breadsticks, 234
Breakfast, menu, 40; leftovers, 27; see *Cereals, Eggs*
Brewer's yeast, 64
Brown rice, 75-76; recipes, 221; 220-25
Browning food, 177-78
Buckets, 107; versatility, 100; for RV's, 133; as seats, 133
Budget, see *Economizing*
Bulgur, 220-26; cereal, 239; salad, 249-50; pudding, 255
Bulk foods, buying, 55-56
Burns, 173
Burritos, 205
Butcher knife, 107
Butter, 77-78
Butter Buds, 78
Buttermilk, 189

- C -

C, Vitamin, 39; infections, 173
Cabbage, storing, 180; 83; salad, 248-49
Cabinets, in RV's, 132-34
Cake, rice, 225
Calcium, 173; 39
Calories, table of, 45-49
Calorie Counter, 37
Camp Cooking Styles, 20-28; No Food At All, 21-22; A Crust of Bread, 22-23; Cold Cooking, 23-24; Heat n' Serve, 24-25; Homestyle Camp Cooking, 25-27; Combinations, 27; Variations, 27-28; Variety, 28-29; Seven-Pot Meal, 139-48
Campfires, 157-61
Camp Kitchens, 97-138
Camp Kitchen Skills, 139-73
Camp Stoves, 125-28; see *Stoves*
Campesino flashlight, 164-65

Cans, as pots, 100-2
Can opener, 104; 98
Candle lantern, 164-65; 138
Canteens, 110-11
Car Kitchens, 129-38
Carbohydrates, 35-38
Cargo bags, 114
Carnivores and Vegetarians, 32-34
Carrots, 82; 83; salad, 250
Cashew Noodles with Cauliflower, 219
Celery, 82; 83
Ceramic sharpening rod, 122
Cereals, 66-68; cooking, 237-39
Chairs, 135; bucket, 133
Chapattis, 66
Charts, Nutritional Table, 45-50; cooking cereal, 238
Cheese, 68-70; and beans, 198; noodles, 217-19; rice, 221-25; sauce, 242; sandwich, 201-2; food co-ops, 55; storing, 68-69
Chile Sauces, 240-41
Chili, bean, 197-98
Chocolate, anecdote, 13-16; obsession, 29; beverage, 64
Chopsticks, 104
Clams, chowder, 195; sandwich, 201-2; linguini, 219
Clipboard, 128
Cocktail, 65
Coffee, 63-64; Cowboy, 257
Cold Cooking, 23-24
Coleman, stove, 126-27; cleaning, 167-69; oven, 122-23; see *White Gas*
Colonizer's Kitchen, 107; 103
Comal, 118; 104
Condiments, 80-82; see *Spices*
Containers, 111-16; in RV's, 132-34; canteens, 110-11; water in RV's, 136; baskets, 133; 'shelf curtain', 134; oil, 78; spice, 81-82; fuel, 128; food co-ops, 55-56; dime stores, 102
Convenience foods, 24-25
Cook Fires, 157-61; tips, 177

Cooking gear, 97-138; impro-
vised, 100-2
Cooking Kits, 116-17
Cooking Methods, 177-79
Cooking styles, 20-28
Cooking times, 177-79; pota-
toes, 178; cereals, 237-39
Cooking tips, 175-89
Co-ops, 55-56
Corn Energy Drink, 259-60
Corn Meal Cakes, 236
Cowboy Coffee, 257
Crab sandwich, 201-2
Crackers, 235
Cramps, 173; lack of salt, 186
Crates, storage containers, 132-
33
Cravings & Snacks, 29-31
Cream, 73-74; substitutions, 189
Creamed Eggs, 209
Crockpot, 118
Croutons, 254
Crumb Topping, 254
Crust of Bread, 22-23
Cucumbers, 180; 83
Cups, 117; 104; size of yours,
176; plastic, 102; for swil-
ling Gran Marnier, 24; see
Measuring Cups
Curtains, as shelves, 134
Cutting board, 128-29; 105

- D -

D, Vitamin, 39
Dehydrators, food, 246-47
Delis, 58
Desert, water, 19; 110
Desserts, 254-56; recipe book,
261
Diarrhea, 170-72; cocktail, 172
Diet For a Small Planet, 261; 35
Dips, recipes, 242
Dishes, plates, 123; plastic,
102; washing, 153-54
Dish pan, 107
Dish towels, 117; 104
Double boilers, 102
Dressings & Croutons, 252-54
Dried eggs, 70
Drift, The, 133
Drip cooler, 156-57
Drying, fruit, 245-48; meat &
seafood, 212-15; vege-
tables, 245-48

Dumplings, 234-35
Dutch oven, 107
Dysentery, 170-72

- E -

E, Vitamin, 39; burns, 173
Eating Well, 34-43
Economizing, meal planning,
18; snacks, 31; tips, 59-62
Eggs, 70; recipes, 206-10;
sandwiches, 201; con-
tainers, 105
Electrical Appliances, 118;
skillet, 107
Elephant bladders, 110-11
Emergency food, 25-26
Empty calories, 36
Enchiladas, 204-5
Energy & Food, 35-38
Energy Drinks, Yeast & Broth,
257-58; Atole, 259-60
Emily Post and The Great Out-
doors, 181
Equipment, kitchen, 97-138

- F -

Fasting, 21-22
Fats, 36; see *Oil*
Fatigue, lack of salt, 186; see
Energy
Fires, cook, 157-61; smoker,
213
Fire fan, 107
Fire grate, see *Grates, Grills*
Fire Pit, 158-60
Fish, recipes, 210-11;
smoking, 212-14; and rice,
224; hash and potatoes,
230; salad, 251
Fish Head Soup, 195
Fishing, 86-89
Flashlights, 118; kept handy,
134; *Campesino*, 164-65
Flask, backpacker's, 102
Flour, substitutions, 188
Foil, see *Aluminum Foil*
Food & Shopping, 62-84
Food Complements, 36-37; en-
ergy, 35-38; poisoning,
170-72; storage, 179-81;
suppliers, 54-59
Food co-ops, 55-56
Food mill, 118; 107

Footlockers, kitchen, 107; 133
Foraging, 85-96
Forks, 125; 105
Fred, 89
Freeze-dried, 24-25; limited
fuel, 19; expensive, 18;
needed? 56
French Dressing, 253
French Fried Potatoes, 228-29
Frisbee, 118; 104
Fruit, dried, 70-71; drying,
245-48; with rice, 31-32;
Gobbler, 256; Punch, 258-
59; Salad, 251-52; from
food co-ops, 55
Fruitcake, 31-32
Frying, 177-78
Frying Pans, 123-25; 104
Fuel, for stoves, 126-28; 165-
66; containers, 128; 104
Furniture, in RV's, 135

- G -

Garbage, 155
Garlic, 83; soup, 194; take lots,
82; cure and preventative,
171; infections, 173; in stuff
sacks, 114-15
Gasoline, see *White Gas*
Gear, Kitchen, 97-138
Generic food, 60
Ginseng tea, 64
Glop, 184
Gobbler, fruit, 256
Golden Noodles, 218
Golden Sauce, 241
Goldenseal, 173
Gookinaid®, 65
Gorditas, 205-6
Gourmet Picnic, 23-24
Grains, see *Cooked Cereals: Rice
& Bulgur: Rice Pudding*
Granola, 66-67; 24
Grape juice, 65
Grate, 104; 107; see *Grills*
Grater, 105
Gravy, 239-44; in stew, 193
Green Chile Sauce, 240-41
Green pepper, 82; 83
Griddles, 118-19
Grills, 119; see *Grates*
Gypsy Stoves, 162-64

- H -

Hardboiled Eggs, 206
Hardtack, 66
Headache, salt deficiency? 186
Headlamp, 118
Health, 169-73
Health Food Stores, 57-58
Heat n' Serve Cooking, 24-25;
    in snow, 19
Herbs, 80-82; see *Spices*;
    Cheese, 69; Garden, 130
Hibiscus Punch, 258
High Altitude Cooking, 188
Hobo Kitchen Gear, stove,
    162-63; oven, 163-64;
    lantern, 164-65; cooking
    pots, 100-2
Hollandaise Sauce, Mock, 242
Homestyle Camp Cooking, 26-
    27
Homestyle Gravy, 241
Honey, 185-86; substitutions,
    189; snacks, 31; see
    Sweeteners
Hot chocolate, 64
Hot pads, 119-20
Hot plate, 118
Hydrogen peroxide, 173

- I -

Ice, 120-21
Ice Chests, 120-21; sleeping
    bag, 155-56; drip cooler,
    156-57
Infections, 173
Instant foods, 24-25; in snow,
    19
Inventory food, 41-42
Iodine, purifying water, 171;
    vegetables, 180

- J -

Jam Gobbler, 256
Jars, plastic, 104; see *Containers*
Juice, grape, 65; freeze-dried,
    64
Junk food, snacks, 29-31; 35

- K -

Kayaking, planning, 13-16;
    oil, 17

Kayaking Kitchen, 103-4
Kerosene, 127; 165-66
Kettles, 107; see *Pots*
Key Lime Pie & Pudding, 256
Kitchens, Backpacker's, 103-4;
    Camping, 97-138; RV,
    129, 131-38; improve-
    ments, 151-73
Kitchen Equipment Discussion,
    108-29; Gear, 97-138
Kitchen sink, 100
Kitchen Skills, 139-73
Knives, 121-22; 104; butcher,
    107

- L -

Lanterns, 125-28; tin can 164-
    65
Lard, 77-78
Leavening, 230-31; 188; 189
Leftovers, for breakfast, 40-41
Lemons, see *Limes*
Lentils, 72; soup, 199-200
Lights, flashlight, 118;
    lanterns, 125-28; RV's,
    137-38; cord, socket and
    bulb, 118
Lighter, 104
Lima Bean Soup, 194-95
Limes, 180; disinfectant, 171
Linguini, 219
Lists, 53-54; 51
Litter, 155
Lunch, 40

- M -

Macaroni, & Cheese, 217-18;
    salad, 250
Mail Order, equipment, 102;
    suppliers, 263
Margarine, 77-78; see *Oil*
Marinades, 243
Mashed Potatoes, 227-28
Masher, bean and potato, 107
Matches, 104
Mayonnaise, 253; 147
Meal Planning, 13-50; Ques-
    tionaire, 17-20; table of
    nutritional values, 45-50
Measuers & Weights, 43-45
Measuring cups, 107; your cup?
    176; for meal planning, 43-
    44; at food co-ops, 55-56

Measuring spoons, 107; your
    spoon? 176
Meat, 72-73; smoking & jerky,
    212-15; in cheese, 69;
    canned, 20-21
Menstrual Cramps, 173
Menu, daily, 39-43; review, 21
Mess Kits, 116-17
Mexican foods: donut, 232;
    noodles, 215, 217; Potato
    Cakes, 229; Rice, 221-22
Milk, 73-74; in bread, 231
Minerals, 39
Miracle Bean Ball, 198-99
Miso, 64
Mixing whisk, 105
Mold, on cheese, 68-69; on
    dried fruit, 71
Moveable Feast, 148-50
Muscle Cramps, 173
Mush, 66-68; cooking, 237-39
Mushrooms, foraging, 86-87;
    with Steve, 89-96; dried,
    82; with rice, 224-25
Mustard, Golden Sauce, 241;
    Sashimi, 242; for munchies,
    31

- N -

Nalgene containers, 112-13
Nancy's Dressing, 253
Naptha, see *White Gas*
NATO Cooking School
    Method, 185
Navy Bean Soup, 194
No Food At All, 21-22
No Kitchen At All, 107-8
Noodles & Pasta, 74; recipes,
    215-19, 28; snacks, 31;
    cooking with seawater, 187
Nuts & Seeds, 76-77; toasted,
    255; 21
Nutrition, 34-43; table, 45-50;
    supplements, 38-39
Nutritionally dense foods, 57

- O -

Oatmeal, 66-68; cooking, 237-
    39; pudding, 255; energy
    drink, 260
Oil, 77-78; containers, 102;
    conserving, 177-78; substi-
    tutions, 189

Oil & Vinegar Dressing, 252
Olive oil, 78
Omelettes, 207
Onions, 82; 83; soup, 194
Open Larder, 43
Oriental Fried Rice, 222-23
Outdoor kitchen, 131
Outdoor Shops, 102-3
Oven, 122-23; 107; tin can, 163-64
Oven grill, 119
Over-equipping, 100
Oyster Chowder, 195

- P -

Pans, 123-25
Pan Bread, 233-34; 66
Pancakes, 233-34
Paper Plates and Towels, 123; 105
Paring knife, 121-22; see *Knives*
Parmesan cheese, 69; with leftover rice, 184-85; with leftover potatoes, 185
Pasta, see *Noodles*
Pepper, bell, 82; 83; see *Chile*
Pero, 64
Phoenix bags, 114
Picnic, Gourmet, 23-24
Pita bread, 66
Pizza, 204
Plastic Bags, 113; to carry: beverages, 64; spices, 81; fresh vegetables, 84; not for cheese, 69
Plastic bottles, 102; see *Containers*
Plastic spoons, 125
Plates, 123; 104; plastic, 102; paper, 105
Poached Eggs, 207-8
Poaching, 178
Pocket Purifier, 171
Poisoning, food, 172; 62
Popcorn, 254-55
Portion Control, 41-45
Postum, 64
Pots, 123; 104; dime store, 102; tin can, 100-2
Pot Grabbers, 125; 104
Pot holders, 119-20
Pot scrubber, 104

Potatoes, recipes, 226-30; chowder, 195; sandwich, 202; salad, 250-51; dried, 82; as snack, 31
Potato masher, 107
Pre-packaged Portions, 42-45
Preservatives, in food, 57
Pressure Cooker, 125; 107; your style? 97-98
Primer, stove, 104; 100
Produce, 83-84; 18-19
Propane, 126-27; cautions, 166
Protein, 35-38
Provisioning, 51-84; at restaurant, 23; see *Shopping*
Puncture wounds, 173
Pudding, Rice, 255; Key Lime, 256
Punch, 258-59
Purifying, water, 170-71; Pure! Pure! Pure!, 171; pills, 104; vegetables, 180

- Q -

Quesadillas, 203-4

- R -

Rabbits In Their Holes, 209
Radishes, 83
Raisins, 31, 71
Ramen noodles, 74
Recipes, 191-260
Red Chile Sauce, 240
Reflector Oven, 122-23; 107
Refrigerators, 120-21
Refrigerator grills, 119
Refritos, 197
Reserve Food, 25-26
Restaurants, for provisioning, 23
Rice, 75-76; recipes, 220-25; with eggs, 208; Energy Drink, 260; Pudding, 255; cooking with seawater, 187; snacks, 31
River Bags, 114
Rob, chocolate, 13-16; dried fruit, 71; ABC kitchen, 149-50; Seven-Pot Meal, 139-48
Routines, 150
RV Kitchens, 129-35

- S -

Safflower Oil, 77-78
Salads, 248-52; storing, 179; Sandwich, 202
Salad Garden, 130
Salami with Eggs, 208-9
Salt, in diet, 39; needing more, 186; using saltwater, 186-88; in bread, 231; sesame, 242-43; keeping dry, 179; making toast 118
Salt shaker, 105; keeping dry, 179
Saltwater, cooking with, 186-88
Sand, in food, 176-77
Sandwiches & Tacos, 200-6
Sashimi Dips, 242
Sauces, 239-44
Sausage with Eggs, 208-9
Sauté, 177
Scout Mess Kit, 116-17
Scrambled Eggs, 206-7
Seafood, 210-14; linguini, 219; sandwich, 201-2
Seafood Dips, 242
Seats, 135; bucket, 133
Seawater, cooking with, 186-88; in bread, 230
Seeds, 76-77; toasted, 255; 21
Sesame Salt, 242-43
Seven-Pot Meal, 139-48
Sharpening rod, 122
Shelf curtain, 134; spice rack, 81
Shops, outdoor, 102-3; see *Shopping*
Shopping, 51-84; see *Lists*; Styles, 51-52; Suggestions, 62-84; Tips, 59-62
Shopping bags, 107
Shrimp Sandwich, 201-2
Simmer, 177; with seawater, 187
Simplicity, 184
Sink, kitchen, 132; 100
Skills, camp kitchen, 139-73
Skillet, 118
Sleeping Bag Ice Chest, 155-56
Sleepytime Tea, 64
Small Touches, 181-82
Smoked Fish, 212-15; with rice, 224; salad, 251

Smoker, 212-14
Smoking Fish & Meat, 212-15
Snacks & Desserts, 254-56; 29-31; recipe book, 261
Snow camping, fuel, 19; plastic bags, 17
Soap, 104
Solid Fuel Stoves, 162
Soups & Stews, 192-95; 199-200
Sour milk, 189
Soy milk, 74
Soy Proteins, 78-80
Spaghetti, 217
Spatula, 104
Spices, 80-82; using, 184-85
Spice Rack, 81
Split Peas, 72; soup, 199-200
Spoilage, 179-81; beans, 63; cheese, 68-69; eggs, 70; meat, 72
Spoons, 125; 104; measuring, 107; 176
Sprouts, 249-50
Squash seeds, toasted, 255
Staples, co-ops, 55-56
Steaming, 178
Steve, spices, 20; mushrooms, 89-96; Seven-Pot Meal, 139-48
Stews, 192-95
Stomach Cramps, 173
Storage Containers, 133-35
Stores, 54-59
Stoves, 125-28; 104; backpacking, 127-28; brass, 99-100; cleaning a Coleman, 167-69; cold weather, 98; 19; cook fires, 157-61; feeding, 165-66; kitchen range? 97; tin can, 162-63; tips, 177
Strainer, 105; for coffee, 257
Stretching food, 43; spices, 31
Stuff Sacks, 114-16
Styles, cooking, 20-28
Sugar, see *Sweeteners*
Suitcase Kitchen, 105-6; 103
Sun Drying, 247
Supermarkets, food, 56-57; 51; for gear, 102
Supper, 40-41

Supplements, nutritional, 38-39
Suppliers, restaurant, 59; stores, 54-58
Survival, Evasion & Escape, 86
Sweeteners, 185-86; substitutions, 189; high altitude, 188; bread, 231

- T -

Tables, 128-29; in RV's, 134-35
Table of Nutrition, 45-50
Tablecloths, 117; 24
Tacos, 203-6
Tarps, 136-37
Tarts, 235
Teas, 64
Teapot, 104
Techniques, cooking, 175-89
Tempura, 211
Teresa's Lima Bean Soup, 194-95
Teriyaki Sauce & Marinade, 243
The Drift, 133
Tin Can Lantern, 164-65; Oven, 163-64; Pots, 100-2; Stoves, 162-63
Tin cups, see *Cups*
Tin foil, see *Aluminum Foil*
Tina, 139-48
Tips, cooking, 175-89; shopping, 59-62
Toast, 118
Toasted Nuts & Seeds, 255
Tomato Sauce, 239-40
Tomato Soup, 192-93
Tortillas, 66; making, 230-33; filled, 203-6; made with seawater, 187
Tortilla *Comal*, 118
Towels, 107; paper, 123

- Y -

Universal Sauce & Marinade, 243
Unleaded Gas, 168
Utensils, see *Spoons. Forks. Knives*

- V -

Vacuum Bottle, 129; 107
Variations and Variety, 27-29; 182-85
Vegetables, fresh, 83-84; dried, 245-48; 82; recipes, 244-48; soup, 192; salads, 248-52
Vegetable broth, 57; beverage, 64
Vegetable peeler, 105
Vegetarians, 32-34
Ventilation, 138; 131
Vitamins, 38-39; C, 173; E, 173
Voyageur bags, 114

- W -

Washing Dishes, 153-54
Water, containers, 110-11; flavoring, 64-65; purifying, 170-71; seawater, 186-88; survival minimum, 63; 19
Water Jugs, 110-11; in RV's, 136
Water Tanks, 136
Weights & Measures, 43-45
Wheat, see *Bulgur*
Whining & Dining, 89
White Bean Soup, 194
White gas, 126-27; cautions, 166; containers, 128; substitutes, 168
White Sauce, 241
Whole foods stores, 55-56
Wine, 65
Wine boxes, 132-33
Wish List, 30
Wood gathering, 157-58
Wounds, 173

- XYZ -

Y & B Energy Drink, 247-58
Yeast, baking, 189; 230-31; brewer's, 64; energy drink, 257-58
Yogurt, 243-44
Yukon Spuds, 229-30
Zip-Loc® bags, 113, for beverages, 64; see *Plastic Bags*

Complete your collection of Carl Franz's informative and hilarious guides—and save a buck (or more) by using the order form below...

The People's Guide To Mexico (8th printing)

The Whole Earth Epilog called it "The best 360° coverage of traveling and short-term living in Mexico that's going... A fantastic book, well written and really interesting..."

The People's Guide To Camping in Mexico

Steve Birnbaum of *CBS Radio* said "...for visitors to Mexico interested in camping, I've seen no guide that's more valuable...absolutely indispensible..."

Send your order with a check or money order to:
John Muir Publications • P.O. Box 613 • Santa Fe, NM 87501